D0405997

WITHDRAWN
UTSA LIBRARIES

DELINQUENCY IN A BIRTH COHORT

STUDIES IN CRIME AND JUSTICE

Editorial Committee

Sanford H. Kadish

Norval Morris (Chairman)

James Vorenberg

Stanton Wheeler

Marvin E. Wolfgang

DELINQUENCY IN A BIRTH COHORT

Marvin E. Wolfgang
Robert M. Figlio
Thorsten Sellin

THE UNIVERSITY OF CHICAGO PRESS
Chicago and London

The University of Chicago Press, Chicago 60637
The University of Chicago Press, Ltd., London
© 1972 by The University of Chicago
All rights reserved. *Published 1972*
Printed in the United States of America

International Standard Book Number: 0-226-90553-5
Library of Congress Catalog Card Number: 75-187929

LIBRARY
University of Texas
At San Antonio

Contents

Foreword

This book launches the Studies in Crime and Justice series. *Delinquency in a Birth Cohort* is one of those turning points in criminological research in the United States – like the Shaw-McKay area studies of the 1930s – which would have been welcomed for publication by the University of Chicago Press quite apart from its inaugurating a new publishing venture. But it is a great stimulus to the series to step off so powerfully.

Knowledge of the incidence of juvenile delinquency and of crime in this country has been gained from reported and recorded police, court, and correctional statistics; from a few self-report sample studies; and from a few victim sample studies. There are, too, prospective and retrospective studies of groups of offenders and sometimes of their "matched" controls. What has been completely lacking until this book is an analysis of delinquency in a substantial cohort of youths, the cohort being defined *other* than by their contact with any part of the criminal justice system. Wolfgang, Figlio, and Sellin here provide a lucid and concise analysis of all available official data on nearly ten thousand boys who lived in Philadelphia from their tenth to their eighteenth birthdays. They follow the youths through their school records, through Selective Service lists, and, of course, in all their recorded contacts with police, court, and correctional agencies. Of the ten thousand, 65 percent had no police contacts; the remainder are the "delinquents" of this study, being further divided into "one-time offenders," "multiple offenders," and "chronic offenders."

The cohort study, the group being defined like a census independently of what is being studied, is an essential tool of criminological research, indeed of all social science research. It is strange that it has lain idle in this country, though tested in the United Kingdom, Norway, Denmark, and quite possibly in other countries. The lack of comparable social research in the United States, despite its obvious theoretical and practical value, was a serious reflection on our scholarship in relation to a problem of very much greater gravity in this country, particularly in the cities, than in those countries where such studies have been pursued. But Wolfgang, Figlio, and Sellin have not merely emulated overseas cohort studies; they have deployed a methodological sophistication and a precision that makes their book a contribution to research methodology in this field.

Practical conclusions for social action emerge. A basis is laid for a more precise cost-benefit analysis of various strategies of intervention in delinquent careers in relation to age, race, socioeconomic circumstances, and past patterns of delinquency than has previously been available. It becomes clear that, for some defined groups of offenders, intervention of a control or treatment nature by the juvenile court seems quite pointless, a costly futility, while for others a much greater allocation of resources and effort is required – and the cohort study provides guidance to the definition of these groups.

A depressing aspect of this study is the light it throws on the tendency of all official agencies of delinquency control to deal more harshly with black youths than with their matched white delinquent brothers.

The book is mercifully free of preaching and polemic. It is a precise and scholarly work which will figure prominently in the ensuing decades of juvenile delinquency research; and will maintain a longer significance in the history of delinquency studies.

NORVAL MORRIS

Preface

Longitudinal studies of a birth cohort, or of persons born during the same year, are uncommon in all fields, particularly in crime and delinquency. We are especially pleased, therefore, to present this volume as the first phase of our research on approximately 10,000 boys born in 1945.

With the cooperation of the Philadelphia public, parochial and private schools and of the Philadelphia Police Department, we have been able to determine which members of the cohort had official contacts with the police, to compare delinquents with nondelinquents, and to trace the volume, frequency and character of delinquent careers up to age 18. Examining these careers as a stochastic process and applying weights of seriousness to acts of delinquency and to the boys who committed them constitute a major part of this research and, we hope, a contribution to the field.

The National Institute of Mental Health has been our principal sponsor for this study.[1] During the early stages of our work, a fire destroyed almost all of our records and much of the progress we had

1. Our research was supported by PHS Training Grant No. 1-R11 MH-01252-01 NIMH (Center for Studies of Crime and Delinquency).

made. The Insurance Company of North America, with whom the University of Pennsylvania had a contract at the time, reimbursed us for our loss, and we are indeed grateful to the company.

Many persons contributed to the success of this study, most of whom were graduate students at the time, working on their doctorates in sociology, specializing in criminology: Stanley Turner, now at the University of Delaware; Bernard Cohen, Queens College; William Hohenstein, Haverford College; Dogan Akman, Memorial University of Newfoundland; Albert Cardarelli, Boston University; Frank Cannavale, George Mason College; Satyanshu Mukherjee, United Nations Social Defense Research Institute in Rome; Robert Silverman, University of Western Ontario; Charles Wellford, University of Maryland; Barry Schwartz, University of Chicago; German Otalora, University of Monterrey, Mexico; Terence Thornberry, from our Center. Janet Novak, Gila Hayim, and Beatrix Simon are still with us at the University of Pennsylvania.

We wish also to express our gratitude to Alfred Blumstein, Richard Larson, Philip Sagi, and Leslie Wilkins for their comments and consultations on several stages of the project.

Members of the secretariat of the Center for Studies in Criminology and Criminal Law were most patient and helpful in the various phases of typing, collecting materials and handling administrative tasks. Jean Wilmot Figlio, Elaine Silverman, Marjorie Silbey, and Rhoda Piltch have our kindest thanks for their care and concern for the many aspects of the research project that required their services.

As this volume goes to press, we are in the process of following up a 10 percent sample of the original cohort. Interviews with them should augment much of the information we report here, and we look forward to a subsequent publication with further insights that a longitudinal analysis can provide.

MARVIN E. WOLFGANG
ROBERT M. FIGLIO
THORSTEN SELLIN

DELINQUENCY IN A BIRTH COHORT

1 The Project

Of writings on juvenile misconduct there is no end. Articles in professional journals, research studies, books written for the general public, newspaper stories and editorials about it, multiply; official commissions and unofficial conventions debate endlessly on what can or should be done to prevent or reduce it, and social action programs are planned, instituted, tried, or transformed in the hope that they will stem what appears to be a mounting tide of delinquency. All these activities testify to the importance increasingly attached to the problem and pose a challenge to the behavioral scientist who is expected to furnish valid explanations.

The research described in this book grew out of an earlier project in which we attempted to discover, conceptualize, and describe a technique of measuring the social harm of juvenile delinquency and to provide qualitative indices to it that would be more useful to criminologists and the public administrators than the existing, traditional indices exemplified in *Uniform Crime Reports* or derived from criminal statistics generally.[1] The research described in our earlier study

1. Thorsten Sellin and Marvin E. Wolfgang, *The Measurement of Delinquency* (New York: John Wiley and Sons, 1964).

was based on a representative sample of offensive events involving juveniles during a single year (1960) in Philadelphia. The analysis of the amount and severity of personal injury to victims and/or loss of or damage to property caused by these events, and an evaluation of the comparative seriousness of the events by means of attitude tests given to many hundreds of students, juvenile court judges, and policemen permitted us to arrive at a new kind of weighted delinquency index, which we believed to be superior to the ones traditionally used.

Being concerned with events, we subordinated our interest in the delinquents involved and dwelt chiefly on their modus operandi, the manner in which the police disposed of them, and the factors affecting such dispositions. Questions of etiology did not arise because they were extraneous to the task. But we speculated on the possibility of applying our scoring system to delinquents and how it could be most profitably used when a juvenile offender is given the same score as that assigned to the event in which he was involved. We assumed that such a procedure would yield more meaningful results in, for instance, the study of recidivism in offenders of different racial and social groups whose living conditions varied. That assumption played a significant role in our decision to design the research which is the subject of the present book.

Most studies of recidivism have been retrospective, that is, based on selected groups of offenders – such as juveniles committed to correctional schools, or persons convicted of crimes or committed to penal institutions – whose prior history of delinquency or crime could be analyzed. Prospective studies have been much less common, that is, studies of the conduct of selected groups of offenders during a period of considerable length usually beginning at the adjudication of a person as delinquent, his conviction of crime, or his commitment to or release from a correctional institution.

Because neither of these two types of research can arrive at more than partial information about recidivism, we thought it would be worthwhile to approach the problem in a different manner: namely, by a study of the history of the delinquency of a birth cohort – a population born in a particular year, whose conflicts with the law could be examined during a segment of the cohort's lifetime, ending with entry into adulthood. Such an inquiry would permit us to note the age of onset and the progression or cessation of delinquency. It would allow us to relate these phenomena to certain personal or social characteristics of the delinquents and to make appropriate comparisons with that part of the cohort that did not have official contact with the law.

We therefore decided to study delinquency and its absence in a cohort consisting of all boys born in 1945 and residing in Philadelphia from a date no later than their tenth birthday until at least their eighteenth. Girls were excluded, partly because of their low delinquency rates and partly because the presence of the boys in the city at the terminal age mentioned could be established from the record of their registration for military service. The fact that no large-scale study of this particular kind had been done previously in the United States gave an additional stimulus to the project and aided us in securing financial support for it from the National Institute of Mental Health.

The Recognized Need for Cohort Studies

The desirability of investigating the offensivity of cohorts has been recognized for a long time. As early as 1890, H. von Scheel, director of Germany's National Bureau of Statistics, wrote:

> Ideal criminal statistics that would follow carefully the evolution of criminal tendencies in a given population should work not with crude annual contingents but with generations. They should start with the first offenders of a given year and continue to observe these persons, showing their later convictions, instead of counting them as new individuals each time they are convicted.[2]

Later, Otto Köbner noted that "correct statistics of offenders can be developed only by a study of the total life history of individuals."[3] Still later, Georg von Mayr argued that

> a deeper insight into the statistics of criminality is made possible by the disclosure of developmental regularities which must be sought through a study of the manner in which criminality develops in the course of a human lifetime. To do this it is necessary to identify the offender and his offense in the population and to keep him under constant statistical control so that it is possible, for each birth cohort entering punishable age and until all its members are dead, to study

2. H. von Scheel, "Zur Einführung in die Kriminalstatistik, insbesondere diejenige des Deutschen Reichs," *Allgemeines statistisches Archiv* 1 (1900): 191.

3. O. Köbner, "Die Methode einer wissenschaftlichen Rückfallsstatistik als Grundlage einer Reform der Kriminlstatistik," *Zeitschrift gesamter Strafrechtswissenschaft* 13 (1893): 670.

> statistically its participation or nonparticipation in criminality and the intensity of such participation in its various forms ... . This is the task of the "criminality table" of the future, as one might call it by analogy with the "mortality table" or the "marriage table," etc. This also has significance for the important problem of recidivism.[4]

More recently, Trenaman and Emmet suggested that,

> in order to estimate the incidence of delinquency, one needs to know more than just the annual ratio of offenders to population. One needs to consider the outcropping of crime throughout the lifetime of a whole generation. One needs to know the probability of any child born at any given time becoming a delinquent sometime during his life. To estimate such a probability, we must consider the number of children born each year – numbers which may conveniently be referred to as "generations" – and count year by year the individuals of each generation who are convicted in the courts for first offenses. When all the members of a particular generation are dead, it will then be possible to express the probability as a ratio of the total number who were convicted at least once to the total number of the generation at birth.[5]

In 1960 at a conference on research into causes of delinquency held at Sunningdale, England, D.V. Glass advocated studies of birth cohorts, and Sir Aubrey Lewis said that "one advantage of cohort studies was that they were not to any great extent dependent on retrospective data, as some other types of research are."[6]

In our work on the measurement of delinquency, we noted how students of juvenile delinquency had often observed that "a true index of delinquency or delinquents must be based on an assessment of conduct during the entire time that juveniles are subject to the law" because "indices based on annual data give no hint of the number of juveniles who become delinquents before they reach adulthood"; and we suggested that a study of the delinquency history of birth cohorts could provide a test of "the relative value of preventive action programs ... by investigating changes in patterns of delinquent conduct, reduction of recidivism, etc., in successive age cohorts as they progressively come under the influence of such programs."[7]

4. Georg von Mayr, *Statistik und Gessellschaftslehre,* vol. 3: *Moralstatistik mit Einschluss der Kriminalstatistik* (Tübingen: Mohr, 1917), pp. 425–26.

5. Joseph Trenaman and B.P. Emmet, "An Estimate of the Incidence of Delinquency in England and Wales," in Joseph Trenaman's *Out of Step* (New York: Philosophical Library, 1952), pp. 204–5.

6. *Report of the Conference on Research into Causes of Delinquency* (mimeograph; London: Home Office, 8 February 1960), p. 2. (CHN 95/2/43).

7. Sellin and Wolfgang, *The Measurement of Delinquency,* pp. 66–67.

Most recently, Hirschi and Selvin, in discussing causal order – the criterion for judging the claim that one variable causes another – said that a solution to this problem, at least in principle, is the longitudinal or panel study. "In an ideal version of this design, the investigator would select a sample of infants and continually collect data on them until they became adults. The practical difficulties of panel studies are undoubtedly the major reason for their infrequent use in delinquency research."[8]

The term *cohort* is used for a variety of groups. An author recently stated that it

> may be defined as an aggregate of individuals (within some population definition) who experienced the same event within the same time interval. In almost all cohort research to date the defining event has been birth, but ... the approach can be generalized beyond the birth cohort to cohorts identified by common time of occurrence of any significant and enduring count in life history. Cohorts may be defined in terms of the year in which they completed their schooling, the year in which they married, the year in which they migrated to the city, or the year in which they entered the labor force full time.[9]

It is, in fact, most uncommon to find analyses of single birth-year cohorts.[10] Usually, the cohort is a population born within a bracket of years (three, five, or ten) as in the case of recent demographic studies of fertility time series, migration differentials, or residential and occupational mobility.[11] The term has even been used to designate "an aggregate of individuals" of widely different ages who experienced the same event such as arrest, prosecution or conviction of crime, or release on parole – within the same time interval.

8. Travis Hirschi and Hanan C. Selvin, *Delinquency Research: An Appraisal of Analytic Methods* (New York: The Free Press, 1967), p. 53.

9. Norman B. Ryder, "The Cohort as a Concept in the Study of Social Change," *American Sociological Review* 30 (December 1965): 845, 847–48.

10. Except, of course, in the construction of life expectancy tables.

11. Cf. Hope T. Eldridge, "A Cohort Approach to the Analysis of Migration Differentials," *Demography* 1 (1964): 212–19. N.B. Ryder, "The Influence of Declining Mortality on Swedish Reproductivity," in *Current Research in Human Fertility* (New York: Milbank Memorial Fund, 1955), pp. 65–81. C.T. Pihlblad and Dagfirm Aas, "Residential and Occupational Mobility in an Area of Rapid Industrialization in Norway," *American Sociological Review* 25 (June 1960): 369–75. Pascal K. Whelpton, "Trends and Differentials in the Spacing of Births," *Demography* 1 (1964): 83–93. Beverly Duncan, Georges Sabagh, and Maurice D. Van Arsdol, Jr., "Patterns of City Growth," *American Journal of Sociology* 67 (January 1962): 418–29.

Some Previous Studies

For the sake of brevity we propose to mention here only some earlier delinquency studies based on single birth-year cohorts. That the earliest study of the delinquency of such a cohort with which we are familiar was published in 1952 shows how recent is this type of research. We refer to Thomas Ferguson's *The Young Delinquent in his Social Setting.*[12] A year earlier, he and J. Cunnison had published, under the title *The Young Wage-Earner,* an account of the home and social background of the entire group of 1,349 "ordinary" Glasgow boys (excluding the physically handicapped, mentally retarded and those in approved schools) who left school in January 1947 at the age of 14 years. That study dealt generally with the well-being of those boys at home, at school, and in their early post-school years and, in particular, with such questions as health, employment and unemployment, use of leisure, and social adaptation. "The incidence of delinquency was one of the yardsticks used in an attempt to assess the well-being of the lads. ... Information was obtained about the police court convictions of these young persons between their 8th and 17th birthdays and the records were set against the general social background disclosed by the study. In the three post-school years contact was lost with only 35 of the 1,349 boys."[13] In *The Young Delinquent in his Social Setting,* Ferguson concentrates on delinquency, which was only an incidental aspect of the earlier study, and adds data on offenses committed during the fourth post-school year. In the research for a later work, which Ferguson and Cunnison again coauthored,[14] they singled out for further study 346 of the lads who had been called up for military service and 222 who had been rejected for service on medical grounds. These men were followed up until most of them had reached the age of 22; their criminality from their eighteenth birthday was analyzed incidentally.

By the time the boys had reached 18 years of age, 165 (12.2 percent) had been convicted on 268 occasions, of which all but 28 involved theft or housebreaking. Forty percent of the offenders were convicted a second time, and, of these, 61 percent had three or more convictions. Ferguson proceeds to analyze the relation between their

12. Thomas Ferguson, *The Young Delinquent in his Social Setting* (London: Oxford University Press, 1952).

13. Ibid., p. 15.

14. Thomas Ferguson and J. Cunnison, *In Their Early Twenties* (London: Oxford University Press, 1956).

delinquency and a whole series of social and environmental factors, the relative importance of these factors in the production of delinquency, and the influence of the presence in the home of another member of the family who had been convicted. But he omits making comparisons with the boys in the cohort who had received no convictions. In a summary statement he says:

Even when furnished with a comprehensive range of data about a large series of young people, as in this present investigation, it is difficult to unravel the many interwoven social and environmental factors bearing on juvenile delinquency. But some circumstances stand out by reason of the frequency of their occurrence and, particularly, because of the frequency of their association with cases marked by more than one conviction; and it is possible to recognize a group of circumstances which, when they occur together – as often happens – must make it difficult for some lads to keep clear of crime.

The boy who is poor in scholastic attainment, unreliable at school, and inclined to truancy, lives in a slum area, or in a "rehousing" slum-clearance area, and is drawn from a large family, living in a home poor in background and severely overcrowded; who, in the process, is still in a stopgap employment when he comes to be 18 years old, in unskilled or semi-skilled work, having undergone no vocational training or perhaps having fallen through an apprenticeship on which he embarked – such is the kind of lad likely to have come into the hands of the police during school days or in the years immediately after leaving school.

If, in addition to these adverse factors, he is the son of a father engaged in unskilled work, irregularly employed; if he is of poor physique, undersized and underweight, if he comes from a home disrupted by circumstances other than the death of a parent, if he is a nonattender at church, is not a member of an organized youth group or club, and is earning big wages early in his career, then the likelihood that he will get into trouble is still greater.[15]

In England in the mid-1940s, the Institute of Child Health, the Society of Medical Officers of Health, and the Population Investigation Committee launched a National Survey of Health and Development. After locating the 12,268 legitimate single births occurring throughout England, Wales, and Scotland during the week of 3–9 March 1946, a sample of 5,362 births was selected for continuous longitudinal study. Since April 1962 this study has been directed at the London School of Economics by the Medical Research Council's Unit for the Study of Environmental Factors in Mental and Physical

15. Ferguson, *The Young Delinquent,* pp. 41–42.

Illness. The sample drawn included all the children born to wives of agricultural workers and to nonmanual workers (referred to as middle class) and one-fourth of all the other children. Approximately half of the children were from middle-class families. This distortion could, according to the staff of the survey, be eliminated in reconstituting the structure of the original sample by giving the middle-class and agricultural workers' children a weight of unity and the rest a weight of four. When this was done, population estimates of mortality, grammar school education, etc., were found to check closely with those from national sources, suggesting that the survey children gave an undistorted picture of those of their age group.

To date, two studies of delinquency in the sample have appeared. One deals with the boys who had been convicted of at least one indictable offense before their 16th birthday and compares them with the nondelinquents with respect to the presence or absence of symptoms of maladjustment – specifically nervousness, aggressiveness, or both.[16] The other is concerned with the 2,402 boys in the sample who were living in Great Britain in 1963. Of these boys, 288 (12 percent) had been cautioned or sentenced for an offense, indictable or nonindictable, before the age of 17, and 67 (2.8 percent) had committed more than one indictable offense. The study focuses on the social class origin of the delinquents as revealed by the occupation of their fathers and the education and social origins of their parents.[17]

In 1960 Nils Christie published a doctoral dissertation which contained the results of a very extensive study of a birth cohort.[18] With the cooperation of the military, he was able to locate the names of all males born in 1933 who had registered in Norway for compulsory military service (about 20,000) and a considerable amount of information about them, such as their residence, education, occupation, and health. A search for any criminal records of these men up to 1958 was made by locating in the national penal register the names of all men born in 1933 and checking these names against the mili-

16. Glenn Mulligan, J.W.B. Douglas, W.A. Hammond, and J. Tizard, "Delinquency and Symptoms of Maladjustment: The Findings of a Longitudinal Study," *Proceedings of the Royal Society of Medicine* 56, no. 12 (December 1963): 1083–1986.

17. J.W.B. Douglas, J.M. Ross, W.A. Hammond, and D.G. Mulligan, "Delinquency and Social Class," *British Journal of Criminology* 6 (July 1966): 294–302.

18. Nils Christie, *Unge norske lovovertredere* (Oslo: Universitetsforlaget, 1960).

tary files. In his sample, Christie found that about 20 percent had been reported to the penal register. The offenders were then compared with a sample of 20 percent of the nonoffenders. Not all offenders were captured by the research, however, because the penal register had no information on offenses committed by the men before their fourteenth birthday except those resulting in commitment to a correctional school; nor did the register contain information on petty crimes. The author analyzes the data on the first offense registered, recidivism, place and character of home, family environment and social status, education, occupation, health, intelligence, personality, and military offenses.[19]

Two near-birth cohort studies have been published recently. One, dealing only incidentally with delinquency, concerns children in the sixth grade of the public schools of a midwestern city who were followed for a nine-year period. Although most of the 247 boys and 240 girls were born in 1940, the study group included a considerable proportion of children (30 percent) born in five earlier or later years. The authors relied on police records and were, so far as delinquency is discussed, interested in social class differences and in developing a prediction instrument based on social maladjustment scores derived from tests given to the boys when they were in the sixth or seventh grades.[20] The second study deals with 271 boys (out of 2,348) who entered the tenth grade of high schools in Denver, Colorado, in 1956, and who resided continuously in the city at least until their eighteenth birthday. The authors relied on juvenile court records. A control group of nondelinquent boys, individually matched with the delinquents on six factors, was secured. Most boys were born in 1939 or 1940. Their history of delinquency until they reached 18 years of age was studied. The principal purpose of the investigation was "to determine (1) whether personality traits manifested by boys in various age-grade periods from kindergarten through the end of the ninth grade were significantly related to future delinquency after the potential effects of other factors had been controlled through a match-

19. An international study of adolescent delinquency, still continuing and being conducted by Jackson Toby, deals with birth cohorts in Tokyo and Stockholm. The Tokyo part is based on two cohorts of boys born in 1942 and 1950 and selected from boys in the graduating classes of 40 junior high schools in 1957 and 1965.

20. Robert J. Havighurst, Paul Hoover Bowman, Gordon P. Liddle, Charles V. Matthews, and James V. Pierce, *Growing Up in River City* (New York: John Wiley and Sons, 1966), chapter 6, "Delinquency – Dead End Street."

ing technique, and (2) whether the nature, extent, and direction of such relationships in each period might vary, depending on the intelligence and social class status of the child."[21]

The cohort studies mentioned above have focused on the delinquent history of cohort members as related to various and often numerous circumstances pertaining to the offender and his environment. Another approach began in 1960 with Leslie T. Wilkins's work *Delinquent Generations,* which examines and tests "the theory that children born in certain years (for example, during war-time) are more likely to commit offenses than are others, and that this tendency remains from childhood to early adult life."[22] The basic data were obtained from official criminal statistics of persons convicted of indictable offenses in England and Wales from 1946 through 1957 and from ages 8 through 20. Crime rates per 100,000 related population were computed. The author concludes that children who reached their fifth year of age during the war were most crime-prone and that all born during the war had higher crime rates than expected.

The Wilkins study prompted Christiansen to replicate it in Denmark,[23] and others to do so in Poland[24] and in New Zealand.[25] Critical analyses of the parent study by Walters and Prys Williams[26] led to a rejoinder by Wilkins,[27] which failed, however, to stifle further criticism.[28]

This brings us to our own project. Our first task was to decide which birth cohort to study. For reasons to be discussed later, we

21. John Janeway Conger, Wilbur C. Miller, et al., *Personality, Social Class and Delinquency* (New York: John Wiley and Sons, 1966), p. 183.

22. Leslie T. Wilkins, *Delinquent Generations,* Home Office Studies in the Causes of Delinquency and the Treatment of Offenders (London: H.M. Stationery Office, 1960).

23. Karl O. Christiansen, "Delinquent Generations in Denmark," *British Journal of Criminology* 4 (January 1964): 259–64.

24. Jerzy Jasinski, "Delinquent Generations in Poland," ibid. 6 (April 1966): 170–82.

25. S.W. Slater, J.H. Darwin, and W.L. Ritchie, "Delinquent Generations in New Zealand," *Journal of Research in Crime and Delinquency* 3 (July 1966): 140–46.

26. A.A. Walters, "Delinquent Generations," *British Journal of Criminology* 3 (April 1963): 391–95. G. Prys Williams, *Patterns of Teen-age Delinquency, England and Wales, 1946–1961* (London: Christian Economic & Social Research Foundation, 1962).

27. Leslie T. Wilkins, "Delinquent Generations: A Rejoinder," *British Journal of Criminology* 4 (January 1964): 264–68.

28. Cf. G.N.G. Rose, "The Artificial Delinquent Generations," *Journal of Criminal Law, Criminology and Police Science* 59 (September 1968): 370–85.

wanted to use the offense reports of the Juvenile Aid Division of the Philadelphia Police Department on apprehended offenders to ascertain the delinquency of the cohort. In order for us to do so, these reports had to be both adequate and continuous. Until 1953, the reporting system had not been perfected, but after 1953 it was complete and reliable. We therefore decided to study the boys born in 1945, who would reach adulthood in 1963. This procedure would ensure that complete information on their police contacts would exist at least from their eighth birthday in 1953.

The problem was how to find the boys. Because the law of Pennsylvania requires children to attend school until they are 16, barring some valid excuse, we assumed that an examination of records available in the city's schools would make possible the establishment of the cohort. Valid as was this assumption, the work involved proved to be very time-consuming and complicated, mostly because of the existence in the city of a parochial school system, paralleling the public one, and of numerous private schools.[29] The manner in which this initial process was carried out will be described in chapter 2.

Identifying Delinquents

Having located the boys to be included in the cohort, we next had to identify those among them who had a police record. Fortunately, the Juvenile Aid Division, in response to a plea which we had made as early as 1960, had saved their files of offense reports for all the years we needed instead of destroying them according to an otherwise firm schedule of obsolescence. These files were made available to us, but we shall reserve for chapter 2 the description of the process of identifying the delinquents and of assembling the offense reports pertaining to them. Here we propose to discuss only the reason for our reliance on police data to determine the delinquency of the cohort, and a couple of important problems in that connection. One of these is a problem which affects all research in this area, namely, the hidden or unknown delinquency; another is more specifically linked to the use of police rather than court records, namely, the question of the innocent, though apprehended, person.

In the past, nearly all studies of juvenile delinquents were based on children disposed of by juvenile courts or committed to correc-

29. In 1960, for instance, 35.2 percent of boys of school age in Philadelphia were enrolled in parochial schools, and 4.2 percent in private schools.

tional institutions. This happened in part because these agencies have the greatest wealth of information about their wards, but also because of traditional belief that, until a person is duly found guilty by a court of justice, he should not be considered a delinquent or a criminal. If a defendant was absolved by discharge or acquittal, the conduct which had originally caused him to become a defendant could then no longer be a blot on his record – or be included in a study of his criminal history, for instance.

Were such a view the only tenable one, we would have had to ignore police data except when they applied to boys whose involvement in delinquent events was subsequently affirmed by a court decision, which in nearly all cases would have been handed down by a judge of the juvenile court. Another consequence of using such official judicial decisions for defining the delinquents in the cohort would necessarily have been the inclusion of all other boys, with no matter how many police contacts, among our nondelinquents. This procedure would have been proper, of course, had we been convinced that guilt or innocence could be settled only in court. We knew, however, from past experience that there were two administrative agencies which did not have the official status of courts but nevertheless assumed and exercised judicial functions: the police department and the intake service in the detention center for juveniles, known in Philadelphia as the Youth Study Center. These agencies extrajudicially dispose of a large proportion of juveniles apprehended for delinquency – in Philadelphia about three-fourths of them. Had we ignored these cases, we would have lost a very significant part of the history of our cohort's illegal conduct.

Failure to submit an apprehended juvenile to court determination of his guilt does not mean that he is innocent of misconduct. If the police officer decides merely to warn him or to do so in a joint interview with his parents, this disposition simply means that the officer does not consider it wise or necessary to arrest him and send him to the detention center. The reason may be single or multiple: the offense may be insignificant, the offender may be very young or without previous contact with the police, his parents may appear to be quite capable of disciplining him, the victim may refuse to prosecute him,[30] etc. In other words, in most cases closed by the police with a

30. In the 1,313 delinquent events which we examined in our previous research on the measurement of delinquency, the police arrested the delinquents in 93 percent of the cases when the complainant insisted on prosecution, but in only 4 percent of the cases when the complainant opposed it.

so-called "remedial" disposition instead of arrest, the "guilt" of the juvenile is well established by his confession or by other evidence. The inclusion of such delinquencies in a study of recidivism, for instance, is clearly justifiable. As a matter of fact, it is generally admitted today that to limit oneself to court-determined delinquency would result in a highly biased view of the problem.[31] Juveniles brought into court are a selected group: boys, Negroes, older children, those with many previous arrests, those from high-rate delinquency areas, and those who have committed serious offenses dominate. The very young, the petty offender, and children from advantaged homes are underrepresented in the court group. Therefore it becomes necessary to exploit the procedurally earliest source for information about delinquency and delinquents – namely, the records of the police – because we are closer in time to the offender's specific conduct and are not disturbed by the series of often unpredictable administrative decisions which intervene between the discovery of any given offender and his ultimate disposition by a court.

We are not unaware of some problems which inhere in the study of delinquency, no matter what official sources of data may be used. One problem is that of hidden delinquency, which writers on criminal statistics have discussed ever since Quetelet called attention to it in the 1830s,[32] long after it must have been known to people generally, for it is a far from obscure social fact. The term "hidden delinquency," or the "dark number" as Oba called it,[33] has several meanings, however.

31. Cf. Nathan Goldman, *The Differential Selection of Juvenile Offenders for Court Appearance* (New York: National Research and Information Center, National Council on Crime and Delinquency, 1963), where a review of opinions in the matter is presented and documented by a study done in several counties of Western Pennsylvania.

32. Adolphe Quetelet, *Recherches sur le penchant au crime aux différents âges* (Brussels, 1831). Of theoretical or general discussions in the last few decades, the following are of interest: Veli Verkko, "Kriminalstatistiken och den verkliga brottsligheten," *Nordisk Tidsskrift for Strafferet* 8 (1930): 95–128; Kurt Meyer, *Die unbestraften Verbrechen* (Leipzig: Wiegandt, 1941); Bernd Wehorer, *Die Latenz der Straftaten* (Wiesbaden: Bundeskriminalamt, 1957); C.N. Peijster, *De unbekende misdaad* (The Hague: M. Nijhoff, 1958); Gunnar Fredrickson, *Kriminalstatistiken och kriminologin* (Stockholm: Almquist & Wicksell, 1962); Hans v. Hentig, *Die unbekannte Straftat* (Berlin: Springer-Verlag, 1965); Inkeri Anttila, "The Criminological Significance of Unregistered Criminality," *Excerpta Criminologica* 4 (1964): 412–14; Albert D. Biderman and Albert J. Reiss, Jr., "On Exploring the 'Dark Figure' of Crime," *Annals of the AAPSS* 374 (1967): 1–15.

33. S. Oba, *Unverbesserliche Verbrecher und ihre Behandlung* (Berlin, 1908).

1. In its proper sense it means conduct contravening a criminal law proscription but unknown to all but the person engaging in that conduct, whether he knows that it is forbidden by law or not. It is fair to assume that few, if any, persons escape being a hidden delinquent or criminal at least once or, what is more likely, many times during their lifetimes. The findings of the growing number of "self-reporting" studies lend ample support to this assumption.[34]

34. A bibliography of American studies prior to 1965 is found in Robert H. Hardt and George E. Bodine, *Development of Self-Report Instruments in Delinquency Research* (Syracuse, N.Y.: Youth Development Center, Syracuse University, 1965). The following items supplement that bibliography. They fall into two broad types, those based on anonymous questionnaires distributed to various groups of persons, and those based on personal interviews.

Among the questionnaire studies are: Austin L. Porterfield, *Young in Trouble* (Fort Worth, Texas: Leo Potishman Fund, 1946); James S. Wallerstein and Clement J. Wyle, "Our Law-Abiding Law-Breakers," *Probation* 25 (March-April 1947): 107–12; Johs. Andenaes, Knut Sveri, and Ragnar Haige, "Kriminalitetshyppigheten hos ustraffede. I. Nork undersökelse," *Nord Tidsskrift for Kriminalvidenskab* 48 (1960): 97–112; Ola Nyquist and Ivar Strahl, "Kriminalitetshyppigheten hos ustraffede. II. Svensk undersökning," ibid., pp. 113–17; Hans Forssman and Carl-Fredrik Gentz, "Kriminalitetsförekomsten hos presumptivt ostraffade. En enkätsundersökning," ibid. 50 (1962): 318–24; Nils Christie, Johs. Andenaes, and Sigurd Skirbekk, "A Study of Self-Reported Crime," *Scandinavian Studies in Criminology* 1 (1965): 86–116; Kerstin Elmhorn, "Study in Self-Reported Delinquency among School-children in Stockholm," ibid. pp. 117–46; David A. Smith and Desmond S. Cartwright, "Two Measures of Reported Delinquent Behavior," *American Sociological Review* 30 (August 1965): 573–76; Inkeri Anttila and Risto Jaakkola, *Unrecorded Criminality in Finland* (Helsinki: Kriminologinen Tutkimuseaitos, 1966); Lamar T. Empey and Maynard L. Erickson, "Hidden Delinquency and Social Status," *Social Forces* 44 (June 1966): 546–54; Edmund Vaz, "Self-Reported Juvenile Delinquency and Socio-Economic Status," *Canadian Journal of Corrections* 8 (January 1966): 20–27; R.A. Kettel, *A Comparative Study of Detected and Undetected Violational Behavior among Students and Inmates* (Res. Study 67-3. Florida Division of Corrections, Research and Stat. Sec., April 1967).

Interviews were used by Martin Gold: "Undetected Delinquent Behavior," *Journal of Research in Crime and Delinquency* 3 (January 1966): 27–46.

Other devices have also been used to estimate the amount of hidden delinquency. Delinquent acts known to social agencies have been studied to discover how many of them were reported to the police. The pioneer study was Sophia M. Robison's *Can Delinquency Be Measured?* (New York: Columbia University Press, 1936). See also Fred J. Murphy, Mary W. Shirley, and Helen L. Witmer, "The Incidence of Hidden Delinquency," *American Journal of Orthopsychiatry* 16 (1946): 686–96; and Edward E. Schwartz, "A Community Experiment in the Measurement of Juvenile Delinquency," *NPPA Yearbook* (1945), pp. 157–81.

Finally, victims of criminal acts have been interviewed to discover the extent to which they reported their victimization to the police. An early example is Roland Bejke, "Prykiatriska synpunkter pa problemet dold kriminalitet och anonyma brottslingar, med särskild hänsyn till exhibitionism," *Nordisk Psy-*

2. Even though the offense may be known to the victim of it or to some bystander, it may remain hidden from the law enforcement authorities because no one, the victim included, is, for personal or other reasons, willing to report it or lodge a complaint.

3. The offense may be known to the police, but if the police end the matter by ignoring it for some reason or by making a remedial disposition of the offender, the offense and its perpetrator will remain hidden from the judicial authorities.

When one relies on police data for a study of delinquency, one realizes, therefore, that the delinquencies charged to boys apprehended by the police represent only the visible illegal conduct, that the total record of their delinquencies during their juvenile years contains only their officially recorded misbehaviors, and that an unknown number of illegal acts which they may have committed have escaped official notice. At present, we have no satisfactory way of estimating this number with confidence. Our research is based, then, on the officially recorded delinquencies of the cohort. We have been compelled to adopt this policy, fully conscious of the fact that its effect on the findings of our research is not calculable. We do know that there are differences in the willingness of victims to bring an offender to public notice, depending on the social class of the offender, the degree of tolerance toward delinquent conduct in different areas and social groups in a community and toward different kinds of delinquency, the relative strength of the victim's belief in the ability or desire of the police to find the offender, etc. If, for instance, a delinquent's family indemnifies the victim for his loss of property and as a result the offense is not reported, a juvenile from a wealthy family would not have as full an official record of delinquency as one from a poor family, who lacks this means of covering up his misconduct. On the other hand, if poor people have less confidence in the police than have the middle and upper classes, they will fail to report offenses that would be reported by the well-to-do. We can only point to the

---

kiatri Medlemsblad 1951, pp. 26–36. The most recent such studies are reported by the President's Commission on Law Enforcement and Administration of Justice, 1967. A summary of the extensive data in its Field Surveys 1–3 is found in Albert D. Biderman, "Surveys of Population Samples for Estimating Crime Incidence," *Annals of the AAPSS* 374 (November 1947): 16–33.

The National Council on Crime and Delinquency has abstracted studies in *Crime and Delinquency Literature, Hidden Crime,* vol. 2, no. 5 (October 1970), compiled by Eugene Doleschal.

existence of differential reporting of delinquency and admit that we cannot estimate its effect on our research.[35]

Another important problem arises when the offense reports of the police are used to establish the delinquency record of a juvenile. It would not arise, presumably, if only the records of the juvenile court were used, because the court would have determined the guilt of the juvenile. When a boy is apprehended by the police and made the subject of an offense report, which would cause him to be listed among the delinquents in our cohort, he may be innocent. If this were the case in a high percentage of instances, the results of our research would be unreliable.

Little is actually known about this particular problem. A recent study of 1,068 juveniles, representing a sample of all referrals (excluding traffic violations and dependency cases) to the juvenile court of Washington, D.C., during the fiscal year 1965 contains some pertinent data. Six hundred and ninety-four of the juveniles had been apprehended for offenses of personal violence or against property. Of the former (316), 25.9 percent denied guilt, and of the latter (378), 11.4 percent did so. Information was lacking in 7.1 percent of these two groups combined. The rate of denial also varied by type of charge. Those apprehended for rape denied involvement in 44 percent of the cases. Corresponding percentages were 24 for robbery, 28 for aggravated assault, 9 for housebreaking, 11 for grand larceny, and 18 for unauthorized use of a motor vehicle. For the entire sample the rate of denial was 16.9 percent, and for the number of cases where information was lacking, 9.3 percent.[36]

The above data would certainly throw doubt on the validity of the findings of studies using police offense reports for establishing the record of any juvenile's delinquencies. Fortunately, we can cast some further light on the matter by examining our experience with the data derived from the 2,094 juvenile involvements[37] in 1,313 events which we analyzed in our earlier research on the measurement

35. For a recent study that uses self-reported and officially known acts of delinquency, although not in a cohort longitudinal analysis, see Travis Hirschi, *Causes of Delinquency* (Berkeley, California: University of California Press, 1969).

36. *Report of the President's Commission on Crime in the District of Columbia: Appendix.* (Washington, D.C.: United States Government Printing Office, 1966), pp. 465–67.

37. We speak of involvements rather than of individuals because there were 1,936 individuals concerned.

of delinquency. In these 2,094 involvements, 265 (12.6 percent) denials of guilt were made. In 15 instances, the police believed that the juvenile was telling the truth, but they nevertheless entered a "remedial" disposition on the report, except in the case of one boy who was actually arrested because he was present at a fight in which his gang was engaged and which led to the arrest of all the participants. In the remaining 250 instances, the police did not believe the denial and charged an offense against the juvenile, arresting him in 186 and remedialing him in 64 of the cases. In 183 cases (73.2 percent) these dispositions were made because the juvenile had been observed in the act by the police, the complainant, or some other witness or had been implicated by his partners in the event. In 21 cases (8.4 percent) indirect evidence led to 17 arrests and four remedials, and in 46 cases (18.3 percent) 36 arrests and 10 remedials occurred after the juvenile had been apprehended on suspicion or for no reason stated in the offense report; altogether, those 97 cases represented 3.2 percent of the 2,094 involvements.

Table 1.1 shows that a large majority of denials came from juveniles involved in events resulting in physical injuries to victims or in property loss or damage. One out of five children apprehended claimed to be innocent, and the rate was as high as 30.3 percent in the personal injury cases. In other types of events, only 6 percent of the juveniles denied involvement, but it is worth noting that 58 out of the 62 whose denials were disbelieved were taken into custody on the basis of eyewitness declarations. Such evidence also led to apprehension in 84.4 percent of the juveniles involved in personal injury events, 73.8 percent of those accused of theft, and 51.4 percent of those charged with property damage. The fact that 49 of the 63 juveniles involved in these more serious offenses – but taken into custody on suspicion or indirect evidence or for no stated reasons – were arrested and sent to the detention center, suggests that the probability of their actually being involved was high.

If we were to classify the above events according to the traditional labels of the criminal law, the highest rates of denials of guilt would occur in cases of robbery (45.7 percent), aggravated assault (37.7 percent), rape or attempted rape (27.3 percent), malicious mischief (30.8 percent), and sex offenses (24.5 percent). Yet 98 percent of the juveniles who denied these offenses were charged on eyewitness evidence, except in the case of malicious mischief, where 9 out of 37 were apprehended on suspicion or for no stated reason.

TABLE 1.1

Juvenile Involvements in Delinquent Events, Denials of Guilt, and Police Reaction

Offenses	Juvenile Involvement	Juvenile Denies Guilt				Police Believe Denial			Juvenile Apprehended Because: observed by police, complainant, other witness or other offender			of indirect evidence			suspect or for no stated reason		
		A[a]	R[b]	Tot.	%	A	R	Tot.	A	R	Tot.	A	R	Tot.	A	R	Tot.
Events involving:																	
Physical injury to victim	254	64	13	77	30.3	1	1	2	57	8	65	1	0	1	5	4	9
Theft	569	61	23	84	17.8	0	3	3	27	15	62	14	4	18	20	1	21
Property damage	127	20	15	35	27.5	0	3	3	11	7	18	1	0	1	8	5	13
Total	950	145	51	196	20.6	1	7	8	95	30	125	14	4	20	33	10	43
Juvenile status offenses	415	12	19	31	7.5	0	6	6	8	13	21	1	0	1	3	0	3
Other offenses	729	30	8	38	5.2	0	1	1	30	7	37	0	0	0	0	0	0
Total	1144	42	27	69	6.1	0	7	7	38	20	58	1	0	1	3	0	3
Grand total	2094	187	78	265	12.6	1	14	15	133	50	183	17	4	21	36	10	46
Percent				100.0				5.6			69.0			8.0			17.4

[a]A = Arrests [b]R = Remedials

TABLE 1.2

Juvenile's Explanation of Denial, and Police Reaction

Explanation of Denial	Police Believe Denial			Police Observed Delinquent			Juvenile Observed by: other offenders			Juvenile Observed by: complainant or witness			Indirect Evidence of Guilt			Suspicion or no reason given			Total		
	A[a]	R[b]	Tot.	A	R	Tot.	A	R	Tot.	A	R	Tot.	A	R	Tot.	A	R	Tot.	A	R	Tot.
No offense committed	0	1	1	6	2	8	0	0	0	5	3	8	1	4	5	3	0	3	15	10	25
Present but not involved	1	13	14	13	1	14	19	6	25	49	20	69	12	0	12	26	10	36	120	50	170
Involved in different offense	0	0	0	2	0	2	1	4	5	11	3	14	1	0	1	2	0	2	17	7	24
Not present	0	0	0	1	0	1	6	3	9	20	8	28	3	0	3	5	0	5	35	11	46
Total	1	14	15	22	3	25	26	13	39	85	34	119	17	4	21	36	10	46	187	78	265

[a]A = Arrests [b]R = Remedials

Table 1.2 illustrates the manner in which the police reacted to the juvenile's claim of innocence and to his explanation of that claim. The juvenile, in most instances, admitted being present on the occasion but disclaimed actual involvement, although in 104 out of 170 cases he was implicated by eyewitnesses.

One must admit, then, that establishing the history of a juvenile delinquent from police offense reports introduces a possibility that he may be charged at some time with an offense of which he is innocent. The likelihood is not very great, and illegal arrest appears to occur mostly in cases of theft, simple assault, and malicious mischief. But these are types of conduct in which police clearance rates are very low, which suggests that in a great many such events juveniles escape detection completely. In a study of a delinquent's history, therefore, there is a slight chance that an offense of which he is not guilty may be recorded against him, but there is a much greater likelihood that the records of the police inadequately show his real involvement in delinquency.

Given these circumstances, it is understood that when we constantly refer to the delinquency of our cohort, we are, in fact, dealing with police contacts with juveniles resulting in their being taken into custody by the police, no matter what disposition the police made of their cases. Because delinquency was present in all but a very small percentage of cases, we have preferred to use the term *delinquency* to designate the conduct of our cohort members that brought them into contact with the police.

In our prior research aimed at the establishment of an index of delinquency we developed a system for assessing the degree of social injury caused by a delinquent event. By this system we were able to assign a score value to an event, depending on weights given to certain of its elements. For instance, a simple physical assault resulting only in an injury requiring temporary medical attention would receive a score of 2, while a complex event of, let us say, an assault requiring the hospitalization of two victims after their being intimidated by a dangerous weapon and beaten and their wallets stolen might receive a score of 23 or more depending on the amount stolen. Whereas in traditional criminal statistics these two offenses would each be given a score of 1 and separated by assigning the milder assault case to the class of simple assaults and the more serious one to that of aggravated assaults in accord with a classification based on the definitions in the criminal code, under our system both events would fall into a class of offenses causing physical injury to a victim and not merely be counted as two crimes but given a combined score of at least 23. In other words, an event was not merely counted; its socially harmful quality was assessed in a manner different from that used in a criminal code in which crimes carrying the same label may vary greatly in their actual harmfulness.

It seemed obvious to us that in studying the history of delinquency in a birth cohort we should profit from what we had learned about the qualitative assessment of delinquent events. Imagine a boy who has a long series of recorded misconducts stretching over several years, a mélange of thefts, burglaries, sex offenses, assaults, as the law defines them. These labels do not in themselves give any evaluation of the seriousness of his offenses. Scoring them by our system would show more clearly, for instance, whether as he grew older his offenses increased in harmfulness or, in spite of the legal labels attached to them, actually decreased in that respect. Other examples could be adduced which consider more than the mere aging process of the cohort. Would the scoring system reveal differences, otherwise unperceived, among delinquents from different racial and social groups, groups with different intelligence, school achievement, residential mobility, socioeconomic status, etc.? We did not know, but we wanted to learn if our scoring system would be helpful in finding answers to such questions, and we therefore decided to score each delinquent event on a boy's police record and to use that score as a measure of his involvement in the event. The basic assumption of such a procedure is that the degree of social harm produced by the event just as accurately measures the degree of harmfulness of the delinquent or delinquents who cause that harm.

One might well question the validity of this assumption. When one shifts from the evaluation of harm produced by a delinquent event to the evaluation of a participant's involvement, can one ignore subjective aspects of his conduct? Let us suppose that three boys have committed a burglary. They range in age from 12 to 16 years. The oldest is the instigator and leader who actively committed the offense with one of the others; the youngest is an unwilling partner who was ignorant of the plan but was present because he happened to be with the others at the start of what began as an idle saunter through the streets of a neighborhood. Suppose the event is given a score of 4. Does this score, when applied to each participant, accurately measure the involvement of each? Should the oldest boy and his active partner be assessed this score, but the youngest given a lower one? From a legal point of view they are all equally guilty, but are they so from a social or psychological viewpoint?

We were not unaware of this problem when we were working on the development of a delinquency index. We speculated (see pp. 315 and 317 of *The Measurement of Delinquency*) on how to distribute the score value of an event among its participants, we referred to the possible value of the legal definition of principals in the first and second degree, and we thought about the importance of leadership in groups of different size, "but under the present circumstances we chose to assign the same seriousness score for the event to each of the participants in the event." The "circumstances" were, of course, the fact that we were preoccupied with the objective features of delinquent *events* and *not* with the participants.

We have found no completely satisfactory solution to this problem. Even if we had wished to find it, the offense reports on delinquent events prepared by the police, although adequate for a description of the objective character of an event, leave much to be desired when the description of participant involvement is required. Our decision to apply in our cohort study the score value of an event to each participant in it was heuristic. In future research some way of refining this procedure might be attempted. This issue is important whether cross-sectional or longitudinal studies of delinquents are undertaken.

The Generalizability of a Cohort

We have noted that longitudinal studies of birth cohorts have been strongly recommended as superior, for some purposes at least, to cross-sectional studies as means of acquiring a greater understanding of the circumstances and forces that condition delinquent conduct. Still, cohort research poses problems. The most interesting one is implied in Ryder's observation that

> the members of any cohort are entitled to participate in only one slice of life – their unique location in the stream of history. Because it embodies a temporally specific version of the [social] heritage, each cohort is differentiated from all others, despite the minimization of variability by symbolically perpetuated institutions and by hierarchically graduated structures of authority.[38]

38. Ryder, "Influence of Declining Mortality" (see n. 11 above), p. 844.

In other words, each cohort is unique, time-bound. As it passes through infancy, adolescence, youth, middle age, and declines to its ultimate extinction, its members are reared by their elders, go to school, get jobs, marry and raise families, retire and decay, not in isolation from other cohorts but in constant contacts and relationships with their members; and, because our society is not static, the impact of dynamic changes in social life undoubtedly differs from one cohort to another, especially when several years separate them.

How representative a single cohort may be for other, similar urban communities can only be conjectured. The criteria of geography, sex, age limits, and birth year would seem to be quite replicable items elsewhere, and with the same rationale employed as in the present study. Larger or smaller regions could be used to embrace a cohort, females could be added, 12 years or 16 years of age could replace the lower and upper age limits, and more recent birth years could readily be substituted. The requirement of residential stability over eight years' time might be more difficult to retain per se, but to retain it without heavy mortality of cases would be disturbing in some places where migration patterns are very different from those in Philadelphia. A shorter span of residence in the region would then be the only constraint on the criterion, but even so, intercity cohort comparisons could still be made on the reduced range of time.

Cohort subset comparisons, as, for example, delinquents with nondelinquents, on the basis of social, economic, and personality variables, may be representatively valid and reliable beyond the single cohort itself. Moreover, the career patterns of the delinquent group, the character of their delinquency, a probability model that forms a dynamic typology of movement from one stage to another – all of these empirical findings may be converted to conclusions for other cohorts. Minimally, every finding from the cohort used in this project has the posture of a hypothesis for testing on other cohorts elsewhere and at other times.

For some findings there is concordance with past research based on cross-sectional studies that have simply taken a group of delinquents of varying age at a specific moment and in a specific setting like an institution, child guidance clinic, or probationary period. But there are other findings that only a cohort analysis can yield, such as a cohort rate of delinquency, or delinquency seriatim by a group passing together through the same time period. The question to be raised is whether any probability figure derived from a cohort has any measure of generality beyond the cohort itself. If in accord with non-cohort studies, the findings would appear to have universality. If non-cohort studies either disagree with, or fail to contain data relevant to, cohort findings, generalizability may be in question until other cohorts are formed and analyzed.

For example, if in our cohort we were to find that boys from the lower socioeconomic class have a higher probability of becoming delinquent than do boys from the middle or upper classes, we should register no surprise, because this is a regularly confirmed finding in cross-sectional studies. However, if we were to find that, among those who have committed a first offense, the probability of committing a second is lower than is the probability among those who have committed a second offense of committing a third, and if we then described the probability of moving from an offense of violence to an acquisitive offense, we should have no firm knowledge, from cross-sectional studies, of how generalizable these findings were. Yet the absence of such knowledge does not deny the power of generalization, and other studies would be needed.

In short, findings from the present project must be treated with the usual caution of the scientific approach, and their empirical and theoretical transferability should be seen as a matter for further research. We present the results with the firm hope that other scholars will find value in the questions raised and hypotheses formed from a cohort analysis.

2 Capturing the Cohort

The cohort used in the present study is composed of all males born in 1945 who resided in the city of Philadelphia at least from their tenth until their eighteenth birthday.

Philadelphia has over two million inhabitants in the city proper and approximately five million in its metropolitan area. Social agencies of record – schools, police, courts, etc. – maintain a first-rate system of files. The police system of recording offenses has been recognized as one of the best in the country,[1] and since 1952 the Juvenile Aid Division has maintained a consistent and standardized style of describing, filing, and tabulating delinquencies.

Theoretically, a sample of a birth cohort could be drawn in the United States as a whole, in Pennsylvania, or in Philadelphia without the residence restriction. But even if such a sample were drawn, population mobility and the resultant variety of environmental exposure experienced by the cohort over time would make the understanding of delinquency patterns difficult. Moreover, record keeping for subjects in general, let alone police recordings of delinquency, would vary so much that comparisons would be virtually impossible. At the

1. For a full description of this system, see Sellin and Wolfgang, *The Measurement of Delinquency,* chapter 7.

least, so many cases would be lost because they could not be traced that the residue used for any kind of analysis would be unrepresentative of the originally drawn sample of the cohort.

We could have begun our search for a cohort by using birth registration data on all persons born in Philadelphia during a specified year. With an upper age limit for inclusion, and after accounting for infant and child mortality, we could have obtained a cohort that resided in the city a sufficient length of time to permit us to analyze its delinquency. However, using this approach to cohort selection, we would not have included juveniles born outside the city who moved in during early childhood. Aware of a considerable immigration, particularly of Negro families from the South, with residential instability within the city after arrival, we were unwilling to use a method of selection that would eliminate what we believed to be no small portion of the juvenile population capable of committing delinquent acts.

We sought a set of principles for cohort selection that would yield a large number of juveniles who were born during the same year and who lived within the Philadelphia community over a sufficiently long period to provide a cohort rate of delinquency. The Pennsylvania Juvenile Court Act establishes age limits to delinquency of 7 to 17 inclusive. The incidence of delinquency in the early years is known to be low, so that it was felt to be unnecessary to require residence in the city at age 7. Considering what is known of psychosexual stages of development, we could have justified the use of a minimum age of 12, but an examination of the cross-sectional age distribution of delinquents recorded by the Philadelphia police indicated that the largest leap in the rate occurs at age 10. We believed that few cases would be lost by setting our minimum age for inclusion at 10. Indeed, nearly all of our cohort members had started their schooling before reaching their seventh birthday; only 3.4 percent entered during their eighth, ninth, or tenth year of age.

The upper age limit for inclusion in the cohort was set by the juvenile court statute of the state. At age 18 a young person is no longer examined by the juvenile court, should he commit an act that is prohibited by criminal law. With this restraint, we early determined that the cohort was to be one that included subjects born in the same year and who lived in the city for at least eight years before reaching the age of 18.

The birth year of the cohort was dictated by several circumstances. Research on the project began in the fall of 1964. In order to have for prospective study a cohort that met the age criteria, the latest birth cohort reaching age 18 was the one born in 1945. A cohort that reached maturity nearest the year the research was begun had several advantages, the most important of which was recency of data files in the agencies to which we would necessarily turn for information. Whatever conclusions might emerge from the study would have currency and greatest transferability. Even if good records had been available back to the turn of the century, we still would have used the most recently matured cohort because of our interest in describing and explaining delinquency in the present culture. The availability of valid and reliable records over the years of our concern was a fortunate convenience, of course. As has been mentioned, the Juvenile Aid Division of the police department had a consistent record system dating from 1953, a year in which a 1945 birth cohort was 8 years of age, young enough to fall within our 10-year lower limit for the cohort. Reform in the record keeping system began in 1952, when the cohort was age 7, so that we could with confidence even go back that far for good data on delinquency. Finally, 1945 was the year during which the Second World War ended. Any social variables of significance to delinquency that may be due to wartime did not intervene directly in a cohort that grew up between 1945 and 1963.

The advantages of studying a cohort born at the time a research is initiated are obvious. If we knew in advance those whom we wanted to study, we could carefully keep records on all such subjects, control the transcription process, obtain more data relevant to a theoretical framework, and more easily select a sample for detailed analysis. Patience would be required, for we would have to wait for the cohort to grow up. We believe that samples of current birth cohorts might be drawn for various kinds of such types of prospective research. If a current crop of a matured cohort can be studied on a sufficient number of meaningful independent and dependent variables, and if the expected empirical yield may make new contributions to knowledge, including the applicability of social action, this kind of prospective research is worth doing.

The cohort used in our project was limited to males. If our primary focus had been on child-rearing practices, or marriage, then obviously females would have been equally relevant. But delinquency is predominantly a male phenomenon. Anywhere from five to ten times more males than females are involved in delinquency and crime. Recidivism, or persistent delinquency and adult crime, is more characteristic of males. Boys and men commit more serious violative behavior and acts that range over a larger spectrum than do girls and women. Thus, the greater incidence, frequency, heterogeneity, seriousness, and persistency of male delinquency have caused most criminological researchers to concentrate on the one sex and have justified, we believe, our own exclusion of females. If the variables and explanatory theories associated with male delinquents are different for female delinquents, exclusion of the latter is justified, for a separate study should then be done on a female cohort. If similar variables and theories are sometimes useful for understanding both male and female delinquency, the exclusion of females does not mean that conclusions derived from the present study have no applicability to a female cohort and to female delinquency.

The choice of specific lower and upper age limits has been explained; the reason for our requirement of sustained residence in the city between those limits needs further amplification. To be included in the project's cohort, a boy had to be resident in the city during the entire period from age 10 or earlier until age 18. Only by imposing this criterion could we be relatively sure of obtaining valid and consistently recorded information about any contact he may have had with the police over the entire span of eight years. A lad born in South Carolina who moved with his family to Philadelphia when he was 15 years of age could have committed a delinquent act before arriving in the city. Similarly, a boy born in Philadelphia who moved with his family to California when he was 15 years of age could commit delinquency after he left the city. Obtaining data on the presence or absence of delinquency for such boys would be an enormously difficult if not impossible task. School, police, and other records would be different in different locales, even if the information could be located. Moreover, the agents of response to deviance would be different in kind and degree, thus vitiating comparison. Even if our interest had been only in the delinquent subset of a cohort, the labor involved in collecting information on several thousand children would have been prohibitive. But it still would have been necessary to have determined whether a boy not in the city for the whole eight years was in fact delinquent or nondelinquent elsewhere. With the criterion of constant residence in Philadelphia between ages 10 and 18, all these methodological problems were eliminated.

Our data source for initial search for the cohort was the school records. This procedure meant that some sets of boys of unknown category size were not included in the final cohort used for analysis.

For example, we did not know how many boys born in Philadelphia left the city prior to entering the school system. We knew nothing about the size of this group, nor did it concern us. Some who were born elsewhere may have come to and left the city before reaching the compulsory age for starting school (6). We did know, on the other hand, how many had to be excluded from the cohort, among all boys, wherever they were born, who ever spent any time in the Philadelphia school system. Some boys born in Philadelphia may have lived in the city until age 14 and then moved away. We had data on these boys but excluded them from our cohort because they were not present until their juvenile court age ended at their eighteenth birthday.

The cohort that was present in the city had the same urban environment over a critical span of time, the same general set of culture forces, the same police, school, and other agencies of response to juvenile conduct. Obviously the ambience of each child is different, even with these macroenvironmental similarities. But many factors are conveniently held constant by this criterion. There may be some differential meaning to boys whose infant and early childhood years were experienced in a rural Southern (or Northern) community, compared to boys who were born and raised in the urban environment of Philadelphia. We cannot account for whatever influence these different backgrounds may have, but so few of the delinquents – and nondelinquents – in our cohort were not born in Philadelphia that any differences between those born in Philadelphia and those born outside the city were determined to be insignificant.

In the discussion thus far we have tried to explain why we sought a (male) cohort that was contained within a geographical and political area (Philadelphia), was present over a sustained duration of time (eight years) between specific ages (10 to 18) and was born in the same year (1945). These specifications, we believe, were reasonable for the task at hand and would be applicable, with perhaps minor modifications, in other places and other times. Exactly how the cohort was captured requires a full description because there are no precedents to which we can refer the reader.

Locating the Boys

Because we were looking at the biographies of boys who had reached their eighteenth birthday in 1963, we first thought that the starting point for our search should be that year. Boys who had not survived or who had moved away would not be part of the cohort anyway. We realized that no agency contained a set of files exactly fitting the defined parameters of the cohort we needed. Our first plan was based partly on the work of Christie, whose Norwegian study used military records, and partly on the knowledge that all males must register, under the Selective Service Act, with local authorities when they reach age 18. With permission from federal, state, and local military authorities, we were able to obtain a list by name and birth date of all registrants born in 1945, divided into those born in Philadelphia and those born elsewhere.

There were several limitations to this approach that caused us to seek another, although having the Selective Service list was still valuable, for against it we later checked names obtained elsewhere. A young man registers with the local draft board, which represents a designated district of the community where he resides. Even if he is de facto living out of state, a young man registers wherever his legal residence is located. Under these circumstances, he could have been out of the city for years, yet have registered in the city, and should not be included in the cohort. Moreover, a considerable number do not register with their local draft boards, but instead volunteer for service and sign up at recruiting stations anywhere. The draft boards do not check out all males in their districts to determine who has failed to register with them, and hence do not compare the volunteer list against a list of potential registrants. The burden of registration is placed on each person by the act; consequently, violators are discovered in many and diverse ways. It was evident, therefore, that some males who belonged to our cohort would not be captured by the net of the Selective Service list.

But it was also evident that many boys who were on this list would not belong to the cohort because they did not spend all their years from age 10 to age 18 in the city. The registration files afforded us no means to determine who entered the city after his tenth birthday. More specifically, the only information we were given permission to obtain was the registrant's name and specific date of birth. Thus, although we secured the list originally requested from Selective Service, we did not use it as a basis for deriving the cohort. As described below, the list was used as a device to check the terminal point at 18 of many in our cohort. The list later became a valuable means of identification but at the outset it could provide only those cases meant to comprise the cohort.

While the Selective Service Registration list was being compiled, we approached the Philadelphia Board of Education and obtained permission to use their files, which became our chief source for the cohort. The Philadelphia Public Schools maintain at the Board of Education building a central filing system. Records are kept on each pupil who ever spent any time, however short, in a public school in Philadelphia. An alphabetical file of all pupils can be found for each year of birth. Clearly, this filing system greatly facilitated our task.

Nonetheless, many problems remained. Our main reason for describing the more general ones is not to catalog the difficulties of data collection, for every research involving field investigation has its own peculiar problems, often of only parochial interest. Rather, our intention is to offer guidelines to other investigators who may be in search of a cohort containing similar definitional boundaries, particularly for delinquency research.

Depending on the governing authority, schools in Philadelphia are classified into three major types: (1) public, (2) parochial (Catholic), and (3) private. Throughout this volume we shall refer to the Catholic schools as parochial, for this is the common designation in the city. They are "private" in the sense that they are not currently supported by taxes and are not under the authority of public officials. The private schools are private in this same sense, but as a category for analysis they exclude Catholic schools. Private schools are great in number and variety, and they may be secular or nonsecular.

At the time this study began, the Philadelphia public school system comprised 251 schools: 200 elementary, 29 junior high, 3 senior–junior high, 3 technical high, and 16 senior high. During the school year 1963-64, the public schools had an enrollment of 261,515 full-time students. Philadelphia has a large parochial school population. Within the Roman Catholic archdiocese of Philadelphia there are 150 parishes, 137 of which maintain elementary schools with a total enrollment in 1963-64 of 118,875 students. In addition to the elementary schools, there are 8 senior and 5 junior high schools whose combined enrollment in 1963-64 was 35,784. No central governing body exists for the more than 50 private schools in Philadelphia, and the majority do not have facilities for high school students. In 1963-64, there were 15,627 students enrolled in private schools.

The following major steps in the field investigation were taken to collect the cohort:

The public school system's central file records of all males born in 1945 were xeroxed over a period of three months by four part-time research assistants. Once each year all the school records of those students who graduate or otherwise leave the public school system are placed in these central files. For most male students, a registration form (form EHV 1; see appendix A.1) provided all the information needed to determine whether a boy belonged or did not belong to the cohort, or whether further information was required before a designation could be made. Commonly attached to this form was a second form which gave additional confirming information about the student from grades one through six. In 1957 a third form (form EH 6; see appendix A.2) was introduced, which, added to the others, gave still further confirmation of residence in the city. In some cases, only a brief medical record or an identification card (form EH 62; see appendix A.3) was available, but both these records contained information about one or more schools attended by the student, and permitted a later check of files in the specific schools mentioned.

After the available information on each male born in 1945 had been procured from the central public school system files, a procedure was established for determining whether or not he should be assigned to the cohort. If he did not at once become part of the cohort, he was placed into one of two categories: (1) those boys for whom sufficient information existed to exclude them from the cohort; (2) those for whom further information was needed to make a definite decision.

Information on why each student was dismissed from the public school system made possible a relatively quick scanning of the record in order to determine his category. The main concern was whether he had been in the public school system at least from ages 10 through 17. If he had left the city, the community to which he went was usually indicated; if he had remained in the city but entered a parochial or private school, the specific school was usually indicated. This checking procedure became the most time-consuming phase of the entire data collection process.

After all available relevant information had been obtained from the central files of the Board of Education, our next task was that of collecting data from the parochial and private schools. Neither the Catholic nor the private schools maintain a central filing system, and it was therefore necessary to devise an efficient scheme that would obviate visits to the more than 200 schools in these two school systems. There were two groups of boys born in 1945 who required our searching the non-public school files: (1) those who had no record of ever having attended a public school and whose records therefore were not in our original file xeroxed at the Board of Education; (2) those who had a public school record that was incomplete because of one or more school-term enrollments in a parochial or private school. At this phase of operation, we limited our individual school visits to parochial and private high schools on the assumption that most of the boys in the two categories above who had resided in Philadelphia from their tenth to their eighteenth birthdays would have attended one of the parochial or private schools in the Philadelphia metropolitan area.

With permission from the archdiocese of Philadelphia, research assistants contacted each of the eight parochial senior high schools to examine their records. Unlike the public school system, whose files were arranged by birth year, the parochial school records were ordered alphabetically for all students who had attended a given school since its inception. To obtain the record of a boy who was born in 1945 it was necessary to search each school's entire set of files. A permanent record was kept on each student from the time he entered parochial school (form 1 – Permanent Record; see appendix A.4); and other forms similar to the records used in the public school system were commonly found for each parochial school student. In three of the eight Catholic high schools no information was available on the student's elementary school history if he had not been enrolled in public school during his elementary school years. Approximately 1,500 school records had to be checked later at the various parochial elementary schools in order to obtain the information needed to make a decision about inclusion in the cohort.

All the private schools were visited for the same reasons that parochial schools had been. Filing systems varied somewhat among the schools, and much time was consumed in traveling around the city, but eventually the necessary records were obtained from all schools.[2]

The next step was an examination of the records of the Juvenile Aid Division of the Police Department. This office has maintained since 1953 a Master Record File, which consists of a series of cards arranged alphabetically for all juveniles who have had a police con-

2. Except Girard College, which refused to cooperate. Despite the title, Girard College is an elementary school.

tact that resulted in a written report. The active file is composed of boys under age 18; the inactive file, of "over-age" boys, that is, of boys who were under 18 when they had a police contact but who since have reached their eighteenth birthday. The records of all boys whose year of birth was recorded as 1945 were photocopied. By using name, specific date of birth, address, race, and other identifying information, we were able to match a Master Record File card with a public, parochial, or private school record. There were records from the Juvenile Aid Division for which no school record could be found. They included: (a) boys born in 1945 whose residence was listed as being outside of Philadelphia and who would therefore have no school history in any of the Philadelphia school systems; (b) boys whose residence was listed as being in Philadelphia but for whom no school was indicated because they entered the city after the compulsory school age of 16 years. These two groups were, of course, excluded from the cohort.

At the end of this tedious task of collection, there were still some records from one or more original sources that were incomplete or that could not be collated. At this stage of the operation, the largest single group we possessed was boys who fitted our criteria for the cohort, but there were other sets of approximately 3,700 records that were classified as follows: incomplete public school records (700), incomplete parochial school records (2,000), incomplete private school records (300), unmatched records from the Juvenile Aid Division (700). Incomplete meant simply that we had insufficient information upon which to base a decision of inclusion in or exclusion from the defined cohort. The major reason for incompleteness of any of the school records was the transference of students into the public school system from either a parochial or private school, or vice versa. Most such movement was into the public school during the high school period. The 700 records from the Juvenile Aid Division were cases for which a school was marked on the delinquent's Master Record File card but whose name and record could not be collated with any school record in our possession at the time.

Addressing ourselves to these 3,700 incomplete records, we had first to visit all the high schools indicated on any of the records. In some cases not all forms from the public schools had been forwarded to the central file, although at least some record for each boy was present in the file. Next, we had to contact all elementary schools in each of the three school systems. For most boys with incomplete records some specific elementary school was mentioned. We decided to visit each elementary school that required our obtaining further information for twelve or more boys. For schools with fewer than twelve names, we devised a special questionnaire for the information needed, supplying on the form all the identifying data we possessed thus far – name, address, birth date, etc. Items like I.Q., school achievement level, etc. (which are discussed in the next chapter), were needed in order to complete the data collection process, although we were primarily concerned at this point with making certain that we had all the basic information needed to place a lad in or out of the cohort. A follow-up questionnaire, when needed, yielded sufficient information to make a decision on all but 55 subjects. The number was further reduced by additional personal visits or telephone calls to the schools.

Many of the incomplete records of boys originally secured from the Juvenile Aid Division were found to have inaccurate birth dates. Upon checking the 1944 and 1946 birth year files at the central file of the public school system, or by locating the name and other identifying data of the boy in a specific elementary or high school, we discovered some discrepancies. Because the schools indicate on their records the particular evidence they have for validating date of birth, and because in almost all cases this validation is the birth certificate, it was clear that a school's record of birth year was more accurate than that of the Juvenile Aid Division. Hence, for all boys with a police contact record whose date of birth was different from that on the school record, we accepted the school record. If the boy was recorded by the school as being born in any year other than 1945, he was eliminated from the cohort. There is, of course, an obvious reason for a boy 18 years of age to give a birth date year to the police that places him under the jurisdiction of the juvenile court. Not only does he have a chance of being given a remedial disposition by the police; he also has a chance, if arrested, of being disposed of by the juvenile court instead of by an adult criminal court.

The name and birth date of each boy not eliminated were checked against the Selective Service Registration list obtained from the 29 local draft boards in Philadelphia. This procedure provided additional confirmation of each boy's presence in the city at age 18, if he had left the school system either because he graduated before age 18 or because he obtained employment after reaching the end of the compulsory school age of 16.

In the end, only 31 subjects among the 14,313 investigated by our staff remained with incomplete records. Considering that this amazingly small number could in no way seriously affect the analysis of the cohort, we eliminated them. Our final cohort available for study numbered 9,945.

3 The Availability of Data

Considering the large size of our cohort and the time available, we had to be content with information recorded by the schools. Even there, some selection had to be made, partly to insure comparability, for all the school systems did not always record the same information. Had it been possible to read the boys' dossiers filed in the separate schools, additional data could have been found, no doubt, but this task was beyond our facilities. Therefore, we were limited to data entered on the termination cards of the public school system and to comparable items on the registration records of other schools.

Public School Records

For each boy, the public schools maintained two termination cards (see chapter 2 and appendixes A.1 and A.2). One could be called mainly an identification and school history card (registration card), the other a cumulative performance record. The former gave the name of the boy, his birth date, the nature of the evidence for that date,[1]

1. "Absolute correctness of this item is essential, for upon it are based the pupil's eligibility for admission to school and subsequent legal right to leave school. ... Documentary evidence of age ... should be one of the following ... in

race (white, Negro, other),[2] first names of parents and indication of whether they were living, name of stepparent or guardian, country of birth of each parent, and city and state where the boy was born, if in the United States. A dozen spaces were reserved for the home address or addresses of the boy. Several spaces were provided for recording date of admission or readmission and date of dismissal with indications of where the boy came from (whether he was a beginner or was transferred from some other school or source) and why he left, a later code being used to identify one of the many ways in which he might be removed from the rolls.[3] Numerous spaces were provided – 33 in all – for recording the date of entry into each grade the name of the homeroom teacher, and the name of the school, ending in most cases with the date of graduation from high school.

The cumulative record card gave performance data for each term of the first six years in school, twelve terms in all. Letter symbols (*S* or *U,* for satisfactory or unsatisfactory) or letter grades were entered for conduct (social habits, work habits, health habits) and for school subjects: arithmetic, art, language arts (separately for speaking, reading, written expression, spelling, handwriting), music, physical and health education, and social studies. The card also provided space for information on attendance already available on the registration card. Space was reserved for a column giving the enrollment record (date of entry and name of schools attended and the dates when psychological examinations were given).

One side of the record card presented, for the twelve terms mentioned, a graph showing the achievement level of the boy as revealed by a variety of tests, and scores received on intelligence tests.

Both cards were modified at some time during the period covered by the study, but the changes were chiefly concerned with the form and not with the substance of the data presented; they did not affect the specific information used in our study.

---

the order of preference: official birth certificate, baptismal certificate, passport, other documentary evidence." Office of the Superintendent of Schools, *Administrative Bulletin,* School District of Philadelphia, no. 15 (2 February 1953).

2. After 1954, race was not indicated, but, because all our boys entered school before 1956, this information was on record.

3. For example: enrolled elsewhere; sent to institution; entered armed forces; moved from city; over or under compulsory school age; employment certificate issued; deceased; mentally or physically incapacitated; migrant; runaway; etc.

Parochial and Private School Records

For information about boys who spent all or most of their time in parochial or private schools our sources yielded rather meager comparable data. The private schools, being completely independent of one another, had no uniform system of records on the boys. The eight parochial high schools for boys did have a standard "permanent record" card which contained some of the data found in the records of the public schools. If a boy received all his education in parochial schools, this record card was the only source of information, but, since a considerable number of boys transferred back and forth from parochial to public schools and quite often transferred to the latter for their junior and senior years, the public school records often supplied information which complemented that drawn from the parochial school's permanent record.

We had xerox copies made of the record cards from the public schools, but we devised a special form on which we entered data found in the files of the parochial and private schools. This form enabled us to record the name, race, and birth date of each boy; the first names of his parents; his and his parents' places of birth; the dates, types, and scores of intelligence tests given him; the schools he had attended and dates of entry; and his home address or addresses. Many items found on the "permanent record" card had no counterpart in the public school cards and were therefore ignored, and other items, listed by the public schools, were not found on the permanent record, especially data on achievement. As a result, in later analyses of the information coded and tabulated, some of our findings had to be restricted to the boys on whom we possessed requisite data from the public schools.

No reader will be surprised to learn that many of the record forms used in the various school systems were incompletely filled out.

Most entries on the school cards contained information such as names, addresses, grade placement, and interschool mobility. Two other types of entry recorded information derived from tests administered to the pupils to ascertain their I.Q. or their mastery of certain skills.

I.Q. Scores

The intelligence tests administered to the boys in school varied considerably from one system to another. Group tests predominated everywhere. Of the 8,700 boys (87.5 percent of 9,945) tested, at least 86 percent had been scored on group tests. The most common test in the public schools was the Philadelphia Verbal Ability Test, usually given during the second term of the second and sixth grades. The scores on this test were converted into standard I.Q. scores, which were recorded on the termination cards of 5,168 (79.8 percent) of the 6,472 boys in public school. For an additional 311 pupils (4.8 percent), scores were derived almost entirely from some of the Otis Mental Ability tests (Alpha, Beta, or Gamma Forms), the Wechsler-Bellevue test, the Wechsler Intelligence Scale for Children, or the Stanford-Binet test. No scores were recorded for 993 (15.3 percent) of the public school boys.

Scores were available for 3,138 (93.3 percent) of the 3,362 parochial school pupils, but the type of test was not indicated in 522 cases. Most of the rest (2,616 boys) had scores derived from one of the Otis tests (2,409, or 92 percent). No scores at all were available for 224 (6.7 percent). Of the 95 private school students, scores existed for all but 12 (12.6 percent). For 20, the type of test was not shown. For the remaining 63, about half had scores from Otis or Wechsler tests and the rest from any of eight different tests. Altogether, scores were available for 87.5 percent of all cohort members – for 89.1 percent of the nondelinquents and 84.7 percent of the delinquents.

Achievement Records

The public schools' termination cards noted the results of another series of tests given at different times during early years of attendance. These tests were designed to show the pupil's attainment of basic study and performance skills and whether his attainment was above or below or equal to what could be expected of a person for his age. The norm was determined from the verbal ability tests already mentioned and additional tests of ability to solve arithmetic problems. Tests of reading comprehension, ability to locate information, and map and graph reading revealed basic study skills; and tests of handwriting, spelling, knowledge of arithmetic fundamentals, and English usage showed the degree of basic performance skills achieved. Although the testing program of the schools continued into the junior and senior high school years, termination cards recorded the results only for the first six grades. The results were given by code letter on a diagonal line, which showed to what extent the test results deviated from the norm, if at all. No comparable information was available at the parochial or private schools.

Records of Police Contacts

The offense reports prepared by the officers of the Philadelphia Police Department's Juvenile Aid Division provided our data on the contact or contacts that cohort members had had with the police. Each report included the central complaint number assigned to the delinquent event; the complaint number assigned by the police district; the title of the offense involved in accord with the law; the code number applying to the offense according to a classification based on the Uniform Crime Reporting system, with subcategories of local importance; name, sex, age, race, nativity, address, telephone number, and occupation of complainant; the name of the person reporting the offense and his relationship to the complainant; the date and hour of the report of the offense; the name of the officer receiving the report; and how the report was received (in person, by mail or telephone, or through arrest on sight). Spaces were provided for recording the date and hour that the event occurred; the type of place of occurrence and the objective of the offense; the means used by the offender, such as force, fists, tools, weapons; whether a vehicle was used; and the name, age, race, and address of anyone taken into custody as offender or suspect.

The lower half of the report sheet gave a description of the event; information secured from the victim or others and from the offender or offenders; the date and nature of an offender's previous police contacts; losses or injuries sustained by the victim of the offense; and action taken by the investigating officer in the case, who would note whether the complaint was unfounded or founded, cleared by arrest or by remedial action, i.e., without detention, for juvenile court action; active, in cases where further investigation was needed, or inactive, in cases where the investigation of a reported event had reached a dead end, at least temporarily.

If the juvenile involved was not dismissed by the police, but arrested and taken to the Youth Study Center for action by the juvenile court authorities, the police kept in contact with the case long enough to record what action was taken by the intake service of the center or by the judge. This information was recorded on the folder containing the offense report and enabled us to determine whether the juvenile was dismissed by the intake service or discharged, placed on probation or sent to an institution by the court.

The offense reports, filed by calendar year, police district number, and crime code classification were hidden in the enormous files of offense reports which Juvenile Aid Division had assembled during

1952–63. It was not difficult, however, to locate them, remove them, and place them in the folder we had established for each boy in the cohort, which contained his school reports, because the Juvenile Aid Division had a master card, filed alphabetically by name, for each juvenile who had had any contact with the police. This card was retained in an active file until the person reached his eighteenth birthday, and on it were entered the date of the offense report, the title of the offense involved, the district number assigned to the case, and the date and type of disposition by arrest or other action. The card also carried the name, nickname, race, sex, birth date, and address of the juvenile, the first names of parents, and the names of the school and church attended. These data made it possible to identify a cohort boy with a police record and to subtract from the files of offense reports the ones with district numbers noted on the master card. In many cases, too, the master file card helped to establish the presence in the city of boys who had dropped out of school at age 16, if they had secured an employment certificate, for instance.

Evaluating the Seriousness of Delinquent Events

Much of our research was centered on four questions: when the delinquency of a cohort boy first brought him to the attention of the police; whether he desisted from or persisted in committing further delinquent acts; the extent of harm inflicted to the community by his misdeeds; and whether, as he grew older, the harmfulness of his delinquencies increased or decreased.

In order to evaluate the seriousness of a delinquent act we needed a measuring tool. The offense reports of the police furnished us with the legal title of each offense (burglary, larceny, malicious mischief, etc.) as defined in the Pennsylvania criminal code, and one might assume that these labels would suffice to indicate, both accurately and adequately, the relative seriousness of the acts they designated. But there were two reasons why they could not do so: (1) The same legal label is given to uncomplicated offenses which vary greatly in degree of seriousness; "larceny" could mean the theft of a dollar or of thousands of dollars, and "robbery" could mean an armed holdup by a gang of the proprietor of a store or the taking by force of a few pennies from a young boy by an older and stronger schoolmate. (2) The legal label attached to the offense report designates only the most serious of the offenses that may concur in a given event. Operationally, the Uniform Crime Reporting Classification of offenses requires that, in case of the concurrence of two or more offenses, the degree of seriousness be determined by the rank of the offense in an ordered list of offenses. If the most serious component of a complex event were "aggravated assault," the event would be so labeled even though the assault were an incidental part of the burglarizing of a store and the theft of valuable property, because, in the list mentioned, aggravated assault ranks higher than burglary and theft. Consequently, these "lesser" components of the event would be given no weight in the assessment of the event's seriousness.

It is obvious then that if the delinquency of the members of a birth cohort were to be analyzed only on the basis of the legal labels attached to delinquent events by the police, an incomplete picture would emerge. In order to sharpen that picture, we have had recourse to a technique which we used in our earlier research on the measurement of delinquency. In that research we developed a system of evaluating the comparative seriousness of a delinquent *event,* whether simple or complex.

The procedure we used to secure the basic information required to assess the seriousness of a delinquent event, taking into account its various components and assigning weights to them so that the total event could be given a single numerical score value, has been described elsewhere in detail.[4] Briefly, a series of attitude tests which scaled 141 different offensive events was given to 748 university students, police officers, and juvenile court judges. All events were described objectively without reference to their legal labels. These descriptions were so couched that the maximum number of conceivably objective features of events could be taken note of in different combinations. The results of the tests enabled us to assign differential weights or score values to single events and to the components of complex ones, and to develop a score card that could be used to score any single event.

The score card exhibits two fundamental features. First, it fails to indicate what *legally defined* offense is involved. Second, it involves only events which produced some injury to a victim and/or some loss of or damage to property. Restricting the events to those resulting in such injury or damage was done because the object of

4. Sellin and Wolfgang, *The Measurement of Delinquency,* chaps. 10, 15–17, and appendixes; Sellin and Wolfgang, *Constructing an Index of Delinquency: A Manual* (Philadelphia: Center of Criminological Research, October 1963).

our research at the time was to develop a new index of delinquency. We had adequate reasons for assuming that offenses of these types were the only ones on which such an index could be based. Because we focused on the objective harm to persons and property – and hence to the chief social values of the community – we were less concerned with what name the law gave to the offensive act.

In the testing and scaling procedure on which our scoring of delinquent *index events* was based, we had covered the gamut of delinquency from running away from home to homicide. For the purpose of the present study, which has an aim different from our prior research, we have extended our scoring system to include *nonindex events* in which our cohort boys figured as sole offenders or as participants.

In developing the original scores we had several series of test results to choose from, all highly intercorrelated, whether derived from tests given to students, police, or judges. We selected one series because it contained the fewest internal inconsistencies in judgments. That series comprised magnitude ratio tests given to 82 students at the Ogontz Center of Pennsylvania State University, supplemented by similar but partial tests administered to 195 students at the University of Pennsylvania.

The extension of the scoring system to nonindex events is based upon the logarithmic relationship between the Ogontz mean raw magnitude ratio scores[5] and the set of scores as finally derived for the index of delinquency.[6] The various offense descriptions[7] were analyzed according to the injury, theft, and damage categories and were scored following the scaling system. Thus a set of values was generated using the offense descriptions as source data.

This set of generated values was then entered as the Y component in the regression equation for a power function, $Y = aX^b$, where the Ogontz raw scores formed the X component. The resulting relationship, $\log Y = 1.2117 + 0.9308 \log X$, enabled the assigning of an "extended" score to those offense types which did not involve injury, theft, or damage.[8] All extended values were multiplied by 100 so that decimals would be eliminated, as were all scores which did have elements of injury, theft, or damage.

5. See *The Measurement of Delinquency,* pp. 393–94.
6. Ibid., p. 402.
7. Ibid., pp. 381–86.
8. See appendix B for derived scores.

Thus, by using the Ogontz raw scores for nonindex offenses, an expected score can be computed which is on the same regression line as the values associated with index offenses.

Socioeconomic Data

One object of our study was to investigate the relationship between socioeconomic factors and the delinquency of the cohort. The information available from the schools did not include data on, for instance, the occupation of the father or the income of specific families, but we did know where the boys lived and could therefore locate their homes in appropriate census tracts. Information on the tracts enabled us to score each cohort member in one of several broad socioeconomic groups depending on the median income of families living in his home tract. The choice of this indicator of socioeconomic status was made for the following reasons.

A search of the literature on stratification revealed that in 1964 the Community Renewal Program of the City of Philadelphia (CRP)[9] had developed a socioeconomic status index based on four factors related to housing quality, overcrowding, occupation, and family income.[10] The factors were chosen from a list of thirteen census variables initially used to obtain decile rankings for each Philadelphia census tract listed in the 1950 and 1960 censuses. The CRP staff found that the four factors clearly differentiated the same homogeneous areas selected for residential treatment by an extensive field survey conducted in 1962–64 involving interviews of residents in West Philadelphia.[11] The factors were used subsequently by the CRP staff to isolate socioeconomic areas in Philadelphia that might benefit most from public intervention and urban renewal programs.

Inspection of the distribution of values for the four factors by census tract indicated that income was highly correlated with housing quality, overcrowding, and occupation. Pearson correlation coefficients were computed, and the following relationships emerged:

9. *City of Philadelphia Community Renewal Program Technical Report*, no. 12 (October 1964).

10. The four operational variables were: percentage of housing units sound with all facilities; percentage of housing with 1.01 or more persons per room; number of blue collar employees to every 100 white collar employees; and median family income. Ibid., p. 2.

11. Ibid., p. 1.

1. Income and blue/white collar ratio, $r = -.8143$
2. Income and overcrowding, $r = -.8655$
3. Income and percentage of housing units sound, with all facilities, $r = .8105$

The associations were sufficiently high – even the lowest correlation coefficient of $r = .8105$ between income and percentage of housing units sound with all facilities explained 65 percent of the total variance – that income alone might effectively be employed as an efficient indicator of socioeconomic status.

Research based upon data for the entire nation also has indicated that median income is highly correlated with variables comprising socioeconomic status indices and is adequate for stratifying a population of individuals. Reiss, for instance, has shown that the rank correlation (Kendall's tau) of weighted NORC (National Opinion Research Center) prestige scores for an occupation with median level of income in 1950 was .85. A similar rank correlation of prestige scores with median level of educational attainment produced a value of .83. Income therefore explained approximately 72 percent of the variance in prestige scores as compared to 69 percent by educational attainment.[12]

Similarly, Duncan has shown that when an age adjustment was introduced, income and education for 45 occupational categories appearing in both the NORC list and the census were correlated ($r = .72$).[13] Moreover, Warner has demonstrated that income and occupation produced an $r = .87$, while education and occupation gave only .77.[14]

The high correlation between median income and other variables measuring socioeconomic status found by Reiss, Duncan, and Warner, together with the strong associations resulting from our computations based upon tract values in the 1960 census, convinced us that median family income would be the most adequate and efficient single variable for classifying cohort subjects into broad socioeconomic categories.

Determination of Socioeconomic Categories

The problem of designating specified categories of socioeconomic status inevitably arises when income is employed as the single meas-

12. Albert J. Reiss, *Occupations and Social Status* (New York: The Free Press of Glencoe, 1961), p. 84.

13. Ibid., p. 124.

14. W. Lloyd Warner, et al., *Social Class in America* (Chicago: Science Research Associates, 1949), table 13, p. 172.

ure comprising the index. Almost any cutting points that might be used are to some degree arbitrary, and the specific needs of the research must be kept in mind. The dividing points finally employed in this research emerged after a number of alternative plans were explored.

First, the twelve "planning analysis sections" established by the Philadelphia City Planning Commission in the late 1940s were examined.[15] Each section contains a number of census tracts that roughly correspond to general socioeconomic divisions existing within the city. The boundaries of the statistical areas have remained constant over the years except for some minor adjustments.

Examination of the criteria determining the boundaries of the subsections revealed these criteria to be intuitively rather than empirically derived. For reasons of expediency a large number of census tracts in geographical proximity to one another were grouped together with natural but nevertheless artificial divisions serving as boundaries. Analysis of the boundaries circumscribing subsection B (South Philadelphia), for instance, revealed that it is bordered by South Street to the North, the Delaware River on the south and east, and the Schuylkill River on the west. Needless to say, the heterogeneity of census tracts within this subsection, as well as in the others is enormous, and to designate subsection B as an area of homogeneous socioeconomic characteristics is unjustifiable.

An alternative to the "planning analysis sections" was the quartiles developed by the United States Department of Labor, Bureau of Labor Statistics.[16] On the basis of general levels of income, educational attainment, and unemployment as reported by the 1960 census, cities with populations of 500,000 or more inhabitants were divided into quartiles. Census tracts for Philadelphia were assigned to the appropriate quartile depending upon their socioeconomic values. Although the quartile method is convenient and at the same time employs three variables for a composite measure of socioeconomic status, the divisions it creates lack theoretical meaning. Moreover, it is well known that socioeconomic areas or tracts most likely to fall into the lowest quartile are relatively deprived and usually contain a disproportionate representation of delinquents. For the purposes

15. *Trends in Population, Housing, and Socio-Economic Characteristics* (Philadelphia Planning Analysis Sections. City of Philadelphia Community Renewal Program), 1963.

16. *Income, Education, and Unemployment* (U.S. Department of Labor, Bureau of Labor Statistics, January 1963).

of this research, a plan that assigns 25 percent of the census tracts of lowest socioeconomic status into one category is too encompassing to discriminate adequately among tracts in high-delinquency areas.

Because the dividing points established by each of these methods either lacked a substantive rationale or encompassed areas too broad to discriminate adequately among tracts within such areas, we attempted to establish our own cutting points.

The Federal Bureau of Labor Statistics and the United States Department of Health, Education, and Welfare had issued a series of reports pertaining to general income and welfare levels for various cities in the United States, including Philadelphia.[17] Families of four (working father, mother at home, and two children) whose income was between $3,000 and $4,500 were considered to be living in poverty. The report maintained that families with this minimum level of income could barely subsist and certainly could not afford major medical or other expenses. Similar levels of poverty had been established by other research endeavors. The Conference on Economic Progress, for instance, in a 1962 study entitled "Poverty and Deprivation in the U.S.," used the figure of $4,000 as the minimum income required by a family to subsist.[18]

Our own research identified each census tract in Philadelphia whose median level of family income was below the subsistence level of $4,500. For purposes of maximum discrimination of socioeconomic status within deprived areas these census tracts were further divided into those with a median family income below $4,000 and those with a median income of $4,001–$4,500. Thirty-five or 10.09 percent of the tracts fell into the below-$4,000 category, and 6.05 percent fell into the $4,001–$4,500 category.

Once the limits of the lowest socioeconomic status categories were established, the median income in Philadelphia of all families and unrelated individuals ($5,783) was selected as the boundary for the next highest category.[19]

The figure of $6,779 as the lower limit of the highest category was selected after consideration of a study of the United States De-

17. *Fact Book on Poverty* (Research Department, Health, Education, and Welfare Council, Special Report series no. 23, 1964).

18. Leon H. Keyserling, *Progress or Poverty,* Conference on Economic Progress (Washington, D.C., December 1964).

19. *U.S. Census of Population 1960,* Pennsylvania Detailed Characteristics, Bureau of the Census Final Report PC(1)-40D.

partment of Labor's Bureau of Labor Statistics.[20] As part of a nationwide inquiry of consumer expenditures in urban places the bureau surveyed families and single consumers living in Philadelphia and its environs. The survey was specifically designed to provide data on expenditure patterns in urban areas, particularly for purposes of economic policy, marketing, and academic research.[21] Employing a three-stage sample design, the survey selected 313 families representative of the population residing in the Philadelphia metropolitan area. Analysis of the data revealed that, during the survey year 1960, the average total money income per family before taxes (of all family members from wages and salaries), after deduction for occupational expenses,[22] was $6,779.[23] Further examination of expenditures for current consumption showed that this income was sufficient for medical care, recreation, gifts and contributions, as well as for the necessities of food, shelter, and clothing. In short, the average family residing in Philadelphia was able to maintain a respectable standard of living on $6,779.

Other studies focusing upon living standards for the entire nation report similar figures for modest yet comfortable existence. Keyserling,[24] for instance, constructed socioeconomic status categories derived from data in a 1959 study conducted by the Department of Labor in twenty cities and their suburbs. After converting the 1959 expenditure value into 1962 dollars, he showed that the average income requirement for a "modest but adequate" budget on the current American scene for families of six or more ranged from $6,216 to $9,603.[25] Thus Keyserling designated $6,999 as the upper cutting point between comfort and affluence. This national level is approximately equal to the Philadelphia value of $6,799 reported by the United States Department of Labor.

In sum, our review of the literature resulted in five mutually exclusive socioeconomic status categories.

20. *Consumer Expenditures and Income; Philadelphia, Pennsylvania: 1960–61* (U.S. Department of Labor, Bureau of Labor Statistics BLS-Report no. 237 58, March 1964).

21. Ibid., p. 16.

22. Occupational expenses include such items as tools, special required equipment, union dues, etc. Ibid., p. 5.

23. Ibid., p. 2.

24. Keyserling, *Progress or Poverty*, pp. 15–16.

25. Ibid., p. 11.

I. Below $4,000: poverty
II. $4,001–$4,500: deprivation
III. $4,501–$5,783: semideprivation
IV. $5,784–$6,799: modest but adequate
V. Above $6,799: comfort

Classifying the Cohort

The first and the last census tracts in which each subject in our cohort had resided were determined. The first corresponds to the address at which the subject lived when he initially entered the Philadelphia school system, usually between 1950 and 1952. The last corresponds to the final address entry on any of his data cards.

We used the last address of each subject to determine socioeconomic status because it was at this residence that he was most likely to have performed his delinquent acts. Each address was converted to the appropriate census tract through the use of an alphabetical listing of addresses by census tract. The median family income for the particular census tract was obtained from the 1960 census, and the subject was assigned to the appropriate socioeconomic category.

4 Delinquents and Nondelinquents: School and Social Background Variables

In this and subsequent chapters we shall refer to cohort *subjects* when we mean all boys included in this study, and to cohort *delinquents* when we mean those of the cohort subjects who had a recorded police contact during their juvenile court age from 7 to 18.

In much of the discussion that follows we shall refer to incidence and frequency statistics. The accompanying rates, which express a kind of predictive probability, have two bases: (1) the total 9,945 subjects, used as denominator, and (2) subsets of these subjects, that is, delinquent and nondelinquent groups.

Where the availability of data permits, we have been able to develop further our examination of some background variables by the addition of the socioeconomic status (SES) of delinquents, nondelinquents, whites, and nonwhites. We described in chapter 3 the operational definitions of SES and the method of obtaining the data. For most of the discussion in this chapter we have collapsed the five SES categories into lower SES (I, II, and III) and higher SES (IV and V) to simplify the treatment, because the more refined distinctions among the five categories were minimal and cell size in the upper categories was often small.

The data in this chapter and the next are presented in what we call a static form because they describe the cohort as an aggregate without movement through time. We shall describe the subjects as sets of configurational collectivities, that is, how nondelinquents compare with delinquents, and how certain types of delinquents compare with other types. In later chapters we shall develop a dynamic model of cohort offensive behavior in which we shall analyze in what proportion, how, when, and in what direction boys move through time as delinquents, and when they desist from further delinquency.

Delinquents and Nondelinquents by Race and SES

Of the 9,945 cohort subjects, 6,470 or 65 percent were nondelinquents, while 3,475 or 35 percent had at least one contact with the police at some time over the span of their juvenile court age. Of all cohort subjects, 2,902 were nonwhite and the remaining 7,043 were white. Of the nonwhites, 1,458 or 50.24 percent were delinquent; of the white cohort subjects, 2,017 or 28.64 percent were delinquent.

The high proportion of delinquents among the nonwhite cohort can be further analyzed by considering jointly race and socioeconomic status (table 4.1). Of the total 1,458 nonwhite delinquents, 1,293 or 88.7 percent belong to the lower socioeconomic status (compared to 763 or 37.8 percent of the white delinquents falling in the same category). It should be noted, however, that the concentration of the total nonwhite group, whether delinquent or nondelinquent, occurs in the lower SES (84.2 percent), whereas only 30.8 percent of the white group are in this SES level, regardless of delinquency status. Of the 458 higher SES nonwhites, 165 or 36 percent are delinquent compared to 1,254 or 25.6 percent among the white higher SES category. Also, of the total nonwhite lower SES subjects, 52.9 percent are delinquents, compared to only 35.6 percent in the corresponding white lower SES category. These findings indicate that race is strongly related to delinquency status regardless of SES level.

The higher proportion of nonwhite delinquents, whether in the lower or the higher SES level, constitutes one of the major statistical dichotomies running throughout the analysis of the cohort. In this static descriptive model and the subsequently discussed dynamic model no other variable emerged quite so clearly as did race as a determinant of contrast.

TABLE 4.1

Number and Percentage of Delinquents and Nondelinquents by Race and SES

	Delinquents			Nondelinquents			Total		
	N	%	%[a]	*N*	%	%[a]	*N*	%	%
White:									
Lower SES	763	37.83	(35.65)	1377	27.40	(64.35)	2140	30.38	(100.00)
Higher SES	1254	62.17	(25.58)	3649	72.60	(74.42)	4903	69.62	(100.00)
Total	2017	100.00	(28.64)	5026	100.00	(71.36)	7043	100.00	(100.00)
Nonwhite:									
Lower SES	1293	88.68	(52.91)	1151	79.71	(47.09)	2444	84.22	(100.00)
Higher SES	165	11.32	(36.03)	293	20.29	(63.97)	458	15.78	(100.00)
Total	1458	100.00	(50.24)	1444	100.00	(49.76)	2902	100.00	(100.00)
Grand Total	3475		(34.94)	6470		(65.06)	9945		(100.00)

[a]Percentage across within each row category.

Place of Birth

By region and size of birthplace, 82 percent of the cohort (81.5% delinquents and 82.5% nondelinquents) were born in Philadelphia. Almost twice as many delinquents (6.1%) as nondelinquents (3.5%) were born in Southern states. The proportion of subjects born in other regions of the United States or outside the country (1.3% delinquents; 1.5% nondelinquents) is too small to be of significance for further analysis.[1]

Approximately 85 percent of the cohort parents were born in this country; only 7.2 percent of the fathers and 5.2 percent of the mothers were foreign born. Finally, a slightly larger proportion of nondelinquents than delinquents had at least one parent of foreign extraction (father or mother of nondelinquents, 8.5% and 6.0% respectively, compared to 4.8% and 3.9% for delinquents). The data on place of birth provide little analytic yield. Even where differences between delinquents and nondelinquents occur, the absolute numbers are so small as to provide little basis for any comment. The fact that similar proportions of delinquents and nondelinquents (about 82%) were born in Philadelphia and in such high numbers permits our dispensing of place of birth in further treatment of the data.

TABLE 4.2

Mean Number of Residential Addresses for Nondelinquents and Delinquents by Race and SES[a]

	Lower SES		Higher SES		Total	
	$\bar{X}$	N	$\bar{X}$	N	$\bar{X}$	N
Nondelinquents:						
Nonwhite	3.04	1,147	2.61	289	2.95	1,436
White	1.78	1,376	1.71	3,641	1.73	5,017
Total	2.35	2,523	1.78	3,930	2.00	6,453
Delinquents:						
Nonwhite	3.64	1,291	3.38	165	3.61	1,456
White	2.32	761	1.87	1,252	2.04	2,013
Total	3.15	2,052	2.04	1,417	2.70	3,469

[a]In some tables the total N does not equal 9,945 because certain items were missing in the school records.

1. The reader is referred to: William R. Odell, *Educational Survey Report for the Philadelphia Board of Education* (Philadelphia: Board of Public Education, 1965), for a general discussion of place of birth and some of the other school variables examined in this chapter.

Types of Schools Attended

Most children enter some form of school between the ages of four and six. For the cohort, this implies entry between the years 1949 and 1951, and 92 percent entered the Philadelphia school system during those years. In general, nondelinquents entered the Philadelphia schools only slightly sooner than the delinquents. The majority of those who entered the system after 1951 were those who came to Philadelphia from a school system outside the city.

For the entire cohort, 96 percent had their first school experience in Philadelphia: 97 percent of the nondelinquents and 92 percent of the delinquents. Fewer than 1 percent (0.3%) of the cohort subjects began school outside the continental United States. Approximately 3 percent of the delinquents and 5 percent of the nondelinquents began their school career in this country but outside the city.

A greater proportion of delinquents than of nondelinquents spent the *major* part of their school years in public schools (72% and 62%). Contrariwise, fewer delinquents (25%) than nondelinquents (37%) had most of their formal education in parochial or private institutions. The proportion of nondelinquents in various types of educational institutions (public, private, disciplinary, etc.) remained constant throughout their progression from elementary to senior status. Eighty-two percent of the cohort attended public school at some time. A large proportion (38%) attended parochial school at some time. More than twice as many nondelinquents (5.67%) as delinquents (2.79%) had ever attended private institutions.

The percentage of delinquents designated as having a disciplinary status increased from elementary to senior high school (elementary: 0.1%; junior: 1.0%; senior: 4.1%). Thus, by the time the delinquents reached their senior year, at least 4 percent of them, compared to only 1 percent of the nondelinquents, obtained some part of their education in a public disciplinary institution. The increase reflects the peak age of delinquency proneness for juveniles and corresponds to the span of years most students attend senior high school.

The bulk of the cohort subjects (93%) were not sent to disciplinary schools or to juvenile reformatories. Of the 7 percent who were, 3.4 percent attended one or more of the public educational system's disciplinary schools (Boone, Shallcross, Catto, and City Center), and an even smaller proportion (2.5%) were institutionalized. Only 1.3 percent experienced both disciplinary and correctional school training. As expected, there is a considerable difference between delinquents and nondelinquents enrolled in these schools, for over 12 percent of the delinquents and only slightly more than 2 percent of the nondelinquents were so enrolled. Eighty-eight nondelinquents sent to juvenile institutions were disposed of by juvenile courts on private petition as dependent, neglect, or incorrigible cases but did not acquire a juvenile arrest record.

From school records, information was also obtained on the number of cohort subjects designated as retarded or physically handicapped. The categories are not mutually exclusive, but indicate that there is no significant difference in the proportion of delinquents and nondelinquents among the physically handicapped. There were 143 subjects (1.4%) who were in some way physically handicapped, and 635 (6.4%) who were retarded. (Some of the 143 handicapped are included in the 635 retarded.) Nearly twice as many delinquents (9.4%) as nondelinquents (4.5%) had a retardation status. The small numbers involved in these two categories of handicapped precludes further treatment.

Residential and School Moves

Using the dichotomy of race as a basis of comparison we find that nonwhite families in the cohort moved 1.8 as many times, on the average, as white families, regardless of delinquency status and SES level (respectively, $\overline{X} = 3.3$ and $\overline{X} = 1.9$). Considering jointly the variables of race and delinquency (table 4.2) we find that the greatest mobility occurs among racial and delinquency status groups. Families of nonwhites and of delinquents made more moves on the average than did families of whites and of nondelinquents. Families of white nondelinquents made 2.0 moves on the average, whereas the nonwhite delinquents' families moved an average of 3.6 times. But even nonwhite nondelinquents ($\overline{X} = 3.0$) moved more often than did the white delinquents ($\overline{X} = 2.0$), thus indicating that nonwhite intracity migration rates are higher than white rates, regardless of the delinquency status of the children.

Over the school age span of the cohort, about twice as many delinquents' families as nondelinquents' families, 40 and 20 percent respectively, moved more than twice. At every mean number of address changes above two, delinquents are represented in higher proportion than nondelinquents. At the extreme of intracity mobility, 67 delinquents, but only 35 nondelinquents, changed address nine or more times. However, delinquency status as a variable of contrast produces the least difference in mean moves (0.7) in comparison to the variables of race or SES. The mean number of moves for the total delinquents in the cohort, holding the other two variables constant, is 2.7, while it is 2.0 for the nondelinquents. When race is employed as the statistical dichotomizer, the difference in the average moves of whites and nonwhites is larger.

Second in importance to race as a variable of contrast is SES level. The higher SES boys made fewer residential moves. Lower SES families made 2.70 moves on the average, compared to 1.87 moves in the higher SES level, regardless of race or delinquency status.

Among lower SES boys, whether white or nonwhite, nondelinquents moved less frequently ($\bar{X}$ moves = 2.35) than did delinquents ($\bar{X}$ = 3.15). However, as table 4.2 indicates, nonwhite nondelinquents in the higher SES moved more often ($\bar{X}$ = 2.61) than did white delinquents in the lower SES ($\bar{X}$ = 2.32).

To conclude, among the variables considered in table 4.2, the race differential produces the most variant values and thus appears to be more importantly related to mobility than delinquency status or SES level. Nonetheless, when race, socioeconomic status, and delinquency status are considered, residential mobility is inversely related to socioeconomic status and the relation is higher for delinquents, regardless of age.

The number of residential moves is reflected in the number of school changes. Even if a boy's family makes no move during his school years, he normally passes through three district schools from elementary to junior high to senior high school. But he could, without a residential change, also go from parochial or private school to public school, then back to parochial or private school. The school movement potentials can be considerably varied, of course, but there is, in the aggregate, much stability. Usually, a large number of school moves reflects residential changes, and/or school changes required by the school system.

The largest number of school moves is made by nonwhite delinquents ($\bar{X}$ = 4.90) and the smallest number is made by white nondelinquents ($\bar{X}$ = 3.21) regardless of SES (table 4.3). Race rather than delinquency is more directly related to the number of school changes, for all nonwhite boys in the cohort move somewhat more than four times – again regardless of delinquency status or SES level. Even lower SES white delinquents ($\bar{X}$ = 3.76) change schools less frequently than nonwhite higher SES nondelinquents ($\bar{X}$ = 4.09).

TABLE 4.3

Mean Number of School Moves
for Nondelinquents and Delinquents by Race and SES

	Lower SES		Higher SES		Total	
	$\bar{X}$	N	$\bar{X}$	N	$\bar{X}$	N
Nondelinquents:						
Nonwhite	4.42	1151	4.09	293	4.35	1444
White	3.21	1377	3.21	3649	3.21	5026
Total	3.76	2528	3.27	3942	3.46	6470
Delinquents:						
Nonwhite	4.89	1293	4.94	165	4.90	1458
White	3.76	762	3.55	1252	3.63	2016
Total	4.42	2055	3.72	1419	4.16	3474

If there is any disadvantage to frequent residential and school changes, nonwhites experience this disadvantage more frequently than do whites. We have no data on the effect of such residential instability, but our findings do show that, within each racial group, delinquents' families move more often than nondelinquents' families.

Highest School Grade

Virtually the same race, SES, and delinquency status patterns occur with respect to the highest school grade completed. That is, white nondelinquents are more likely to have attained a higher grade, especially those in the higher SES ($\bar{X}$ = 11.67), while the opposite is true of nonwhite delinquents, especially those in the lower SES ($\bar{X}$ = 8.92). The message here is neither new nor surprising. But once again the most comfortable set of nonwhites – nondelinquents in the higher SES – attain an average completed grade ($\bar{X}$ = 10.48) that is about the same as that of the worst positioned white delinquent ($\bar{X}$ = 10.10) in the lower SES, and lower than that of white delinquents in the same SES ($\bar{X}$ = 10.94). If SES is held constant, nonwhites average about one grade lower than whites.

Nearly 80 percent of the white boys completed twelfth grade, but half this amount, or only 42 percent, of the nonwhite boys did. Nondelinquents come close to completing the twelfth grade ($\bar{X}$ = 11.24) and attained on the average an additional year over the delinquents ($\bar{X}$ = 9.96). But more white delinquents (57%) finished twelfth grade

TABLE 4.4

Mean Highest School Grade Completed for Nondelinquents and Delinquents by Race and SES

	Lower SES		Higher SES		Total	
	X̄	*N*	X̄	*N*	X̄	*N*
Nondelinquents:						
Nonwhite	9.92	1005	10.48	263	10.04	1268
White	11.26	1284	11.67	3481	11.56	4765
Total	10.67	2289	11.59	3744	11.24	6033
Delinquents:						
Nonwhite	8.92	1103	9.65	139	9.00	1242
White	10.10	649	10.94	1138	10.63	1787
Total	9.36	1752	10.79	1277	9.96	3029

than did nonwhite delinquents (54%). Fewer nonwhite delinquents finished twelfth grade (29%) than did any of the other delinquency status specific groups, and nonwhite delinquents have the lowest mean number of grades completed, especially in the lower SES group (8.92).

I.Q. and Achievement Level

As table 4.5 indicates, the average I.Q. for nondelinquents is 107.87, and for delinquents, 100.95. By dividing the cohort into race, SES and delinquency status, we find the same pattern as we did with respect to the previous variables: namely, that the lower SES, delinquent whites have a higher mean I.Q. score (101.87) than the higher SES, nondelinquent nonwhites (100.26). The lowest mean I.Q. score is found among nonwhite delinquents in the lower SES (93.84). The biggest difference between the races is that between white high SES nondelinquent and nonwhite low SES delinquent – 17.55 points. If we disregard the variables of delinquency status and SES level, however, this difference between the races decreases to 13.28 points. The racial difference is still the highest compared to the difference in mean I.Q. score between total delinquents and nondelinquents, holding SES and race constant (6.92), or the difference between total high SES and low SES subjects, holding delinquency status and race constant (9.22). Race appears then as the most important variable of dichotomization yielding the highest variant values. SES level stands second in importance, followed by delinquency status.

TABLE 4.5

Mean I.Q. Scores for Nondelinquents and Delinquents by Race and SES

	Lower SES		Higher SES		Total	
	$\bar{X}$	N	$\bar{X}$	N	$\bar{X}$	N
Nondelinquents:						
Nonwhite	97.04	892	100.26	229	97.70	1121
White	107.45	1239	111.39	3391	110.34	4630
Total	103.09	2131	110.69	3620	107.87	5751
Delinquents:						
Nonwhite	93.84	1040	97.42	137	94.26	1177
White	101.87	650	107.47	1117	105.41	1767
Total	96.93	1690	106.37	1254	100.95	2944

The greatest difference, within each race, is between higher SES nondelinquents and lower SES delinquents. And this difference is constant for each race; for example, nonwhite higher SES nondelinquents have a mean I.Q. (100.26) that is 6.42 points greater than nonwhite lower SES delinquents (93.84); and white higher SES nondelinquents have a mean I.Q. (111.39) that is 9.52 greater than white lower SES delinquents (101.87). These are the largest differences within each race, but they do not match the I.Q. differences between the races, even when the delinquency status and SES levels are held constant. The difference between the races among nondelinquents or delinquents is about the same. For example, among nondelinquents, whites are again higher in each SES level (lower SES: 8.03 points higher; upper SES: 10.65 points higher). It is clear again that race is the most important variable of contrast rather than delinquency-nondelinquency status or SES level. The latter two variables become important only within each race.

Achievement level is a designation noted in the public school records (see chapter 3). The five categories (very low, low, average, high, very high) show considerable and not surprising correspondence to I.Q. frequencies among whites and nonwhites, delinquents and nondelinquents. It is perhaps clearest and most convenient to refer to the modal groupings, which reveal the disconcerting position of nonwhites. Among them, both nonwhite delinquents and nondelinquents are more likely to reside in the very low achievement level (43% and

TABLE 4.6

Achievement Level of Nondelinquents and Delinquents by Race

Achievement Level	Nondelinquents		Delinquents		Total	
	N	%	*N*	%	*N*	%
Nonwhite:						
Very low	217	38.48	277	43.08	494	40.93
Low	151	26.77	209	32.50	360	29.82
Average	137	24.29	128	19.91	265	21.96
High	47	8.33	27	4.20	74	6.13
Very high	12	2.13	2	.31	14	1.16
Total	564	100.00	643	100.00	1207	100.00
White:						
Very low	105	5.38	89	12.90	194	7.34
Low	215	11.01	153	22.17	368	13.93
Average	529	27.10	253	36.67	782	29.60
High	625	32.02	122	17.68	747	28.27
Very high	478	24.49	73	10.58	551	20.86
Total	1952	100.00	690	100.00	2642	100.00
Both Races:						
Very low	322	12.80	366	27.46	688	17.87
Low	366	14.56	362	27.16	728	18.91
Average	666	26.47	381	28.58	1047	27.20
High	672	26.71	149	11.18	821	21.33
Very high	490	19.48	75	5.63	565	14.68
Grand Total	2516	100.00	1333	100.00	3849	100.00

38%), compared to white delinquents (13%) and white nondelinquents (5%) in this "very low" category. The modal category for white nondelinquents is "high" (32%), and for white delinquents, "average" (37%).

Among the delinquents for whom information about achievement level is available, there is an almost equal number of whites (690) and nonwhites (643). Yet, only two nonwhites are recorded as "very high" in achievement level compared to 73 whites.

Another contrast is the fact that 65 percent of nonwhite nondelinquents are classified as low or very low in achievement level while 57 percent of white nondelinquents are classified as high or very high. About 76 percent of delinquent nonwhites are low or very low in contrast to 28 percent of delinquent whites who are high or very high. The importance of race in this variable is inescapable.

Summary

In this chapter we have examined several variables available from school records. In general, the major observation is that racial differences form more clearly distinctive groups and patterns in the variables than any other basis used here for comparison. The delinquency-nondelinquency dichotomy, while yielding consistent directional differences of what might be deemed disadvantaged positions, does not exhibit striking differences within each racial grouping.

The major variables that we have examined in some detail – residential and school moves, highest grade completed, I.Q. and achievement level – by delinquency status, race, and socioeconomic status indicate that the values for each of these variables are most likely to be related to race, then to socioeconomic status, and finally to delinquency status. In eight-cell analyses of white and nonwhite, delinquent and nondelinquent, lower and higher socioeconomic status, the white higher SES nondelinquent contrasts most with the nonwhite lower SES delinquent. The white nondelinquent possesses the highest I.Q., the highest achievement level, makes the least residential and school moves, and most frequently completes the twelfth grade of school. In contrast, the nonwhite delinquent has the lowest I.Q., the lowest achievement level, makes the most residential and school moves, and least frequently completes the twelfth grade.[2]

2. Several of these variables were entered in a multiple regression procedure with rather unstartling results. We have not discussed the outcome of this investigation here because of the resulting lack of any additional information. It seemed that a simple discussion of the frequency distributions would suffice. Nonetheless, the intercorrelation matrix for some of these variables may be found in appendix C. There are no surprises in this matrix; for example, I.Q. is moderately negatively related to being a nonwhite, as are highest grade completed and income level. The number of moves is obviously positively related to the number of schools and to being nonwhite. Of the other variables, highest grade completed is positively related to I.Q. and income level. Additional analysis by means of a multiple classification configuration technique was also undertaken. Again little significant information was gained.

5 The Delinquency Status

In this chapter we discuss the distinction between one-time offenders and those who have had two or more recorded police contacts – multiple offenders. The degree of seriousness of these delinquencies is reviewed, with special attention to an even more dramatic group of delinquents, the "chronic" offenders or "hard-core" delinquents who have five or more recorded delinquencies in their biographies.

The rate of delinquency of our birth cohort was 349.4 per 1,000 subjects. About 54 percent, or 1,862 offenders, committed more than one offense, while the remaining 46 percent, or 1,613, were one-time offenders.

When we analyze the school and social background variables of the cohort by the one-time-multiple classification, we find that recidivists are more likely to be nonwhites in the lower SES, have lower I.Q. scores, fewer school years completed, and lower achievement levels than one-time delinquents. One-time offenders and nondelinquents show less variance than one-time compared to multiple offenders in any combination of the race-SES-delinquency frequency matrix that includes these school variables. The complexity only serves to underscore the differences that were reported in chapter 4. For each variable, the lower SES nonwhite delinquent cell appears in

TABLE 5.1
Delinquency Status by School Variables

	Nondelinquents	One-time Delinquents	Recidivists
	(N = 6,470)	(N = 1,613)	(N = 1,862)
Mean number of residential address changes	2.0	2.2	3.1
Mean number of school moves	3.5	3.6	4.6
Mean I.Q. score	107.9	104.2	98.1
Mean highest grade completed	11.2	10.8	9.2
Modal achievement level	High	Average	Very low

the most disadvantaged position. Table 5.1 shows the simple trichotomy of nondelinquents, one-time delinquents, and recidivists by the most relevant school variables.

About 54 percent of the offenders in the cohort are recidivists, and their rate per 1,000 cohort subjects is 187.2, compared to 46 percent one-time delinquents, whose rate is 162.2. When considering SES level, this proportion is maintained for lower SES boys but is reversed for higher SES boys. Thus, in the lower SES group, the rate for one-time delinquents is 175.0, whereas for recidivists it is 273.6, with a general class-specific rate of 448.6. Among the higher SES boys, the overall class-specific delinquency rate is 264.7; but here one-time delinquents have a higher rate (151.3) than recidivists (113.4). The amount of recidivism among the lower SES boys is such that their recidivism rate alone (273.6) is higher than the total class-specific delinquency rate for all higher SES boys (264.7). (See table 5.2.)

This same kind of generalization can be made for race as well as socioeconomic status. The white delinquency rate (286.7) is about three-fifths that of the nonwhite group (501.7). Among nonwhites the rate of one-time delinquency (173.3) is much lower than the rate of recidivism (328.4). But among whites, the one-time rate (157.6) is higher than the rate of recidivism (129.1). The rate of nonwhite recidivism is higher than the total delinquency rate of whites.

Race-SES-specific rates were computed to assess the combined influence of these variables relative to the delinquency status split.

TABLE 5.2

Delinquency Status by Race and SES

	One-Time Delinquents			Recidivists		
Race and SES	*N*	%	Rate per 1,000 Cohort Subjects	*N*	%	Rate per 1,000 Cohort Subjects
Both Races:						
Lower SES	802	39.01	175.0	1254	60.99	273.6
Higher SES	811	57.15	151.3	608	42.85	113.4
Total	1613	46.42	162.2	1862	53.58	187.2
Nonwhite						
Lower SES	430	33.36	175.9	859	66.64	351.5
Higher SES	73	43.71	159.4	94	56.29	205.2
Total	503	34.55	173.3	953	65.45	328.4
White						
Lower SES	372	48.50	173.8	395	51.50	184.5
Higher SES	738	58.95	150.5	514	41.05	104.8
Total	110	54.98	157.6	909	45.02	129.1

Forty-eight percent of lower SES whites are one-time delinquents (rate = 173.8), and 52 percent are recidivists (rate = 184.5); while 58 percent of higher SES whites are one-time delinquents (rate = 150.5). On the other hand, nonwhite boys do not reverse across SES levels. Of lower SES nonwhites, one-third are one-timers (rate = 175.9), two-thirds are recidivists (rate = 351.5); of higher SES nonwhites, 44 percent are one-timers (rate = 159.4), and 56 percent are recidivists (rate = 205.2).

Table 5.2 displays these frequency distributions and rates for one-time and multiple delinquents. Nonwhite lower SES recidivists exhibit the highest rate (351.5), and white higher SES recidivists the lowest (104.8). So pervasive is the race variable that higher SES nonwhites exhibit a total delinquency rate slightly higher than that of lower SES whites. The rate reduction from lower to higher SES boys is considerable for both racial groups, but is greater for nonwhites. This rate reduction across the racial groups is even more than that for SES and is greater among lower SES than higher SES boys.

TABLE 5.3
Type of Offense by Race of Delinquents

	Nonwhites		
Offense	*N*	%	Rate per 1,000 Cohort Subjects
Homicide	14	.24	4.8
Rape	38	.66	13.1
Robbery	173	3.01	59.6
Aggravated assault	181	3.14	62.4
Burglary	394	6.84	135.8
Larceny	802	13.93	276.4
Auto theft	187	3.25	64.4
Other assaults	365	6.34	125.8
Forgery and counterfeiting	4	.07	1.4
Fraud and embezzlement	1	.02	.3
Stolen property	23	.40	7.9
Weapons	212	3.68	73.1
Prostitution	1	.02	.3
Sex offenses	84	1.46	28.9
Narcotics	0	0	0
Liquor law violations	108	1.88	37.2
Drunkenness	117	2.03	40.3
Disorderly conduct	851	14.78	293.2
Vagrancy	15	.26	5.2
Gambling	49	.85	16.9
Road violations	0	0	0
Other traffic violations	12	.21	4.1
All other offenses	2,123	36.88	731.6
Hospital cases	0	0	0
Investigations	0	0	0
Minor disturbance	1	.02	.3
Missing persons	1	.02	.3
Reports affecting other city departments	0	0	0
Total	5,756	100.00	1,983.5

Types of Offenses

The 3,475 boys in the cohort who are recorded delinquents were responsible for 10,214 delinquent acts through age 17. Whites were involved in 4,458, or 44 percent, and nonwhites in 5,756, or 56 percent, of these offenses.

Whites			Total		
N	%	Rate per 1,000 Cohort Subjects	*N*	%	Rate per 1,000 Cohort Subjects
0	0	0	14	.14	1.4
6	.13	.9	44	.43	4.4
20	.45	2.8	193	1.89	19.4
39	.87	5.5	220	2.15	22.1
248	5.56	35.2	642	6.29	64.6
387	8.68	54.9	1189	11.64	119.6
239	5.36	33.9	426	4.17	42.8
172	3.86	24.4	537	5.26	54.0
1	.02	.1	5	.05	.5
3	.07	.4	4	.04	.4
7	.16	1.0	30	.29	3.0
58	1.30	8.2	270	2.64	27.1
2	.04	.3	3	.03	.3
63	1.41	8.9	147	1.44	14.8
1	.02	.1	1	.01	.1
165	3.70	23.4	273	2.67	27.5
102	2.29	14.5	219	2.14	22.0
883	19.81	125.4	1,734	16.98	174.4
6	.13	.9	21	.21	2.1
40	.90	5.7	89	.87	8.9
4	.09	.6	4	.04	.4
25	.56	3.5	37	.36	3.7
1,974	44.28	280.3	4,097	40.11	412.0
1	.02	.1	1	.01	.1
9	.20	1.3	9	.09	.9
0	0	0	1	.01	.1
2	.04	.3	3	.03	.3
1	.02	.1	1	.01	.1
4,458	100.00	633.0	10,214	100.00	1,027.0

The offense rate is, of course, different from the offender rate. We have noted earlier that when the rate of delinquency is computed on the basis of the number of boys ever recorded as having had a delinquency contact with the police, the offender rate is 349.4 per 1,000 cohort subjects. However, this kind of computation ignores the number of offenses committed and statistically treats alike each boy who ever was recorded as a delinquent, regardless of the number or types of acts committed and when they were committed. An offense rate was computed for the birth cohort by using the number of events as numerator and the 9,945 boys as denominator, times the constant, 1,000, yielding a cohort rate of 1,027. The nonwhites' rate is three times as high as the whites' rate (1,983.5 as against 633.0).

Table 5.3 shows frequency distribution and race-specific rates of offenses in terms of the Philadelphia Crime Code. The crime classification most often violated by members of both races is the residual "all other offenses" category, which consists of 54 specific crime designations ranging from criminal abortion to keeping a vicious dog.

All 14 criminal homicides recorded for the entire cohort were committed by nonwhite boys, yielding a rate of 4.8 per 1,000. This is a rate similar to the national average for all ages, both sexes and all ethnic groups combined.

For nearly every offense category listed in table 5.3, nonwhites have higher rates than whites. The exceptions are fraud and embezzlement, of which there were only 4 offenses for the entire cohort; and prostitution, of which there were 3. Other labels, like "incorrigibility," are commonly used for prostitution committed by juveniles. As will be noted in more detail below, the rate differentials between whites and nonwhites are most pronounced for assaultive offenses.

Because there were 1,613 delinquent acts committed by one-time offenders, 8,601 offenses were committed by only 1,862 recidivists. The mean number of offenses committed by the recidivists was 4.62; nonwhites 5.51, and whites 3.68. The offense rate for nonwhite repeaters (1,810.1) is over three times the offense rate for white repeaters (475.4); the 953 nonwhite repeaters were responsible for 5,253 offenses while the 909 white repeaters committed 3,348 offenses. The one-time delinquents were usually involved in petty offensive behavior, including "juvenile status" offenses such as running away from home, truancy from school, or incorrigibility. Nearly three-fourths of their offenses were in this category.

Race differentials are most pronounced in the serious assaultive and property offenses from homicide to auto theft, called "index" here (see table 5.3). Nonwhites are 13 times as high in rape, 20 times as high in robbery, over 10 times as high in aggravated assault, 4 times as high in burglary, 5 times as high in larceny, and about twice as high in auto theft.

In order to determine the relationships between race, socioeconomic status, and delinquency status (one-time versus recidivists) among offense types in this static model, we have concentrated on offenses involving assaults on the person, property offenses, and robbery. The assault category includes the subcategories of homicide, rape, aggravated and simple assault and battery. Property offenses include burglary, larceny, and auto theft. We have retained robbery as a separate category because it is in the anomalous position of being an offense against the person and/or against property. First, we shall consider the relationship between this compressed offense classification and race in general, and then SES and delinquency status. As we proceed, we shall examine the interrelations of these variables by offense type. The variables are displayed in table 5.4

The nonwhite rate (742.2) is higher than that of the white (157.8) for all three categories combined. Nonwhites commit assault offenses at a rate 6 times that of whites (206.1 to 30.9), while their rate is 4 times as great for property offenses (467.6 to 124.1). But clearly the greatest difference is in robbery, where nonwhites have a rate 20 times as high as that of whites (59.6 to 2.9). The SES levels, without regard to race, show similar differences. For example, the lower SES rate for robbery is about six times as great as the higher SES rate (35.3 to 5.8).

One-time delinquents committed relatively few index offenses, compared to recidivists. In fact, recidivists committed over twice as many assaults alone (N = 726) as the total number of assaults, property offenses, and robberies committed by one-time offenders (N = 330). One-time offenders were responsible for only 10 robberies compared to recidivists, who committed 183. All told there were nearly 9 times as many index offenses committed by recidivists (2,935) as by one-time delinquents (330), with about the same proportion for property offenses. The assault-property-robbery rate of offenses for one-time offenders was 204.6, and for recidivists, 1,576.3.

It is clear from the rates shown in table 5.4 that, regardless of race or SES, juveniles who commit only one major offense are rarely involved in the serious kinds of disturbing offenses. Comparing the more extreme cases, the rate for higher SES white recidivists (92.4) is about twice the lower SES nonwhite rate for one-time offenders (49.9), but it is more than 4 times the rate of higher SES white, one-time offenders (21.8). The ratio of the rates for recidivists and one-time offenders ranges from about 3 (assaults committed by higher SES whites) to about 50 (robberies committed by lower SES non-

TABLE 5.4

Assault, Property, and Robbery Offenses by SES, Race, and Delinquency Status

	Assaults			Property Offenses			Robbery Offenses			Total		
Delinquency Status	*N*	%	Rate	*N*	%	Rate	*N*	%	Rate	*N*	%	Rate
Lower SES nonwhite:												
One-time delinquents	35	28.69	14.3	84	68.85	34.3	3	2.46	1.2	122	100.00	49.9
Recidivists	509	27.68	208.3	1180	64.17	482.8	150	8.16	61.4	1839	100.00	752.5
All	544	27.74	222.6	1264	64.46	517.2	153	7.80	62.6	1961	100.00	802.4
Lower SES white:												
One-time delinquents	24	30.00	11.2	54	67.50	25.2	2	2.50	0.9	80	100.00	37.4
Recidivists	85	18.05	39.7	379	80.47	177.1	7	1.49	3.3	471	100.00	220.1
All	109	19.78	50.9	433	78.58	202.3	9	1.63	4.2	551	100.00	257.5
Higher SES nonwhite:												
One-time delinquents	5	23.81	10.9	13	61.90	28.4	3	14.29	6.6	21	100.00	45.9
Recidivists	49	28.49	107.0	106	61.63	231.4	17	9.88	37.1	172	100.00	375.5
All	54	27.98	117.9	119	61.66	259.8	20	10.36	43.7	193	100.00	421.4
Higher SES white:												
One-time delinquents	25	23.36	5.1	80	74.77	16.3	2	1.87	0.4	107	100.00	21.8
Recidivists	83	18.32	16.9	361	79.69	73.6	9	1.99	1.8	453	100.00	92.4
All	108	19.29	22.0	441	78.75	89.9	11	1.96	2.2	560	100.00	114.2
Lower SES, both races:												
One-time delinquents	59	29.21	12.9	138	68.32	30.1	5	2.48	1.1	202	100.00	44.1
Recidivists	594	25.71	129.6	1559	67.49	340.1	157	6.80	34.2	2310	100.00	503.9
All	653	26.00	142.4	1697	67.56	370.2	162	6.45	35.3	2512	100.00	548.0

Higher SES, both races:												
One-time delinquents	30	23.44	5.6	93	72.66	17.3	5	3.91	0.9	128	100.00	23.9
Recidivists	132	21.12	24.6	467	74.72	87.1	26	4.16	4.8	625	100.00	116.6
All	162	21.51	30.2	560	74.37	104.5	31	4.12	5.8	753	100.00	140.5
Both SES groups, nonwhite:												
One-time delinquents	40	27.97	13.8	97	67.83	33.4	6	4.20	2.1	143	100.00	49.3
Recidivists	558	27.75	192.3	1286	63.95	443.4	167	8.30	57.6	2011	100.00	692.9
All	598	27.76	206.1	1383	64.21	476.8	173	8.03	59.7	2154	100.00	742.2
Both SES groups, white:												
One-time delinquents	49	26.20	7.0	134	71.66	19.0	4	2.14	0.6	187	100.00	26.6
Recidivists	168	18.18	23.9	740	80.09	105.1	16	1.73	2.3	924	100.00	131.2
All	217	19.53	30.9	874	78.67	124.1	20	1.80	2.9	1111	100.00	157.8
Both SES groups, both races:												
One-time delinquents	89	26.97	8.9	231	70.00	23.2	10	3.03	1.0	330	100.00	33.2
Recidivists	726	24.74	73.0	2026	69.03	203.7	183	6.24	18.4	2935	100.00	295.1
All	815	24.96	82.0	2257	69.13	226.9	193	5.91	19.4	3265	100.00	328.3

whites). The overall proportion is 9 to 1 (295.1 for recidivists and 33.2 for one-time offenders).

The comparison of one-time offenders and recidivists shows also the significance of the race and SES variables. In general, the differential in rates between one-time offenders and recidivists is about 3 times as large for nonwhites as for whites, but it is twice as great when we look at SES. This more pronounced effect of the race variable obtains all through the table, even more noticeably for recidivists than for one-time offenders. The ratio of rates for similarly positioned one-time offenders is seldom larger than 2, while in the case of recidivists it only occasionally goes under 10.

The results of our comparison of one-time offenders to recidivists, whites to nonwhites, and higher to lower SES are, we believe, a finding of social significance.

Under the generally accepted assumption that the index offenses are the most serious, that they are the ones which any deterrence or prevention program should attempt to reduce, and that most of the other forms of delinquency are relatively trivial, our study indicates at this stage that the critical moment of social cost reduction occurs when juveniles have committed their first offense. To produce delinquency desistance at this stage in the biography of the child might thus be considered a primary goal. Since more nonwhites than whites commit further delinquent acts after the first offense, the major concern should perhaps be with this racial group. Of the 2,017 white delinquents, 55 percent were one-time offenders and desisted thereafter; whereas, of the 1,458 nonwhite delinquents, only 35 percent were one-time offenders. At the other extreme, as we shall show later in greater detail, nearly 30 percent of the nonwhite boys as compared to only 10 percent of the white boys fall into the chronic offender category (five or more offenses).

Seriousness Scores and Weighted Rates

By using the judgmental scale of seriousness described in *The Measurement of Delinquency,* a quantitative measure of the amount of social harm inflicted on the community by our birth cohort can be obtained. The seriousness scores which were assigned to each cohort delinquent for each delinquent act committed during the age span of exposure to potential delinquency involvement has provided the basis for this and subsequent discussion of the gravity of delinquency committed by the cohort.

TABLE 5.5

Race-specific Rates of Delinquency Weighted by Seriousness of Offense

	Weighted Rate per 1,000 Cohort Subjects	Weighted Rate per 1,000 Delinquents
Both races	1,172.4	3,355.2
Nonwhite	2,594.4	5,163.8
White	587.9	2,052.8

Table 5.5 shows the weighted rates for the cohort, with race-specific weighted rates per 1,000 cohort subjects as well as per 1,000 delinquents.[1] As is readily observed, the nonwhite weighted delinquency rate per 1,000 cohort subjects is a little less than 5 times as great as the rate for whites. But among delinquents the nonwhite weighted rate is only 2½ times as great as the rate for whites.

Table 5.6 displays the frequency distribution of offenses by race and categories of seriousness.[2] Within each racial group, the percent distributions are generally quite similar. Most of the delinquent acts (87%), regardless of the race of the offender, fall into seriousness score categories below 300 and reflect the fact that youngsters engage mostly in nonindex events and petty thefts. The largest proportion of events in a single category (30%) have a seriousness score of 1, implying that almost one-third of the recorded delinquencies were apprehensions mainly for curfew violations, truancy, and trespassing.

That offenses by whites are less serious than offenses by nonwhites is reflected in the fact that the proportion of whites in each of the 11 categories under score 100 is larger (with two slight exceptions) than that of nonwhites. On the other hand, the proportion of nonwhites in each of the 13 score categories of 100 and above exceeds that of whites (save for one white delinquent with a score of 4,400). There are nearly twice as many nonwhites as whites with a

1. See appendix D.1 for details on the computation of these weighted rates.

2. For a discussion of seriousness scores, see Sellin and Wolfgang, *The Measurement of Delinquency,* and appendix D.2 of this volume. Maud M. Craig and Laila A. Budd have used these seriousness scores in a study of recidivism: "The Juvenile Offender: Recidivism and Companions," *Crime and Delinquency* 13, no. 2 (April 1967): 344–51.

TABLE 5.6

Race of Delinquents by Offense Seriousness Score

Offense Seriousness Score	Nonwhites		Whites		Total	
	N	%	*N*	%	*N*	%
1 –	1,608	27.94	1,480	33.20	3,088	30.23
2 - 18	46	.80	26	.58	72	.70
19 –	605	10.51	565	12.67	1,170	11.45
20 - 29	192	3.34	257	5.76	449	4.40
30 - 39	245	4.26	225	5.06	470	4.60
40 - 49	137	2.38	198	4.44	335	3.28
50 - 59	13	.23	18	.40	31	.30
60 - 69	124	2.15	105	2.36	229	2.24
70 - 79	76	1.32	80	1.79	156	1.53
80 - 89	45	.78	22	.49	67	.66
90 - 99	3	.05	9	.20	12	.12
100 - 199	1,046	18.17	470	10.54	1,516	14.84
200 - 299	771	13.39	566	12.69	1,337	13.09
300 - 399	384	6.67	221	4.96	605	5.92
400 - 499	234	4.07	133	2.98	367	3.59
500 - 599	34	.59	25	.56	59	.58
600 - 699	47	.82	14	.31	61	.60
700 - 799	52	.90	15	.34	67	.66
800 - 899	22	.38	3	.07	25	.24
900 - 999	7	.12	1	.02	8	.08
1000 - 1999	46	.80	20	.45	66	.65
2000 - 2999	18	.31	2	.04	20	.20
3000 - 3999	1	.02	2	.04	3	.03
4000 +	0	0	1	.02	1	.01
Total	5,756	100.00	4,458	100.00	10,214	100.00
Mean score	130.80		92.88		114.15	
Weighted rate per 1,000 cohort subjects	2594.4		587.9		1172.4	
Weighted rate per 1,000 delinquents	5163.8		2052.8		3355.2	

score of 400 or more (8% to 4.8%). The mean seriousness score for all 10,214 delinquencies is 114.15: for white events, 92.88; for non-white events, 130.80.

The important differential noted earlier, when one-time offenders were compared to recidivists by race and SES level, led us to compute weighted rates for this matrix (see table 5.7). Although it is clear

TABLE 5.7

SES and Delinquency Status: Mean Seriousness, Number, and Weighted Rate

	One-time Delinquents			Recidivists			Total		
SES Level	$\bar{X}$	N	WR	$\bar{X}$	N	WR	$\bar{X}$	N	WR
Lower SES:									
Both races	98.74	802	172.8	124.10	6,329	1,713.4	121.25	7.131	1,886.2
Nonwhite	106.00	430	186.5	130.14	4,760	2,534.6	128.14	5,190	2,721.1
White	90.35	372	157.1	105.79	1,569	775.6	102.83	1,941	932.7
Higher SES:									
Both races	62.93	811	95.2	104.12	2,272	441.3	93.29	3,083	536.5
Nonwhite	88.46	73	141.0	135.40	493	1,457.5	129.35	566	1,598.5
White	60.41	738	90.9	95.45	1,779	346.3	85.18	2,517	437.3

that, within each SES level and delinquency status, the mean seriousness scores and weighted rates of offenses committed by whites is consistently lower than the scores for nonwhites, it is also abundantly evident that these same mean scores and weighted rates are most dramatically different between one-time offenders and recidivists. This difference holds for both races and for both SES levels.[3]

For example, among one-time nonwhite offenders, the weighted offense rate difference between lower SES boys (186.5) and higher SES boys (141.0) is minimal, for the former is only 1.3 times as great as the latter. Among nonwhite recidivists, the lower SES weighted offense rate (2,534.6) is but 1.7 times as great as the higher SES weighted rate (1,457.5). The corresponding weighted offense rates for white boys show substantially the same differences, namely, that one-time lower SES offenders (157.1) have a weighted rate 1.7 times as great as one-time higher SES boys (90.9), and that lower SES recidivists (775.6) have a weighted rate 2.2 times as high as higher SES recidivists (346.3). These differences across socioeconomic levels, *within each race and delinquency status category*, are relatively small.

However, when we examine weighted rates *within each race and SES level*, across delinquency status, the differences are much greater. Thus, the weighted rate for nonwhite recidivists in the lower SES is 13.6 times as great as the weighted rate for nonwhite one-time offenders in the same SES; and it is 10.3 times as great for recidivists than for one-time offenders in the same race and higher SES level. Similar comparisons for whites show recidivists 5.0 times as high as one-time offenders among lower SES boys and 3.8 times as high among higher SES boys. Obviously comparison between one-time offenders and recidivists makes for more of a difference among non-white than among white boys. The relevance of stopping nonwhite boys from persisting in delinquency beyond their first offense is again clear.

The Relative Seriousness of Injury Offenses

Most offenses of bodily injury are committed by delinquent repeaters. Less than 10 percent, or 117, of the 1,391 delinquencies with known physical injury involve one-time offenders although one-time offenders make up 45 percent of all delinquents. Nonwhite repeaters, particularly from the lower SES, are responsible for most of

3. See appendix D.3 for note on additional seriousness score classifications.

these offenses. Table 5.8 shows these various data by mean seriousness score and weighted rates.

The highest mean injury score occurs among nonwhite recidivists in the lower SES (241.93), while the lowest mean score is among non-white one-time offenders in the higher SES (100.0). There are only 8 one-time, nonwhite, higher SES delinquents but both this small number and the lowest mean seriousness score for offenses involving physical injury make an interesting commentary. The 39 one-time, white, higher SES boys committing bodily harm still have a slightly lower weighted rate (14.7) than their nonwhite counterparts (17.5).

Perhaps the most striking conclusions revealed by the weighted injury offense rates on table 5.8 are as follows:

1. *There are no significant race differences within each respective SES level for one-time delinquents.* Thus, for example, among lower SES boys who committed only one injury offense and no further delinquency, the weighted rate is 35.2 for nonwhites and 31.8 for whites. And, as we indicated above, among higher SES boys who committed only one offense, nonwhites have a weighted rate of 17.5 and white boys a weighted rate of 14.7. These within-SES rates across racial groups are not significant.

2. *Significant race differences appear among recidivists.* Within the lower SES, the nonwhite weighted rate (779.0) is 4.6 times as great as the white rate (169.4), and within the higher SES, the nonwhite weighted rate (467.3) is about 6.5 times as high as that for whites (72.0).

3. *The greatest difference is not between the races or between the SES levels but between nonwhite one-time offensivity and nonwhite recidivism.* The weighted rate differential for nonwhite lower SES boys shows recidivists (779.0) 22 times as high as one-time offenders (35.2), and that for nonwhite higher SES boys shows recidivists (467.3) 26 times as high as one-time offenders (17.5).

Once again our attention is mostly drawn to the delinquency status difference rather than to race or SES differences. The sheer size of offenses of bodily harm committed by nonwhite lower SES boys who are recidivists is alone a measure of the importance of promoting some kind of intervention as a basis for prevention. The 787 offenses of injury committed in this category alone constitute 56 percent of all 1,388 such offenses.

TABLE 5.8

Injury Offenses: Mean Seriousness Score, Number, and Weighted Rate by Delinquency Status, SES, and Race

	One-time Delinquents			Recidivists			Total		
SES Level	$\bar{X}$	*N*	*WR*	$\bar{X}$	*N*	*WR*	$\bar{X}$	*N*	*WR*
Lower SES:									
Both races	220.00	70	33.6	240.60	942	494.4	239.18	1012	528.0
Nonwhite	209.76	41	35.2	241.93	787	779.0	240.34	828	814.2
White	234.48	29	31.8	233.87	155	169.4	233.97	184	201.2
Higher SES:									
Both races	170.21	47	14.9	172.34	329	105.8	172.07	376	120.7
Nonwhite	100.00	8	17.5	222.92	96	467.3	213.46	104	484.7
White	184.61	39	14.7	151.50	233	72.0	156.25	272	86.7

TABLE 5.9

Race of Delinquent by Type of Injury: Number, Percentage, and Weighted Rate

	Nonwhites			Whites			Total Delinquents		
Type of Injury	*N*	%	*WR*	*N*	%	*WR*	*N*	%	*WR*
Deaths	14	1.49	125.4	0	0	0	14	1.01	36.6
Hospitalized	59	6.31	142.3	22	4.82	21.9	81	5.82	57.0
Treated and discharged	217	23.21	299.1	84	18.42	47.7	301	21.64	121.1
Minor harm	645	68.98	222.3	350	76.75	49.7	995	71.53	100.0
Total	935	100.00	789.1	456	100.00	119.3	1391	100.00	314.71
Unknown	64			11			75		
Grand total	999	68.14		467	31.86		1466	100.00	
Mean seriousness score		244.92			184.21			225.02	

We have provided a further refinement in table 5.9 of the types of physical injury committed by each racial group. The frequency distributions as well as the weighted rates show that more serious forms of harm are committed by nonwhites. We have already pointed out that no whites were responsible for the 14 homicides. The modal weighted rate (*WR*) for nonwhites is in the category involving hospitalization of the victim (although the modal number is in the "minor harm" category). The modal weighted rate and number for white offenders are both in the minor harm category. By using the weighted rate, based on the judgmental scale of the gravity of crime, the 14 homicides represent more social harm to the community during the juvenile life span (*WR* = 125.4) of nonwhite boys than do all the combined 456 acts of physical injury committed by white boys during their juvenile years (*WR* = 119.3). The same can be said about the 59 acts of violence committed by nonwhites that resulted in hospitalization of the victims (*WR* = 142.3).

Weapons

Of the offenses having weapons information, only 263 or 2.58 percent, with a cohort rate of 26.4, involved the known presence of a weapon (table 5.10). It is obvious, therefore, that most of the 1,446 events with physical injury were not performed with a weapon external to the body of the offender. There were 3,813 index offenses (injury, theft, or damage), of which the 263 represent only about 7 percent. Only 17 of the 1,613 one-time delinquents used a weapon; all of the remaining 246 acts with weapons were performed by recidivists; and most of these (185) by nonwhite lower SES boys.

Because most lower SES boys are nonwhite, and most nonwhite boys are lower SES, it is not surprising that lower SES boys in general have a rate of weapon use that is six times as great as higher SES boys (48.2 to 7.8). The nonwhite weapon use is ten times as great as white use (73.4 to 7.1). The high rate of weapon use for nonwhites and lower SES in general is kept high mainly by the nonwhite lower SES group, which has a use rate of 75.7.

Guns were present in 47 offenses – in 43 of the nonwhite and 4 of the white offenses (table 5.11). The most common weapons used by whites were blunt instruments or something other than guns or knives. For nonwhites, knives were used in nearly one-third of all offenses committed with weapons. As might be expected, when a gun is present the probability of more serious harm increases. When

TABLE 5.10

Weapon Present during Offense, by Delinquency Status, Race, and SES

	Weapon Present			No Weapon Present	
	N	%	Rate	*N*	%
One-time Delinquents:					
Lower SES nonwhite	10	2.34	4.1	418	97.66
Lower SES white	3	0.81	1.4	369	99.19
Total	13	1.63	2.8	787	98.37
Higher SES nonwhite	1	1.37	2.2	72	98.63
Higher SES white	3	0.41	0.6	735	99.59
Total	4	0.49	0.8	807	99.51
Recidivists:					
Lower SES nonwhite	185	3.90	75.7	4562	96.10
Lower SES white	23	1.47	10.7	1545	98.53
Total	208	3.29	45.4	6107	96.71
Higher SES nonwhite	17	3.46	37.1	475	96.54
Higher SES white	21	1.18	4.3	1758	98.82
Total	38	1.67	7.1	2233	98.33
Both SES:					
Lower	221	3.11	48.2	6894	96.89
Higher	42	1.36	7.8	3040	98.64
Both Races:					
Nonwhite	213	3.71	73.4	5527	96.29
White	50	1.12	7.1	4407	98.88
Total	263	2.58	26.4	9934	97.42

a gun is present in an offense, the chances that a homicide will occur are higher than for any other weapon involved in an offense. The likelihood of hospitalization is also highest when a gun is present. Among injury offenses with a gun present, 38 percent resulted in death (15%) or hospitalization (23%). If the weapon used to inflict injury is anything other than a gun, the chances are 40 percent or better that only minor harm will result to the victim. Injuries from blunt instruments are the least serious (48% minor or no harm), and among them only 4 percent reached the level of hospitalization.

TABLE 5.11

Type of Weapon by Type of Injury among all Delinquent Events with a Known Weapon Present

	Gun		Knife		Blunt Instrument		Other	
Type of Injury	*N*	%	*N*	%	*N*	%	*N*	%
Death	7	14.89	2	2.56	0	0	0	0
Hospitalization	11	23.40	18	23.08	3	4.41	6	8.57
Treated and discharged	13	27.66	34	43.59	32	47.06	34	48.57
Minor harm	6	12.77	17	21.79	27	39.71	28	40.00
No harm	10	21.28	7	8.97	6	8.82	2	2.86
Total	47	100.0	78	100.0	68	100.0	70	100.0

About 23 percent of injuries caused by knives resulted in hospitalization, and there were two deaths. Table 5.11 summarizes the relationships between weapons and extent of injury.

Theft and Damage

Of the total delinquent events, 3,813 were index events, or those involving injury, theft or damage. Of the latter number, 2,401, or 63 percent, were classified by the police as some form of theft.[4] Of these, 434 were recorded with unknown amounts of theft so that, for purposes of analyzing dollar loss and seriousness scores by race, the known universe of thefts totals 1,967 offenses.

About two-fifths of theft offenses involved amounts less than $10. Half of these offenses committed by nonwhite boys and about a third committed by white boys were thefts under $10. White boys committed fewer theft offenses but stole more per offense. The median dollar values of thefts by whites is $33.84, while for nonwhites it is only $10.52. The cohort weighted rate, using frequency and seriousness scores, is 396.4 per 1,000, with 834.6 for nonwhites and 214.7 for whites.

4. Some damage may have occurred in these theft cases; combinations of theft and damage were thus classified under theft for purposes of analysis in this section.

TABLE 5.12

Property Offenses of Theft, by Race of Delinquent and Dollar Loss

	Nonwhites		Whites		All Delinquents	
Dollar Loss	*N*	%	*N*	%	*N*	%
< 10	599	49.46	236	31.22	835	42.45
10 - 25	185	15.28	126	16.67	311	15.81
26 - 49	87	7.18	51	6.75	138	7.02
50 - 99	87	7.18	60	7.94	147	7.47
100 - 250	91	7.51	85	11.24	176	8.95
251 - 499	27	2.23	25	3.31	52	2.64
500 - 999	39	3.22	59	7.80	98	4.98
1,000 - 1,999	46	3.80	46	6.08	92	4.68
2,000 - 2,999	28	2.31	35	4.63	63	3.20
3,000 - 3,999	14	1.16	25	3.31	39	1.98
4,000 - 4,999	5	.41	4	.53	9	.46
5,000 - 5,999	2	.17	1	.13	3	.15
6,000 - 6,999	0	0	1	.13	1	.05
7,000 - 7,999	1	.08	0	0	1	.05
20,000	0	0	1	.13	1	.05
30,000	0	0	1	.13	1	.05
Total	1,211	100.00	756	100.00	1,967	100.00
Unknown dollar loss	303		131		434	
Median dollar loss	$10.52		$33.84		$17.16	
Weighted rate per 1,000 cohort subjects	834.6		214.7		395.6	

There were 958 cases involving damage to property. These were usually classified by the police under such labels as malicious mischief or disorderly conduct. Nearly half of the nonwhite and about two-fifths of the white offenses were again trivial, or under $10 in value. Another three-tenths involved dollar loss between $10 and $25. As with thefts, the median amount of damage by whites ($14.63) is higher than the median damage by nonwhites ($11.43), but because of high frequency, the weighted rate for nonwhites (408.7) is about four times as high as the weighted rate for whites (103.6).

No important differences are discernible when these data are broken down by delinquency status (one-time offenders versus recidi-

TABLE 5.13

Property Offenses of Damage, by Race of Delinquent and Dollar Loss

	Nonwhites		Whites		Total Delinquents	
Dollar Loss	*N*	%	*N*	%	*N*	%
< 10	280	47.22	151	41.37	431	44.99
10 - 25	173	29.17	102	27.95	275	28.71
26 - 49	37	6.24	21	5.75	59	6.16
50 - 99	38	6.41	30	8.22	68	7.10
100 - 250	46	7.76	43	11.78	89	9.29
251 - 499	6	1.01	4	1.10	10	1.04
500 - 999	5	.84	6	1.64	11	1.15
1,000 - 1,999	5	.84	4	1.10	9	.94
2,000 - 2,999	1	.17	0	0	1	.10
5,000 - 5,999	2	.34	0	0	2	.21
7,000 - 7,999	0	0	3	.82	3	.31
10,000 +	0	0	1	.27	1	.10
Total	593	100.00	365	100.00	958	100.00
Unknown dollar loss	120		91		211	
Median dollar loss	$11.43		$14.63		$12.62	
Weighted rate per 1,000 cohort subjects	408.7		103.6		192.7	

vists), by SES, and by race. The one exception to this generalization might be that within each race the proportion of offenses committed by one-time white offenders (20%) is higher than the proportion by one-time nonwhite offenders (8%). Put another way, 92 percent of the theft and damage offenses involving nonwhite boys are committed by recidivists.

A Summary Implication

Of the 9,945 boys in the birth cohort, 3,475, or 35 percent, were delinquent and responsible for 10,214 delinquents acts from age 7 through age 17. The nonwhites' offense rate is three times as high as that of whites. In general, however, only about 30 percent of these offenses are index crimes, defined in terms of the FBI Standard Classification system or in terms of all acts of injury, theft, and damage.

Although nonwhites and lower socioeconomic status boys have significantly higher crude rates and weighted rates based on the seriousness of their offenses, the differences between one-time offenders and recidivists are among the most striking of any of the multiple ways of analyzing the data. If a question about social intervention is posed in terms of the data available thus far for our cohort in terms of the greatest amount of offense reduction registered among groups, it is clear that preventing the group of nonwhite lower SES boys from continuing delinquency after their first offense would indeed produce the maximum delinquency reduction. If resources and attention were to be focused on the lower SES nonwhite subset of the cohort who have a first delinquency, not only could the general rate of delinquency be affected; the most serious acts – those involving physical violence or assault on others – could also be drastically decreased.

6 Chronic Offenders

In exploring the offenders and their delinquencies in chapter 5, we found the distinction between the one-time offenders and the recidivists to be significant both in understanding the dimensions of delinquency (amount, seriousness, rates) and in exploring the specific influence of the variables of race and income. Interrelationships which appeared weak when we looked at all the offenders together or at one-time offenders alone were more apparent when we considered only those delinquents with more than one offense in the life span under study. We thus concluded that a more detailed analysis of the patterns of recidivism would enhance our knowledge about the delinquent population in the cohort.

Of the 10,214 cohort offenses, 8,601 (84.2%) were committed by the 1,862 recidivists (53.6% of all the delinquents). Those who committed five or more offenses (627 or 18%), whom we here call chronic offenders, were responsible for 5,305 of these delinquent acts (51.9%; see table 6.1).

Throughout this study we have maintained that socioeconomic and race differences are the most significant descriptive variables of the delinquents in the cohort. The chronic offender category gives further support to this position. Table 6.2 presents race-specific data

TABLE 6.1

Offenders and Offenses by Delinquent Subgroups

	Offenders		Offenses	
	N	%	*N*	%
Delinquents:	3,475	100.0	10,214	100.0
One-time offenders	1,613	46.4	1,613	15.8
Chronic recidivists	627	18.0	5,305	51.9
Non-chronic recidivists	1,235	35.6	3,296	32.3
Recidivists:	1,862	100.0	8,601	100.0
Chronic	627	33.7	5,305	61.7
Non-chronic	1,235	66.3	3,296	38.3

TABLE 6.2

Number and Percentage (of Total Cohort) of Delinquents by Frequency Category and Race

	Nonwhites		Whites		All	
	N	%	*N*	%	*N*	%
Cohort	2,902	.....	7,043	.....	9,945	.....
Delinquents	1,458	50.2	2,017	28.6	3,475	34.9
One-time offenders	503	17.3	1,110	15.7	1,613	16.2
Recidivists	953	32.9	909	12.9	1,862	18.7
Chronic	417	14.4	210	3.0	627	6.3
Non-chronic	536	18.5	699	9.9	1,235	12.4

relating to the different delinquent subgroups. The percentages are based on the total white and nonwhite subjects in the cohort.

Table 6.2 reveals the profound effect of the variable race on delinquent behavior. Half of the nonwhite subjects belong in the delinquent group, but only 28.6 percent of the white subjects are in this group. Dividing the delinquent group into one-time offenders and recidivists further highlights the disadvantaged position of the nonwhites. While percentages for the one-time offenders are approximately the same (NW, 17.3; W, 15.7) the differences for recidivists are large indeed. Approximately one-third of the nonwhites in the cohort are recidivists, but only 13 percent of the whites are. Clearly the phenomenon of repeated criminal behavior is of paramount importance in describing the delinquency of the cohort.

Additionally, the recidivist groups can be divided into the two categories of chronic and nonchronic offenders. The data in table 6.2 again indicate that relationship of race to these two delinquency groups is quite strong. The nonwhite boys are overrepresented in both the chronic and the nonchronic offender groups. Nonwhites are twice as likely as whites to be found in the nonchronic group (NW, 18.5%; W, 9.9%) but are 4½ times as likely to be found in the chronic group as are whites (NW, 14.4%; W, 3.0%).

Thus, race is a major determinant of delinquent subgroup membership. Nonwhites are more likely to become recidivists than are whites, and of the recidivists they are more likely to be chronic offenders than nonchronic offenders.

These same variables may be described by using percentages calculated on different bases, as appear in table 6.3

Employing the delinquent group as the base, we can examine the effect of race on delinquency status. Of the 1,458 nonwhite delinquents, only 34.5 percent were one-time offenders. The remaining two-thirds (65.4%) were recidivists. The opposite is true for the white subjects. Of the 2,017 white delinquents, over half (55%) were one-time offenders, and less than half (45.1%) were recidivists. Thus, within the delinquent group the nonwhites are more likely to be re-

TABLE 6.3

Number and Percentage (of Specific Delinquent Subgroup) of Offenders by Frequency Category and Race

	Nonwhites		Whites	
	N	%	*N*	%
Cohort	2,902	.....	7,043	.....
Delinquent	1,458	50.2	2,017	28.6
One-time offenders	503	34.5	1,110	55.0
Recidivists	953	65.4	909	45.1
Chronic	417	43.8	210	23.1
Non-chronic	536	56.2	699	76.9

cidivists and the whites are more likely to be one-time offenders. The recidivist subset shows clearly the relationship to race. Among the 909 white recidivists, the majority (76.9%) are found in the nonchronic group while only 23.1 percent are chronic offenders. Yet the situation is quite different for the nonwhites. Of the 953 nonwhite recidivists, 43.8 percent are chronic offenders and 56.2 percent are nonchronic. Thus slightly over one-fifth of the white recidivists committed five or more offenses, while almost twice that number (over two-fifths) of the nonwhite recidivists committed more than four offenses.

Within both SES groups similar racial differentials hold. In the lower SES group a greater percentage of nonwhites fall into the delinquency group and the recidivist group than do whites. Lower SES nonwhite boys are three times as likely to be chronic offenders than are lower SES white boys. This is the same pattern that was observed when the SES level was not held constant. A similar picture emerges for the higher SES group. Again nonwhites are more likely to be recidivists and, among the recidivists, are more likely to be chronic offenders than are white boys.

We have noted that lower SES boys are more likely to be delinquents, recidivists, and chronic offenders than higher SES boys. These differences are not, however, as pronounced as the differences be-

TABLE 6.4

Offenders by SES and Race

	Lower SES				Higher SES			
	Nonwhites		Whites		Nonwhites		Whites	
	N	%	*N*	%	*N*	%	*N*	%
Cohort	2444	.....	2140	.....	458	.....	4903	.....
Delinquents	1293	52.9	763	35.6	165	36.0	1254	25.6
One-time offenders	434	17.8	368	17.2	71	15.5	740	15.1
Recidivists	859	35.1	395	18.4	94	20.5	514	10.5
Chronic	378	15.5	106	5.0	39	8.5	104	2.1
Non-chronic	481	19.7	289	13.5	55	12.0	410	8.4

tween whites and nonwhites. For example, the greatest difference between lower and higher SES boys occurs among whites, where the lower SES group is twice as likely to have chronic offenders as is the higher SES group. But the smallest difference between whites and nonwhites occurs within the lower SES group, where nonwhites are three times as likely to be chronic offenders as whites. Thus, although SES level does explain to some extent the composition of the chronic offender group, it is not as powerful an indication as the variable of race.

We find that the chronic offenders do not significantly depart from the patterns of race and SES selection found in the previous analyses of offenders. Their recruitment is made along the same lines within race and/or SES groups.

There are background variables that indicate differences between the chronic offenders and other offender groups. However, as with race and income distributions, these differences generally reflect differences that emerged in the comparisons of nonoffenders and offenders, and in the comparison of one-time offenders and recidivists. These variables are: (1) number of moves; (2) measures of school success potential (I.Q., retarded status, and achievement level); and (3) school performance measures (disciplinary placements, remedial-disciplinary placement, highest grade attained, and type of school exit).

Table 6.5 contains the data for the mean number of moves by chronic and one-time offenders divided into race and SES groups. In each of the cells, chronic offenders exhibit a higher mean number of moves than do one-time offenders.

TABLE 6.5

Mean Number of Moves of One-time and Chronic Offenders by SES and Race

	Lower SES		Higher SES	
	One-time	Chronic	One-time	Chronic
White	2.0	3.1	1.8	2.2
Nonwhite	3.1	4.6	2.9	4.2

Analysis of the school potential variables (which are obviously intercorrelated) also discloses differences between the chronic and one-time offenders, but not patterned ones. Table 6.6 displays I.Q. score, percentage retarded, percentage below average, and the mean achievement levels for one-time and chronic offenders by race and SES. In all cases the pattern of relationship described in the discussion of the number of moves persists. Throughout, the chronic offenders have lower mean I.Q. scores and higher percentages of those defined as retarded or as below-average achievers. The within-offender classification ordering also remains the same, with nonwhites in the lower SES occupying the most disadvantaged position in all three instances, and whites in the higher SES the most advantaged position. For example, nonwhite chronic offenders in the lower SES have a mean I.Q. score of 87.4, while nonwhite one-time offenders have a mean of 95.5.

School performance further positions the chronic offenders. Only 9.2 percent of the chronic offenders graduated from high school compared to 74 percent of the nonoffenders, 58 percent of the one-time offenders, and 24 percent of the recidivists. Table 6.7 contains

TABLE 6.6

School Potential Variables of One-time and Chronic Offenders by Race and SES

	Lower SES		Higher SES	
	Whites	Nonwhites	Whites	Nonwhites
I.Q.:				
One-time offenders	103.7	95.5	109.0	99.2
Chronic offenders	93.1	87.4	98.0	90.9
Percent retarded:				
One-time offenders	4.0	11.2	1.8	7.9
Chronic offenders	14.6	30.4	5.8	17.9
Percent below average achievement:				
One-time offenders	39.8	68.1	21.7	66.7
Chronic offenders	73.7	86.0	44.9	78.3

TABLE 6.7

Percentage Graduating from High School by Race and SES: One-time and Chronic Offenders

	Lower SES		Higher SES	
	One-time	Chronic	One-time	Chronic
Whites	50.8	10.1	72.1	17.6
Nonwhites	43.3	6.8	50.0	15.7

TABLE 6.8

Average Grade Completed by One-time and Chronic Offenders by Race and SES

	Lower SES		Higher SES	
	One-time	Chronic	One-time	Chronic
Whites	10.7	8.6	11.4	9.1
Nonwhites	10.0	7.6	10.4	9.0

data comparing the percentage of graduates by race and SES for one-time and chronic offenders. In all categories lower percentages of chronic offenders graduate than do the one-time offenders. The difference between races within SES groups is less than the differences between SES groups within races. The same pattern emerges if we consider the mean grade completed (table 6.8), a variable that is obviously highly correlated with the type of exit from school. As expected, chronic offenders completed fewer grades than did one-time offenders in all classifications. Chronic offenders exhibit many disciplinary designations (51% compared to 4% for one-time offenders) and remedial-disciplinary placements (23.1% compared to 2.1% for one-time offenders). Social class differences between chronic and one-time offenders virtually disappear (see tables 6.9 and 6.10) within each race.

TABLE 6.9

Percentage of One-time and Chronic Offenders with Disciplinary Status by Race and SES

	Lower SES		Higher SES	
	One-time	Chronic	One-time	Chronic
Whites	2.4	38.8	2.4	33.7
Nonwhites	9.1	57.3	9.0	57.5

TABLE 6.10

Percentage of One-time and Chronic Offenders with Remedial-Disciplinary Status by Race and SES

	Lower SES		Higher SES	
	One-time	Chronic	One-time	Chronic
Whites	1.9	17.5	0.5	18.3
Nonwhites	3.9	25.6	2.7	26.8

Type of Offense and Seriousness Score

Now we shall treat the offense, instead of the offender, by considering the various types of offenses and their respective mean seriousness scores, the offenses as classified by the crime code, the use of weapons, and the relationship between the offenders and their offenses.[1]

The mean seriousness score for offenses committed by chronic offenders in our cohort is 127.45. This compares with a score of 80.65 for one-time offenders and 118.83 for the offenses committed by all the recidivists. Within the group of chronic offenders the white boys' mean seriousness score is 106.95, and the nonwhites', 135.47. The relationship is comparable to that for one-time offenders (W, 70.31; NW, 103.33) and all recidivists (W, 100.30; NW, 130.64). The

1. See appendix E for a multiple regression analysis of those variables.

mean seriousness score, we may assert, increases as the number of offenses committed per person increases, and within each group of offenders the nonwhite values are higher than those of the whites. In order to make a more meaningful comparison by race and income, table 6.11 displays the seriousness scores for one-time offenders, recidivists (i.e., 2 to 4 offenses) and chronic offenders (5 or more offenses).

Seriousness scores are higher for nonwhite offenders than for white offenders in all income groups – a pattern comparable to that found among one-time offenders and recidivists. With one exception the scores also increase in seriousness as the number of offenses committed by each offender increases. The exception is in nonwhite income groups IV and V (higher SES), where the recidivist seriousness score is 0.1 points above that of the chronic offenders.[2] The mean seriousness score for the chronic white offender (in this income group) is only 32 points above that for the recidivists. In the lower SES, the difference between the scores of the recidivists and those of the chronic offenders is for nonwhites 13.3 and for whites 18.9. Another pattern that can be seen in table 6.11 is that, with one exception, the seriousness scores for higher SES boys are lower than those for lower SES boys – among all one-time offenders, all chronic offenders, and white recidivists.

2. The scores presented in this table for nonwhite income groups IV and V have been adjusted to take account of an unusual bias in the recidivist category of this group. The category contained two offenses with a high seriousness score (one murder with a score of 2,600 and one case of disorderly conduct – a gang fight – with a seriousness score of 2,400). The number of offenses in this group (142) was less than one-half the number in the chronic group (351); therefore the seriousness score when all offenses were considered was skewed toward a high score (158.2). The score for chronic offenders when all cases were considered was considerably lower (131.8).

The chronic offender group also contained one murder, but because of the greater number of offenses in this group it had little effect on the seriousness score. In order to make the scores more comparable, the seriousness score for the murder was subtracted from the total score for the chronic offenders, and the mean of 124.7 was obtained for the remaining offenses. The scores for the murder and the gang fight were subtracted from the total for the recidivists, giving a mean seriousness score of 124.8 for the remaining 140 offenses. If the second most serious score (1,000) is also subtracted from the total for the chronic offenders, the mean seriousness score for this group becomes 122.2. This small change in seriousness score shown by the subtraction of one or two offenses from the scores of the chronic offenders compared to the large change for the recidivists demonstrates how the latter seriousness score was biased by the inclusion of two high scores in a small number of offenses.

TABLE 6.11

Mean Seriousness Scores by Race, SES, and Type of Offender

Race and SES	One-time Offenders	Recidivists minus Chronic Offenders	Chronic Offenders
Lower SES:			
Nonwhite	106.0	123.1	136.4
White	90.4	96.4	115.3
Higher SES:			
Nonwhite	88.5	124.8	124.7
White	60.4	93.5	96.7

TABLE 6.12

Nonindex Offenses as a Percentage of Total Offenses by Race, SES, and Type of Offender

Race and SES	One-time Offenders	Recidivists minus Chronic Offenders	Chronic Offenders
Lower SES:			
Nonwhite	64	62	55
White	70	69	59
Higher SES:			
Nonwhite	64	63	61
White	78	71	65

From table 6.12 it can be seen that for both race and SES groups the percentage of nonindex offenses decreases as the number of offenses increases. This finding reflects the positive relationship between the number of offenses and seriousness scores. The higher the percentage of index offenses within a category, the greater is the expected seriousness score due to the higher mean seriousness score for index offenses (231.1 for white chronic offenders and 264.5 for nonwhite chronic offenders) than for nonindex offenses (26.4 for white chronic offenders and 33.2 for nonwhite chronic offenders).

The group of index offenses can be further subdivided into offenses involving injury, theft, or damage or any combination of these three (see table 6.13).

TABLE 6.13

Mean Seriousness Score for Chronic Offenders by Race, SES, and Type of Offense

SES and Race	Nonindex	Injury	Theft	Damage	Combi-nation	All Index Offenses
I						
Nonwhite	35.1	426.3	173.7	167.9	313.1	271.8
White	18.8	175.0	193.5	168.5	242.0	201.5
II						
Nonwhite	28.4	450.4	157.8	156.2	329.7	265.7
White	34.9	100.0	50.0	175.0	283.3	180.0
III						
Nonwhite	31.0	311.4	173.4	159.1	287.5	255.1
White	26.5	467.9	190.0	160.8	275.6	242.4
IV						
Nonwhite	40.8	328.5	190.7	139.5	298.8	248.9
White	25.8	252.7	191.0	223.7	292.1	218.9
V						
Nonwhite	48.2	662.0	188.9	0	420.0	401.6
White	27.6	293.3	211.4	160.0	330.8	241.0
Total						
Nonwhite	33.2	413.3	172.2	160.1	306.6	264.5
White	26.4	358.1	192.8	178.1	286.1	232.1

Mean seriousness scores for all income groups and all races taken as a whole yield the following order (from highest to lowest): injury offenses, combination offenses, theft, damage, and nonindex offenses. However, the mean seriousness score for each type of offense varies by race. The nonwhite offenders' seriousness score for injury exceeds that of the whites by 55.2 points, and the nonwhites' score for combination offenses exceeds that of the whites by 20.5 points. The whites' mean seriousness score for theft is 20.6 points above that of the nonwhite, and the whites' score for damage offenses is 18.1 above that of the nonwhites. The nonwhites' score for nonindex offenses is 5.8 points above that of the whites.

The seriousness score for injury does not follow the general pattern in all income groups. The score for white boys in income group III is higher than that for nonwhites. In fact, the offenses committed by whites in this income group all tend to be more serious than those committed by nonwhites. The mean seriousness score for the nonwhite boys in group III remains lower, despite two homicides among nonwhite offenses. The modal seriousness score for the nonwhite offender is 100 (58 offenses), and for whites, 400 (11 offenses). The whites in income group III therefore differ considerably, with respect to injury offenses from whites in other income groups. There is only one offense in income group II, which gives this group its low score of 100, and there are only 4 offenses in group I; the small number of offenses in these groups therefore means that little significance can be attached to their seriousness scores. Nonwhites in group V have a seriousness score far higher than those for all other injury offenses. This group has a low total number of offenses (7) and includes one homicide, so that the distribution is biased toward a high seriousness score. If the homicide is excluded, the mean seriousness score for the remaining 6 offenses is 339.0.

In order of seriousness from highest to lowest, nonwhite offenses for all income groups (with the exception of group V, which has no damage offenses) are: injury, combination, theft, damage, and nonindex offenses. Group V has a seriousness score for combination offenses that is considerably higher than that for the other four groups. However, the significance of this figure is limited, as the number of offenses in this group is small. If the damage score of 0 for group V is excluded, theft, damage, and nonindex offenses have a low range of seriousness for all income groups.

The types of offenses committed by whites do not have the same order of seriousness for all income groups. Combination offenses are the most serious in groups I, II, and IV, and injury offenses are the most serious in groups III and V. The difference between combination and injury offenses in group V is 37.5, but in group III it is 192.3. This large difference is created by the high seriousness score for group III whites.

Table 6.14 indicates that whites not only commit more serious theft offenses but also commit a higher proportion of such offenses than nonwhites in all income groups. Nonwhites commit a higher proportion of assaultive offenses in relation to all offenses as well as having higher seriousness scores for these offenses. Although the seriousness score for injury offenses in income group III is higher than that for the other income groups, the proportion of injury offenses committed by group III is similar to that for the other groups.

TABLE 6.14

Frequency and Percentage of Index Offenses Committed by Type of Offense, SES and Race: Chronic Offenders

Type of Offense	SES I & II[a]				SES III			
	Whites		Nonwhites		Whites		Nonwhites	
	N	%	*N*	%	*N*	%	*N*	%
Nonindex	49	50.5	1097	55.2	420	60.0	794	55.3
Injury	5	5.2	203	10.2	39	5.6	167	11.6
Theft	20	20.6	358	18.0	144	20.6	256	18.5
Damage	8	8.2	81	4.1	39	5.6	61	4.3
Combination	15	15.5	249	12.5	58	8.2	148	10.3
Total	97		1988		700		1435	

[a]Percentages for all offenses are so similar in groups I and II and in groups IV and the following table.

Crime Code

The crime code frequency distribution of offenses by race and socioeconomic status is outlined in table 6.15. The category that contains the greatest number of offenses for both whites and nonwhites is the one termed "all other offenses." It includes 43.4 percent of all white offenses and 36.4 percent of all nonwhite offenses. Disorderly conduct is second in frequency for whites (15.8%) but third for nonwhites. Larceny constitutes 15.5 percent of all nonwhite offenses, and disorderly conduct 15.0 percent. However, within the income groups a somewhat different pattern obtains. Disorderly conduct exceeds larceny in the nonwhite income groups III, IV, and V. In group I–II it is 14.6 for the former and 16.1 for the latter offense type. Burglary is second in frequency of commitment for whites in income groups I and II, but in groups III, IV and V it is exceeded by disorderly conduct. This accounts for the higher seriousness score for white offenses in the lower income groups and is a further example of the predominance of property offenses among white offenders. In income group I–II, larceny also exceeds disorderly conduct in frequency, so that the latter offense appears fourth in frequency.

A similar pattern of offense distributions can be seen when offenses are given as percentages of total offenses for the group of one-

SES IV & V[a]				All SES Groups					
Whites		Nonwhites		Whites		Nonwhites		Total	
N	%	*N*	%	*N*	%	*N*	%	*N*	%
477	65.0	214	61.0	946	61.8	2105	55.8	3051	57.5
37	5.0	33	9.4	81	5.3	403	10.7	484	9.1
148	20.2	52	14.8	312	20.4	675	17.9	987	18.6
30	4.1	12	3.4	77	5.0	154	4.1	231	4.4
42	5.7	40	11.4	115	7.5	437	11.6	552	10.4
734		351		1531		3774		5305	

and V that these four groups have been combined into two for the purposes of this

time offenders and recidivists. The largest number of offenses falls in the category of "all other offenses" (one-time offenders: W, 51.4%; NW, 45.1%; recidivists: W, 41.9%; NW, 36.1%), followed by disorderly conduct (one-time offenders: W, 18.8%; NW, 13.9%; recidivists: W, 19.6%; NW, 14.9%), and larceny (one-time offenders: W, 7.7%; NW, 11.1%; recidivists: W, 9.5%; NW, 14.2%). Larceny exhibits an increasing percentage of total offenses as the number of offenses per person are considered.

A higher percentage of index offenses are committed by nonwhites than by whites in all income group categories (W, 29.4%; NW, 33.7%). However, higher percentages of burglary and auto theft are committed by whites than by nonwhites (8.9% and 7.1% respectively for whites, and 7.6% and 2.9% for nonwhites).

A comparison between white and nonwhite participation in index offenses is given in table 6.16. The nonwhite offenders committed 71.2 percent of all the offenses committed by the total group of chronic offenders. These offenders commit a greater proportion of assaultive index offenses in relation to their proportion of the total offenses and a lower proportion of the property offenses. All the murders, 90.6 percent of the rapes, 92.6 percent of the robberies, and 87.5 percent of the cases of aggravated assault were committed

TABLE 6.15

Crime Code of Offenses by SES and Race of Offender: Chronic Offenders

Crime Code Categories[a]	I & II				III			
	Whites		Nonwhites		Whites		Nonwhites	
	N	%	*N*	%	*N*	%	*N*	%
1.	0	0	7	0.4	0	0	2	0.2
2.	0	0	17	0.9	1	0.1	10	0.7
3.	0	0	77	3.9	4	0.5	36	2.5
4.	1	1.0	68	3.4	12	1.7	54	3.8
5.	20	20.6	158	7.9	69	9.8	105	7.3
6.	13	13.4	321	16.1	92	13.2	214	14.9
7.	3	3.1	47	2.4	41	5.9	52	3.6
8.	4	4.1	116	5.8	24	3.4	101	7.0
12.	2	2.1	70	3.5	7	1.0	41	2.6
14.	1	1.0	20	1.0	9	1.3	21	1.5
18.	0	0	85	4.3	43	6.1	49	3.5
19.	1C	10.3	290	14.6	103	14.8	216	15.1
26.	43	44.4	712	35.8	295	42.2	524	37.3
Total	97		1,988		700		1,435	

[a]The general contents of the crime code categories are: 1. Criminal homicide; theft; 8. Other assaults; 12. Weapons, possessing; 14. Other index offenses; 17–18.

TABLE 6.16

Index Offenses by Race, for Chronic Offenders

Offenses	Whites		Nonwhites	
	N	%	*N*	%
Homicide	0	0	10	100.0
Rape	3	9.4	29	90.6
Robbery	10	7.4	125	92.6
Aggravated assault	19	12.5	133	87.5
Burglary	135	31.9	288	68.1
Larceny	175	23.1	582	76.9
Auto theft	108	49.7	109	50.3
Total	1,531	28.8	3,774	71.2

Note: Income groups for each race are not shown, since percentages for all income groups within each racial category showed little variation.

IV & V				All SES Groups					
Whites		Nonwhites		Whites		Nonwhites		All SES Groups, Both Races	
N	%	N	%	N	%	N	%		
0	0	1	0.3	0	0	10	0.2	10	0.1
2	0.3	2	0.6	3	0.1	29	0.7	32	0.6
6	0.8	12	3.4	10	0.6	125	3.3	135	2.6
6	0.8	11	3.1	19	1.2	133	3 5	152	2.9
46	6.3	25	7.1	135	8.9	288	7.6	423	8.0
70	9.5	47	13.4	175	11.5	582	15.5	757	14.3
64	8.7	10	2.8	108	7.1	109	2.9	217	4.0
22	3.0	19	5.4	50	3.3	236	6.3	286	5.3
12	1.6	13	3.7	21	1.3	124	3.3	145	2.7
9	1.2	7	2.0	19	1.2	48	1.2	67	1.2
44	6.0	18	5.1	87	5.8	152	4.1	239	4.7
127	17.3	59	16.9	240	15.8	565	15.0	805	15.2
326	44.5	127	36.2	664	43.4	1,373	36.4	2,039	38.4
734		351		1,531		3,774		5,305	

2. Rape; 3. Robbery; 4. Aggravated assault; 5. Burglary; 6. Larceny-theft; 7. Auto Drunkenness and liquor law violation; 19. Disorderly conduct; 26. All other offenses.

by nonwhites, but only 68.1 percent of the burglaries and 50.3 percent of the auto thefts were. The proportion of larcenies committed by each racial group closely approximates their respective proportions of the total offenses. Nonwhites also committed a higher percentage of other assaultive offenses than whites – 82 percent as against 17.5 percent. Offenses of this kind constitute 6.3 percent of total nonwhite offenses as against 3.3 percent of total white offenses.

Age of Onset

Table 6.17 shows a negative relationship, in nonwhite offenders, between age of onset and number of offenses committed during their juvenile court age. The earlier the offender commits his first offense, the greater the number of offenses he will have committed by the end of his seventeenth year. There is only one deviation from this pattern. The mean for those who commit their first offense at 12 years is 0.5 percent higher than that for those who commit their first

TABLE 6.17

Mean Number of Offenses by Age of Onset: Chronic Offenders

Age of Onset	Nonwhites	Whites	Total
7	15.6	7.0	13.5
8	12.7	9.3	11.7
9	11.5	8.8	10.6
10	9.5	8.0	9.0
11	8.3	7.2	8.0
12	8.8	7.9	8.6
13	8.4	6.4	7.8
14	7.3	6.8	7.2
15	7.7	6.2	7.1
16	6.5	5.2	6.0

offense at 11 years. White offenders display a less consistent relationship between age of onset and number of offenses. A lower number of offenses are committed by white offenders who began at 7 years than by those who began between the ages of 8 and 12 years inclusive. Those who began offensive behavior at 12 years accumulated a larger mean number of offenses than those who began at 11 years; those who began offending at 14 years committed more offenses than those who began at 13 years. When all offenders are considered together, the only fluctuation in the negative relationship between age of onset and number of offenses committed exists in the age groups 11 and 12.

The mean age of onset for white chronic offenders is higher than that for nonwhites (W, 14.2; NW, 13.3). The age of onset for each race is closely comparable in all income groups. Both white and nonwhite lower SES boys began at a slightly lower age of onset than higher SES boys. The mean age of onset for both whites and nonwhites in the lower SES is 11.7 years. In the higher SES the age of onset is 12.6 years for whites and 12.4 for nonwhites. The mean age of onset for white chronic offenders is lower by a little more than two years than the mean for all white offenders taken together (chronic offenders, 12.0; all offenders, 14.2). The difference between the two groups for nonwhite offenders is 1.7 years (chronic offenders, 11.6; all offenders, 13.3). These differences obtain for all income groups.

Summary

Eighteen percent of the cohort offenders fall into the category of chronic recidivists. Of the 3,475 delinquents, these 627 alone were responsible for more than half of the total number of offenses committed by the delinquent group. The recruitment of the chronics is made along the same general lines as that of the general delinquent group. We found a heavy concentration of chronics in the lower SES.

Chronic offenders, as would be expected, move more often and show a poorer level of ability, performance, and achievement in the school variables.

It is clear, after closer analysis of the chronic recidivists, that any social intervention that could stop these delinquent cases before they go beyond their fourth delinquency would decrease significantly the number of offenses committed by a birth cohort. Such social action, if concentrated on the lower SES chronic offenders, would not only reduce the amount but also the seriousness of the offenses committed. The dynamic analysis offered in the second part of this book will reveal with more precision whether intervention would have to discriminate between types of offenses and patterns of what we may call incipient criminal careers.

7 Age and Delinquency

In 1940 Sellin noted that "the research student who is in pursuit of an answer to the relationship of age to crime [utilizing then available statistical information] is doomed to disappointment."[1] In 1959, following a review of age-related theories of crime and delinquency, Wootton concluded that there had been little significant advance since Sellin's analysis.[2] The material presented in the Task Force Reports of the President's Commission on Law Enforcement and Administration of Justice and other recent research indicate that this condition has not been appreciably altered. It is our suggestion that the relationship between age and delinquency has not been adequately explored, partly because most researchers have considered age an antecedent condition rather than a measure of time.[3]

Consider the three major modes that such analyses have taken: (1) the distribution of delinquent acts within a given period of time, usu-

1. Thorsten Sellin, *The Criminality of Youth* (Philadelphia: American Law Institute, 1940), p. 110.

2. Barbara Wootton, *Social Science and Social Pathology* (London: Allen and Unwin, 1959), pp. 157–72.

3. Our position is not that taken by Hirschi and Selvin. They contend that age itself is an antecedent condition. Age can only be a measure of the type or length of exposure to institutional structure. See Travis Hirschi and Hanan Selvin, *Delinquency Research: An Appraisal of Analysis Methods* (New York: Free Press, 1967).

ally one calendar year, by age-specific categories; (2) the age of onset of delinquency; (3) the effect of early delinquency on later delinquency.

The first is the most common and is usually performed with cross-sectional rather than longitudinal data. In the analysis of persons arrested, the Uniform Crime Reports use this procedure. For example, the 1969 UCR indicated that the modal age of persons arrested under age 18 was 16 (328,733), followed by ages 17 (312,597), and 15 (292,479). The inference is that 16-year-olds comprise the most delinquent group and that a peculiar set of variables (masculine identity, street culture, etc.) accounts at that age for the prevalence of delinquent acts. However, relating age to delinquency in this way does not take into account the fact that many (if not most) 16-year-olds may have entered into delinquency at a much earlier age. The circumstance of being age 16 may indeed be of less consequence than exposure to other and previous factors, or the cumulative impact of participation in earlier delinquency. Age is not the sole factor but is a measure of exposure to other factors. This first method, then, does offer information about the amount of delinquency at a given age for a specific period of time, but it does not provide an opportunity to examine other dimensions of the relationship between age and delinquency.

The second mode of analysis – examining delinquency by attention to the age of onset – has been recognized by several scholars, most notably by the Gluecks.[4] By the use of this procedure it is possible to consider the extent of delinquent careers according to varying ages at the commencement of delinquency, and thus to specify which onset age seems most likely to generate the greatest amount of delinquency over time. The Gluecks have used age of first public misbehavior and age of first police contact in many of their computations. Robin has suggested that the earlier the age of onset the more extensive will be the delinquency.[5] Lerman has observed that attraction to delinquent values at an early age has a more serious effect than attraction at later ages.[6] Consideration of age of onset in delinquency studies has generally led scholars to emphasize the rela-

4. Sheldon Glueck and E. Glueck have utilized this procedure in all their analyses of their data on delinquency and recidivism.

5. Gerald Robin, "Gang Member Delinquency: Its Extent, Sequence and Typology," *Journal of Criminal Law, Criminology and Police Science* 55 (1964): 59–70.

6. Paul Lerman, "Individual Values, Peer Values and Subcultural Delinquency," *American Sociological Review* 33 (1968): 219–35.

tionship between early age of onset and greater amounts of delinquency and criminality.

The cross-sectional approach is unable to describe the relationship between age of onset and delinquency, even if first offenders are separately tabulated. All subjects to be studied must have completed their juvenile careers in order to permit identification of the final extent of delinquency within each age-of-onset category. In cross-sectional studies, neither the child nor delinquent careers have expired. Only longitudinal data can handle this problem.

But there are other problems. The extensiveness of known delinquency may be a function merely of the early age of delinquency and the amount of available exposure time elapsing between the age of the first known delinquency and the juvenile terminal age. Unless some standardization procedure is introduced – which is not commonly done – the fact that boys who began delinquency at age 9 commit more offenses before age 18 than do boys who began delinquency at age 16 adds little to our understanding of the relationship between age and delinquency. Indeed, the number of offenses committed in a late juvenile period may not be related to the number of offenses committed in an earlier juvenile period. The extent to which delinquency at ages 15, 16, and 17 is related to prior delinquency cannot be measured by the average number of offenses committed by age-of-onset categories.

We might encounter the following situation: In a group of juveniles, each commits four offenses between the ages of 7 and 10, and then has a crime-free period until age 17, at which time each commits two more offenses – a total of six offenses per juvenile. In another group, the offenders are first arrested at age 16 and commit four additional offenses before the end of their juvenile court age of 18, for a total of five offenses per juvenile.

Delinquents in the first group committed fewer offenses as they grew older, having in addition a longer crime-free period. Therefore, computing the mean number of offenses for each group from age of onset to age 18 and employing this mean as a measure of subsequent criminality is misleading. The mean number of offenses for the later age-of-onset group is five, while the mean for the earlier age-of-onset group is six. Yet if we were to regard only the period from age 16 to age 18, the second group is by far the more delinquent in this period. Thus, age of onset greatly influences our understanding of delinquency and alters our interpretation of a statistic such as the mean.

Our two groups are not really comparable in terms of such a mean score.

In this volume we compare delinquency patterns in late juvenile years among offenders with varying ages of onset. In effect, we control for age of the offender by exploring the effect of early delinquent patterns on subsequent delinquency. We employ all three modes of age analysis to expose the differences, but consider the third procedure most useful for examining the relationship between age and delinquency.

To appreciate fully the range of delinquency patterns over age, we shall make use of information on the gravity of offenses. In so doing, we are able to relate more precisely the relationship between seriousness of crime and age, and to provide thereby a better answer to the question of whether delinquency is more serious when committed by older teen-agers or by those who are below or close to the age of puberty.

A Review of Rates of Delinquency

Nonwhites have considerably higher delinquency rates than whites. Tables 7.1 and 7.2 are a revealing display of the crude and weighted

TABLE 7.1

Age-Race-Specific Crude and Weighted Rates of Delinquency

Age	Nonwhites		Whites		Difference in *CR*	Difference in *WR*
	CR	*WR*	*CR*	*WR*	*NW/W*	*NW/W*
10 and under[a]	32.39	83.32	7.33	7.33	4.5	11.4
11	97.86	112.80	22.15	17.82	4.4	6.3
12	152.31	170.30	31.95	37.93	4.8	4.5
13	213.65	241.66	48.13	43.34	4.5	5.6
14	284.63	345.68	80.79	72.24	3.5	4.8
15	385.25	445.01	124.66	120.79	3.1	3.6
16	437.28	633.49	180.18	143.65	2.4	4.4
17	282.91	503.34	115.58	122.50	2.4	4.1
Total	1983.46	2585.91	632.97	587.84	3.1	4.4

[a]The rates for this category are expressed as the mean for each of the four ages from 7 to 10 years of age.

TABLE 7.2

Age-Race-Specific Crude and Weighted Rates by Index and Nonindex Offenses

	Index				Nonindex			
	Nonwhites		Whites		Nonwhites		Whites	
Age	*CR*	*WR*	*CR*	*WR*	*CR*	*WR*	*CR*	*WR*
10 and under	15.85	29.53	3.55	6.70	16.54	3.79	3.83	.65
11	54.45	99.25	8.38	15.24	43.42	13.55	13.77	2.58
12	78.91	154.67	17.89	35.17	73.40	15.63	14.06	2.76
13	100.62	211.60	17.75	37.38	113.03	30.06	30.38	5.96
14	114.75	293.87	28.82	59.35	169.88	51.81	51.97	12.89
15	139.90	373.12	40.75	100.73	245.35	71.89	83.91	20.06
16	158.51	539.26	39.33	115.90	278.77	94.23	140.85	27.75
17	120.95	413.29	31.66	92.96	161.96	90.05	83.91	29.54
Total	831.50	2,203.46	198.78	483.63	1,151.96	382.45	434.19	104.21

(by seriousness) race-age-specific rates per 1,000 boys, by index and nonindex offenses.

The nonwhite crude rate (1,983.5) is 3.1 times as great as the white crude rate (633.0), but the rate when seriousness scores are considered is 4.4 times as great for nonwhites (2,585.9) as for whites (587.8). Among index offenses, the nonwhite crude rate is 2.4 times as great as the white rate, but the weighted rate is 4.6 times as great. Among nonindex offenses, nonwhites have a crude rate 2.6 times and a weighted rate 3.7 times as great as the respective white rates. These figures reveal that nonwhites proportionately commit not only more offenses but more serious offenses than do whites.

Among the 5,756 offenses committed by nonwhite cohort boys, 2,413 were index offenses with a mean seriousness score of 265.0. Among the 4,458 offenses committed by white cohort boys, only 1,400 were index offenses, with a mean score of 243.3. Incidence and average seriousness make for the considerable difference in the computed rates for whites and nonwhites. Nonwhites committed 3,343 nonindex offenses, with a mean seriousness score of 33.2; whites had 3,058 nonindex offenses and a mean score of 24.0.

Another way to view the weighted rates is in terms of total cumulative scores for the offenses and the total amount of social harm inflicted on the community. For example, nonwhites inflicted on the city 750,433 units of social harm or seriousness points – 639,455 of which were from index offenses and 110,988 from nonindex offenses. If a 10 percent reduction, not of all nonwhite offenses but of index offenses, were shifted to a 10 percent increase in nonindex offenses, the corresponding reduction in seriousness units would amount to 72,777. That is, index gravity units would dip to 565,501, and nonindex gravity units would increase to 122,087 – a socially favorable trade-off. The overall crude rate of 1,983 would remain the same, but the reduction of 72,777 seriousness units (or a weighted rate reduction from 2,585.91 to 2,403.81) would be equivalent to the elimination of 28 homicides, or 104 assaults that send victims to hospitals for treatment, or 181 assaults treated by physicians without hospitalization.

In short, if juveniles must be delinquent, a major thrust of social action programs might be toward a change in the character rather than in the absolute reduction of delinquent behavior. It could also be argued that concentration of social action programs on a 10 percent reduction of white index offenses (N = 1,400; WR = 483.63) would have a greater social payoff than a 10 percent reduction of nonwhite nonindex offenses (*N* = 3,343; *WR* = 382.45). To inculcate values against harm, in body or property, to others is obviously the major means to reduce the seriousness of delinquency, both among whites and nonwhites. We are simply faced with the fact that more social harm is committed by nonwhites, so that the resources and efforts of social harm reduction should be employed among nonwhite youth, especially the very young.

Age-specific Analysis

An examination of age-specific rates, especially weighted rates, by race clearly reveals that the incidence of nonwhite offensivity at young ages is equal to or more serious than that of whites. For example, the average crude rate per 1,000 nonwhites aged 7 to 10 (32.39) is about the same as the rate for whites aged 12 (31.95). More dramatically, the average weighted rate of nonwhites aged 7 to 10 (83.32) is higher than the rate for whites between 14 and 15 years of age (72.24). In fact, for the single year when nonwhites in this cohort were 16 years old, their weighted rate of delinquency (633.49) was higher than the rate for whites over their entire juvenile careers (587.84). It may be said that nonwhites in their seventeenth year inflict more social harm, through delinquency, on the community than do whites from age 7 to age 18. The incidence (weighted) of nonwhites at age 11 (112.80) is just slightly less than that for whites at age 15 (120.79) or 17 (122.50) – a striking indication of the relatively high rate of delinquency at a very youthful age among nonwhites. Another way of pointing clearly to this fact is to draw attention to the greatest weighted rate difference between whites and nonwhites, which is at ages 7 through 10. Here the average weighted rate for nonwhites (83.32) is 11.4 times as great as the rate for whites (7.33). At age 11, nonwhites have a weighted rate 6.3 times as high as whites; thereafter the difference fluctuates, dropping to a low of 3.6 times as high at age 15.

At age 16 both whites and nonwhites reach their peak in the absolute number of offenses, in crude rates and in weighted rates. This generalization, with only a few exceptions, holds for both index and nonindex offenses and for both races. At this age the absolute value of offenses is exactly the same (*N* = 1,269) for whites and nonwhites. But because there are fewer nonwhite cohort boys and because the mean seriousness score for offenses committed by nonwhite boys ($\bar{X}$ = 144.9) is about twice as high as the mean seriousness score for offenses committed by white boys ($\bar{X}$ = 70.7) at this age, the weighted rate for nonwhites (633.49) is 4.4 times as high as the rate for whites (143.65), which difference exactly reflects the overall white/nonwhite cohort differential.

Turning attention again to the index/nonindex differences between racial groups, we see from table 7.1 that all rates, crude or weighted, are higher for nonwhites. The greatest differential is for index offenses at age 11, where the nonwhite rates are 6.6 times higher than white rates. The lowest differential is at age 17 for nonindex offenses, where the crude rate for nonwhites is only 1.9 times as great and the weighted rate 3.1 times as great as the respective white rates.

The major pattern revealed by these data is that highest crude rates for both races are among the nonindex offenses at ages 16, 15, and 17, in that order. Weighted rates follow essentially the same pattern, age 16 being the peak year. The one exception is found among white nonindex rates: at age 16 the crude rate is 140.85 and the weighted rate 27.75, while at age 17 the crude rate is much lower, 83.91, and the weighted rate 29.54. The greater number of nonindex offenses committed by whites at age 16 (N = 992) compared to their nonindex offenses at age 17 (N = 591) is offset by the lower mean seriousness score of these offenses at age 16 ($\bar{X}$ = 19.7) compared to age 17 ($\bar{X}$ = 35.3).

The weighted rates help to make especially clear the fact that a relatively low incidence of serious offenses in the early ages can produce rates that are higher than the high incidence of minor offenses in the later ages. In short, many petty offenses have a lower quantum of social harm than a few serious offenses. For example, at age 11, nonwhites committed 158 serious index offenses, and had a crude rate of only 54.45 and a weighted, or seriousness, rate of 99.25 per 1,000. At age 16, nonwhites were picked up by the police on 809 quite minor offenses, and had their highest crude rate of 278.77 but a weighted rate of only 94.23.

Whites provide a similar example: at age 12, white boys committed 126 index offenses, and had a low crude rate of 17.89 and a weighted rate of 35.17; at age 16 they committed 992 minor nonindex offenses, and had their highest crude rate at 140.85 but a rate by degree of gravity that was only 27.75.

The average seriousness scores of offenses committed in each specific age group show that nonwhite offenses are in general more serious than white offenses. In table 7.3, which displays mean offense

TABLE 7.3

Number and Mean Seriousness Scores of Index and Nonindex Offenses, by Age and Race

	Index Offenses				Nonindex Offenses			
	Nonwhites		Whites		Nonwhites		Whites	
	N	$\bar{X}$ seriousness	*N*	$\bar{X}$ seriousness	*N*	$\bar{X}$ seriousness	*N*	$\bar{X}$ seriousness
10 and under	184	186.3	100	188.9	192	22.9	108	17.1
11	158	182.3	59	181.9	126	31.2	97	18.7
12	229	196.0	126	196.6	213	21.3	99	19.6
13	292	210.3	125	210.6	328	26.6	214	19.6
14	333	256.1	203	205.9	493	30.5	366	24.8
15	406	266.7	287	247.2	712	29.3	591	23.9
16	460	340.2	277	294.7	809	33.8	992	19.7
17	351	341.7	223	293.6	470	55.6	591	35.3
Total	2,413	265.0	1400	243.3	3343	33.2	3058	24.0

seriousness scores by specific years of age as well as by race and the major dichotomy of offenses (index and nonindex), there are only two inconsequential exceptions to this generalization. With some slight fluctuations, the mean seriousness scores of index and nonindex offenses increase steadily from the younger to the older juvenile ages, for both whites and nonwhites.

A steady increase from ages 10 to 16 in crude and weighted rates (with some variations of the increments in these two types of rates) can readily be seen from examination of the foregoing tables. This pattern is similar for both races and both major offense types. But at age 17 there is a rather sharp decline (except for the white nonindex weighted rate) from the apex reached at age 16. All rates at age 17 are still high and are commonly the second or third highest of any specific race-age category. Nonetheless, the drop is noticeable. Two specific offenses seem to account for the considerable crude rate reduction between age 16 and age 17 among nonindex offenses: these are truancy and curfew violations. After age 16, boys may get working papers upon finding employment and be released from attending school; hence, absence from school that formerly was defined as truancy and labeled delinquency is no longer delinquent behavior at age 17. Moreover, the city ordinance regarding curfew applies only *through age 16*. At age 17 a lad may be on the street at any hour without being taken into custody by the police for a curfew violation. But no similar explanation is available for the rate reductions among index offenses. Whether boys who start working at age 17 are less likely to commit serious delinquencies is not clearly known but may be suspected.

As nonwhites become older they become somewhat proportionately less delinquent, and as whites become older they become somewhat more delinquent (see table 7.4). Nonetheless, the proportion of nonwhite offenses in each age category is always greater than that of the white offenders.

Reviewing the number of offenders in each age category is another way of looking at the relationship between delinquency and age. Table 7.5 shows the number of boys who committed offenses in a specific age category. An individual offender can appear in each age category, but he can be counted only once within a specific age category, for a multiple count would be equivalent to an offense count. The total distribution of offenders is almost the same as that of offenses (table 7.4) with a general pattern of increasing proportions to

TABLE 7.4

Offenses by Race and Age

Age	Nonwhites			Whites			Total		
	N	%		*N*	%		*N*	%	
10 and under	376	6.53	(64.4)	208	4.67	(35.6)	584	5.7	(100.0)
11	284	4.93	(64.5)	156	3.50	(35.5)	440	4.3	(100.0)
12	442	7.68	(66.3)	225	5.50	(33.7)	667	6.5	(100.0)
13	620	10.77	(64.7)	339	7.60	(35.3)	959	9.4	(100.0)
14	826	14.35	(59.2)	569	12.76	(40.8)	1395	13.7	(100.0)
15	1,118	19.42	(56.0)	878	19.69	(44.0)	1996	19.5	(100.0)
16	1,269	22.05	(50.0)	1269	28.47	(50.0)	2538	24.8	(100.0)
17	821	14.26	(50.2)	814	18.26	(49.8)	1635	16.0	(100.0)
Total	5,756		(56.4)	4458		(43.6)	10214		(100.0)

TABLE 7.5

Offender Count by Age and Race

Age	Whites				Nonwhites				Total		
	N	%		$\bar{X}$[a]	N	%		$\bar{X}$	N	%	$\bar{X}$
10 and under	186	5.60	(42.08)	1.12	256	7.67	(57.91)	1.47	442	6.64	1.32
11	135	4.07	(41.03)	1.12	194	5.81	(58.96)	1.46	329	4.94	1.34
12	178	5.36	(38.69)	1.26	282	8.45	(61.30)	1.57	460	6.91	1.45
13	278	8.38	(48.34)	1.22	297	8.90	(51.65)	2.09	575	8.64	1.68
14	423	12.75	(46.02)	1.34	496	14.86	(53.97)	1.67	919	13.81	1.52
15	627	18.90	(50.28)	1.40	620	18.57	(49.71)	1.80	1,247	18.74	1.60
16	881	26.56	(55.97)	1.44	693	20.76	(44.02)	1.83	1,574	23.65	1.61
17	608	18.33	(54.92)	1.34	499	14.95	(45.07)	1.64	1,107	16.63	1.48
Total	3316		(49.84)		3337		(50.15)		6,653		

[a]$\bar{X}$ = The average number of offenses per offender at each age category.

age 16, then a decrease at age 17. When race is introduced, the pattern still closely resembles that of the total offender and offense patterns. When age is examined across the racial categories, we find that white offenses decrease from age 10 and under to age 12, increase to age 16, then have a slight decrease at age 17. Nonwhite offenses display the opposite pattern with increasing proportions from ages 10 and under to 12, decreasing to age 16, and then slightly increasing at age 17.

The last column within racial categories and in the total category of table 7.5 presents the average number of offenses per offender for each age category. There are steady increases for both whites and nonwhites from ages 10 and under to 16, and a decrease at age 17. The only exception is at age 13, where the nonwhite average has a tremendous jump, which decreases at age 14. Within each age category, nonwhites tend to commit more offenses per offender than do whites, with the greatest distance between races at age 13.

Age, Race, and Socioeconomic Status

General patterns previously observed by race and SES are not altered when age-specific rates are introduced. Table 7.6 shows this three-variable complex. Proportionately, most offenses are committed by 16-year-old nonwhite boys in the lower SES (rate per 1,000 = 473.40), and fewest offenses are committed by white boys 10 years old or younger in the higher SES ($\bar{X}$ rate = 4.94). Within each race-SES group, offense rates have a monotonic increase from age 10 to age 16 and a reduction at age 17 to a level that is generally similar to that at age 15.

Rate differences between the races remain higher than rate differences between SES groups. As we earlier observed, lower SES nonwhite boys have a crude rate (2,123.57) that is about 2.4 times as high as the rate for lower SES white boys (907.01); and higher SES nonwhites have a rate (1,235.81) that is also 2.4 times as high as the rate for higher SES whites (513.36). When race is held constant and rates are compared between lower and higher SES boys, the rate for lower SES boys is shown to be about 1.7 times as high for whites as for nonwhites.

Another and more graphic way of saying this would be as follows: Assuming all other things were equal, if nonwhite boys in the lower income group had the social status of being white (acted like and were reacted to as white), a greater reduction in their delinquency would occur than if they retained their nonwhite social status but

TABLE 7.6
Age-Specific Rates by SES and Race

	Lower SES		Higher SES	
Age	Nonwhites	Whites	Nonwhites	Whites
10 and under	35.90	12.97	13.39	4.94
11	103.93	39.72	65.50	14.48
12	157.12	58.88	126.64	20.19
13	230.36	81.78	124.45	33.45
14	301.55	116.36	194.32	65.27
15	417.35	172.43	213.97	103.81
16	473.40	239.25	244.54	154.40
17	296.24	146.73	211.79	101.98
Total	2123.57	907.01	1235.81	513.36

were elevated in income. Age-specific comparisons do not disturb the power of this generalization.

The extremities of the age distribution by SES and race again reveal the enormity of the disparities in rates. For example, nonwhite lower SES boys aged 11 are proportionately committing slightly more offenses (R = 103.93) than are white higher SES boys aged 17 (101.98).

Within each specific age category, as well as for all members of the cohort, the rank order of delinquency rates from highest to lowest remains stable; namely, nonwhite lower SES, nonwhite higher SES, white lower SES, white higher SES.

Another variable of significance in the understanding of our previous work is a division into index and nonindex. Controlling for this variable in the association of age to delinquency has no effect on the original relationship (table 7.7). Holding age constant and examining proportions of index and nonindex offenses across the rows in table 7.7, we note that, for index crimes from age 10 and under to age 12, there is an increase in the number of offenses committed (4.6%), then a sharp decrease between ages 12 and 16 (24.2%), with a 6% recovery at age 17. The nonindex pattern is the exact opposite of the index pattern. As the offenders reached puberty (age 13), they committed proportionately less serious crimes, mainly because of the increase in nonindex offenses.

TABLE 7.7

Index and Nonindex Offenses by Age

Age	Index			Nonindex			Total		
	N	%		*N*	%		*N*	%	
10 and under	284	7.44	(48.63)	300	4.68	(51.36)	584	5.71	(99.99)
11	217	5.69	(49.31)	223	3.48	(50.68)	440	4.30	(99.99)
12	355	9.31	(53.22)	312	4.87	(46.77)	667	6.53	(99.99)
13	417	10.93	(43.48)	542	8.46	(56.51)	959	9.38	(99.99)
14	536	14.05	(38.42)	859	13.41	(61.57)	1,395	13.65	(99.99)
15	693	18.17	(34.71)	1303	20.35	(65.28)	1,996	19.54	(99.99)
16	737	19.32	(29.03)	1801	28.13	(70.96)	2,538	24.84	(99.99)
17	574	15.05	(35.10)	1061	16.57	(64.89)	1,635	16.00	(99.99)
Total	3813	99.96	(37.33)	6401	99.95	(62.66)	10,214	99.95	(99.99)

TABLE 7.8

Index Offenses by Type and Age

Age	Violence		Robbery		Property		Other Index Offenses		Total	
	N	%	*N*	%	*N*	%	*N*	%	*N*	%
10 and under	29	3.56 (10.21)	10	5.18 (3.52)	154	6.82 (54.22)	91	16.64 (32.04)	284	7.45 (99.99)
11	31	3.81 (14.28)	10	5.18 (4.61)	131	5.80 (60.37)	45	8.23 (20.74)	217	5.69 (100.00)
12	34	4.18 (9.58)	14	7.25 (3.94)	250	11.07 (70.42)	57	10.42 (16.06)	355	9.31 (100.00)
13	63	7.74 (15.11)	38	19.69 (9.11)	248	10.98 (59.47)	68	12.43 (16.31)	417	10.94 (100.00)
14	111	13.64 (20.71)	34	17.62 (6.34)	315	13.94 (58.77)	76	13.89 (14.18)	536	14.06 (100.00)
15	160	19.66 (23.09)	23	11.92 (3.32)	426	18.86 (61.47)	84	15.36 (12.12)	693	18.17 (100.00)
16	202	24.82 (27.41)	38	19.69 (5.16)	425	18.81 (57.66)	72	13.16 (9.77)	737	19.33 (100.00)
17	184	22.60 (32.05)	26	13.47 (4.53)	310	13.72 (54.01)	54	9.87 (9.41)	574	15.05 (100.00)
Total	814	100.01 (21.35)	193	100.00 (5.06)	2,259	100.00 (59.24)	547	100.00 (14.34)	3,813	100.00

In table 7.8 we further break down index offenses into the four categories of violence, robbery, property, and other index offenses. Descriptively, crimes of violence, robbery, and crimes against property increase with age, while the category "other index offenses" follows no discernible pattern. Crimes of violence exhibit an increase of 21 percent from age 10 and under to age 17 (except for age 12, which deviates from the pattern). Robbery is not affected by age, while property crimes show a sharp increase from ages 10 and under to age 12 (16.2%) and then an inconsistent decline to age 17 (16.4%). This pattern indicates that property offenses peak prior to puberty, decrease sharply at puberty, and then tend to level off. "Other index offenses" shows a consistent decrease of 22.6 percent from ages 10 and under to age 17. Thus, of the four index offense categories, only violence increases with age, while the three other offense types either decrease or are unaffected by age.

Race and SES each may be independently held constant to determine if some patterns can be distinguished. In table 7.9, when race is held constant, both nonwhites and whites show increasing patterns of violence, but nonwhites fall off at age 17 while the whites continue to increase at this age. A jump at age 13 for nonwhites (12.71) occurs with robbery, but thereafter there is an inconsistent pattern. No pattern exists for whites (perhaps owing to the very small number of robberies). Property crimes increase for both whites and nonwhites, with nonwhite increase being more consistent than the white increase. Both races show a decrease at age 17. Both whites and nonwhites show an inconsistent increase from ages 10 and under to age 15, then a decrease.

When age is held constant, an apparent increase in violence for nonwhites occurs from ages 10 and under to age 17 (14%), while the white proportion of violent offenses increases only half as much (7.8% over the same age period). Robbery remains unchanged for both whites and nonwhites, while property offenses decrease from age 11 to age 17 by 16.6% for the nonwhites, and show inconsistent increases and decreases for the whites. The relationship of "other index offenses" to race is also affected by age. There is a steady decrease from age 10 and under to age 17 (11.1%) for nonwhites, while for the whites, "other index offenses" remain unchanged.

In summary, as nonwhites grow older, they are involved in more violent crimes but less property and other index offenses. As whites grow older, they are slightly more violent, but show no truly distinguishing patterns of crime.

TABLE 7.9

Index Offenses by Race, Age, and Offense Type

Race and Age	Violence N	%		Robbery N	%		Property N	%		Other Index Offenses N	%	
Nonwhites:												
10 and under	22	3.68	(7.75)	7	4.05	(2.46)	111	8.14	(39.08)	44	17.05	(15.49)
11	25	4.19	(11.52)	10	5.78	(4.61)	103	7.44	(47.46)	20	7.75	(9.22)
12	25	4.19	(7.42)	14	8.09	(3.94)	163	11.77	(45.92)	27	10.47	(7.60)
13	52	8.71	(12.47)	36	20.81	(8.63)	173	12.49	(41.49)	31	12.02	(7.43)
14	82	13.74	(15.30)	30	17.34	(5.60)	189	13.64	(35.26)	32	12.40	(5.97)
15	112	18.76	(16.16)	20	11.56	(2.89)	229	16.53	(33.00)	45	17.44	(6.49)
16	154	25.00	(20.90)	32	18.50	(4.34)	240	17.33	(32.56)	34	13.18	(4.61)
17	125	20.94	(21.78)	24	13.87	(4.18)	177	12.78	(30.84)	25	9.69	(4.36)
Total	597			173			1385			258		
Whites:												
10 and under	7	3.23	(2.46)	3	15.00	(1.06)	43	4.92	(15.14)	100	7.14	(35.21)
11	6	2.76	(2.76)	0	0.00	(0.00)	28	3.20	(12.90)	59	4.21	(27.19)
12	9	4.15	(2.54)	0	0.00	(0.00)	87	9.95	(24.51)	126	9.00	(35.49)
13	11	5.07	(2.64)	2	10.00	(.48)	75	8.58	(17.98)	125	8.93	(29.98)
14	29	13.36	(5.41)	4	20.00	(.75)	126	14.42	(23.51)	203	14.50	(37.87)
15	48	22.12	(6.93)	3	15.00	(.43)	197	22.54	(28.43)	287	20.50	(41.41)
16	48	22.12	(6.51)	6	30.00	(.81)	185	21.17	(25.10)	277	19.79	(37.58)
17	59	27.19	(10.28)	2	10.00	(.35)	133	15.22	(23.17)	223	15.93	(38.85)
Total	217			20			874			1400		

TABLE 7.10

Index Offenses by SES, Age, and Offense Type

	Violence			Robbery			Property			Other Index Offenses		
SES and Age	*N*	%		*N*	%		*N*	%		*N*	%	
Lower SES:												
10 and under	25	3.82	(8.80)	9	5.55	(3.16)	134	7.89	(47.18)	64	17.58	(22.53)
11	26	3.98	(11.98)	8	4.93	(3.68)	114	6.71	(52.53)	34	9.34	(15.66)
12	26	3.98	(7.32)	11	6.79	(3.09)	199	11.71	(56.05)	41	11.26	(11.55)
13	51	7.81	(12.23)	35	21.60	(8.39)	203	11.95	(48.68)	46	12.63	(11.03)
14	92	14.08	(17.16)	25	15.43	(4.66)	229	13.48	(42.72)	45	12.36	(8.39)
15	124	18.98	(17.89)	21	12.96	(3.03)	301	17.72	(43.43)	55	15.10	(7.93)
16	176	26.95	(23.88)	33	20.37	(4.47)	299	17.60	(40.56)	43	11.81	(5.83)
17	133	20.36	(23.17)	20	12.34	(3.48)	219	12.89	(38.15)	36	9.89	(6.27)
Total	653		(17.12)	162		(4.24)	1698		(44.53)	364		(44.53)
Higher SES:												
10 and under	4	2.48	(1.40)	1	3.22	(.35)	20	3.56	(7.04)	27	14.75	(9.50)
11	5	3.10	(2.30)	2	6.45	(.92)	17	3.03	(7.83)	11	6.01	(5.06)
12	8	4.96	(2.25)	3	9.67	(.84)	51	9.09	(14.36)	16	8.74	(4.50)
13	12	7.45	(2.87)	3	9.67	(.71)	45	8.02	(10.79)	22	12.02	(5.27)
14	19	11.80	(3.54)	9	29.03	(1.67)	86	15.32	(16.04)	31	16.93	(5.78)
15	36	22.36	(5.19)	2	6.45	(.28)	125	22.28	(18.03)	29	15.84	(4.18)
16	26	16.14	(3.52)	5	16.12	(.67)	126	22.45	(17.06)	29	15.84	(3.93)
17	51	31.67	(8.88)	6	19.35	(1.04)	91	16.22	(15.85)	18	9.83	(3.13)
Total	161		(4.22)	31		(.81)	561		(14.71)	183		(4.79)

Violence increases by 14.4% for offenses committed by lower SES members from ages 10 and under to age 17 and by 7.5% for higher SES offenders (see table 7.10). For the higher SES offenses there are no other clear trends, while for the lower offenses there are interesting results for both property and other index offenses: property offenses increase from ages 10 and under to age 12 by 8.9%, then decrease from age 12 to age 17 by 10.5%. It appears that just prior to puberty there is a decline in property offenses. The category "other index offenses" declines by 16.3% from ages 10 and under to age 17.

These data imply that, while violence increases for lower SES boys when age is held constant, property and other index crimes decrease over the long run. For higher SES offenses, only violent offensiveness increases when age is controlled.

In order to provide some tentative anticipations of the extent of adult criminality in our cohort, we have projected our analysis of index offenses to age 30. We have restricted this analysis to index offenses so as to avoid the inclusion of juvenile status offenses and therefore to provide a more precise estimate of those offenses containing elements of injury, theft, and/or damage.

In table 7.11 and figure 7.1 (for first offense), yearly cumulative probabilities for index offenses are presented. Although the logistic curve $[Y = k \div (1 + e^{a + bx})]$ and the third degree curve fit the data equally well, the logistic expectancies were plotted in order to assess the extent to which the predicted values will correspond to the adult data that are to be collected later.[7] Specifically, we expect the regression of cumulated probabilities of index offenses from age 7 to at least age 30 to be logistic in nature.

Table 7.11 shows that at the end of seventeen years 12.7 percent of the cohort had committed at least one index offense. About 7 percent had committed at least two index offenses; comparable probabilities for at least three to six offenses are 4.7 percent, 3.4 percent, 2.5 percent, and 1.7 percent respectively. Thus, the probability of aggregate recidivism drops sharply from one to two offenses and continues to decline at a decreasing rate, approaching zero as we move from one to six index offenses.

7. At the Center for Studies in Criminology and Criminal Law, University of Pennsylvania, we are following a sample of the birth cohort through age 25. A future publication will describe offense probabilities to that age.

TABLE 7.11

Cumulative Probabilities of at Least One to Six Index Offenses by Age

	First Offense		Second Offense		Third Offense	
Age	Observed	Expected*	Observed	Expected*	Observed	Expected*
7	.0013	.0043	.0001	.0005	.0000	.0001
8	.0040	.0071	.0006	.0011	.0001	.0004
9	.0108	.0114	.0020	.0023	.0006	.0008
10	.0185	.0181	.0046	.0044	.0018	.0017
11	.0296	.0279	.0094	.0083	.0041	.0035
12	.0443	.0414	.0166	.0150	.0072	.0068
13	.0587	.0583	.0259	.0250	.0128	.0125
14	.0765	.0773	.0362	.0372	.0215	.0201
15	.0974	.0961	.0490	.0493	.0315	.0306
16	.1153	.1126	.0598	.0587	.0406	.0393
17	.1269	.1254	.0690	.0649	.0466	.0455
18		.1347		.0684		.0491
19		.1409		.0703		.0511
20		.1450		.0713		.0521
21		.1475		.0718		.0525
22		.1491		.0721		.0528
23		.1501		.0722		.0529
24		.1506		.0723		.0529
25		.1510		.0723		.0529
26		.1512		.0723		.0529
27		.1513		.0723		.0529
28		.1514		.0723		.0529
29		.1515		.0723		.0529
30		.1515		.0723		.0529
	* k = .151521311 a = .867526 b = –.22138033		* k = .07234934 a = 1.188366 b = –.30383666		* k =.052984305 a = 1.479431 b = –.32315700	

If the observed probabilities follow the logistic model, we may expect 15.2 percent of the cohort to have committed at least one index offense by the end of their thirtieth year. The expected probabilities of from two to six offenses follow the same logistic pattern of decline as the observed values which we have examined.

The prediction of delinquency in future cohorts is perhaps the most obvious practical advantage of the age-specific probabilities that we have obtained. To make such a prediction does not necessarily require that the absolute values of the probabilities remain unchanged

Fourth Offense		Fifth Offense		Sixth Offense	
Observed	Expected*	Observed	Expected*	Observed	Expected*
.0000	.0000	.0000	.0000	.0000	.0000
.0000	.0001	.0001	.0002	.0000	.0001
.0003	.0003	.0004	.0004	.0003	.0003
.0009	.0009	.0008	.0008	.0005	.0005
.0017	.0019	.0013	.0015	.0010	.0011
.0044	.0045	.0028	.0029	.0021	.0020
.0083	.0085	.0061	.0056	.0039	.0037
.0122	.0119	.0103	.0097	.0066	.0063
.1790	.0180	.0157	.0151	.0095	.0096
.0273	.0262	.0216	.0205	.0137	.0130
.0335	.0327	.0254	.0248	.0168	.0159
	.0391		.0267		.0178
	.0362		.0292		.0190
	.0374		.0301		.0196
	.0389		.0305		.0199
	.0401		.0307		.0201
	.0407		.0309		.0202
	.0407		.0309		.0202
	.0407		.0309		.0202
	.0407		.0309		.0202
	.0407		.0309		.0202
	.0407		.0309		0202
	.0407		.0309		.0202
	.0407		.0309		.0202

* k = .04076842
a = 1.543926
b = -.31478000

* k = .030903972
a = 1.604226
b = -.31654000

* k = .02023988
a = 1.562055
b = -.30395466

among different cohorts, although such a condition would be of maximum utility for the estimation of future criminality. Minimally, we hope that the ratios among age-specific probabilities across different cohorts would be stable.[8]

8. The problem of stability has been examined by Mildred R. Chaitin and Warren H. Dunham, "The Juvenile Court in its Relationship to Adult Criminology – A Replicated Study," *Social Forces* 45, no. 1 (1966): 114–19. See also, Harold S. Frum, "Adult Criminal Offense Trends Following Juvenile Delinquency," *Journal of Criminal Law, Criminology and Police Science* 49 (May–June 1958): 29–49.

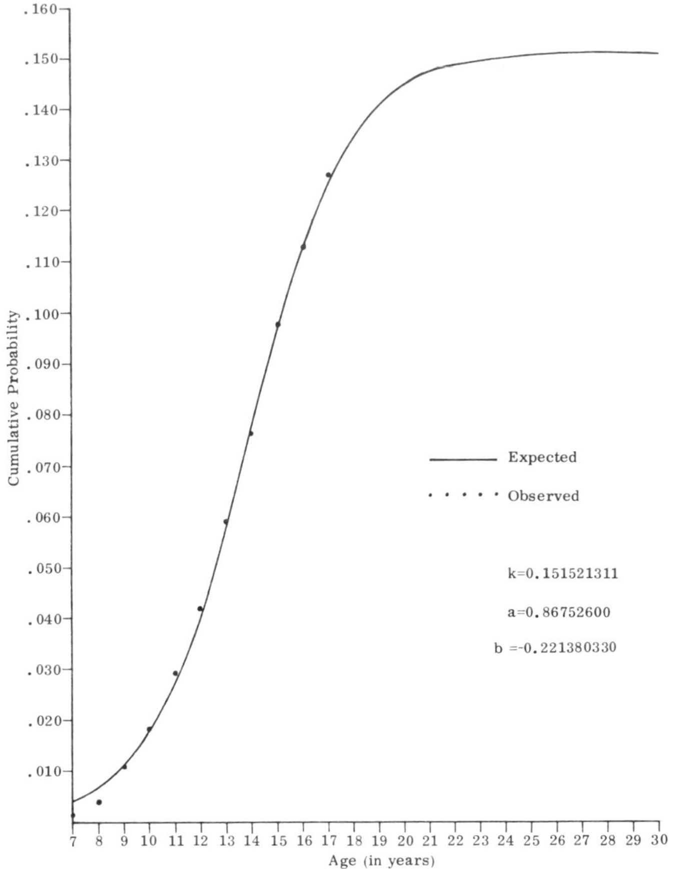

FIGURE 7.1
Cumulative Probability of at Least One Index Offense by Age

Summary

Our discussion of age and delinquency is not complete with this chapter. We have here only described some of the cohort statistics in a static stance. We have sought to show patterns of delinquency and degrees of difference over age, by race and socioeconomic status. Rates per 1,000, when weighted by seriousness of offense, reveal more clearly what happens over age and age-race-distributions. Proportionate distributions by index and nonindex offenses within each specific age have also been shown.

The next chapter deals exclusively with age of onset of delinquency, or the age at which the first offense was discovered and recorded by the police. This is a phenomenon of special significance to a birth cohort study. More findings about age and delinquency will be described in later chapters, when we more thoroughly capitalize on the use of a cohort analysis and examine these careers as a stochastic process.

8 Age of Onset

Age of onset refers to the age at which a child designated delinquent was first taken into custody by the police. In this chapter we examine, for each specific age, the relative probability of beginning delinquency. This process requires the use of a diminishing denominator at each yearly increase in age in order to compute a rate based on the remaining number of boys who, at each age, have not yet been taken into custody for a delinquent act. We also analyze the degree of seriousness of delinquency and relationships between race, SES, and types of offenses committed by boys at varying ages of onset.

Age-of-Onset Probabilities

First, let us examine the pattern of probabilities of becoming delinquent at a specific age of onset (table 8.1). The offender rates for all offenders increase gradually from age 7 to age 11, then rapidly from age 11 to age 16, with a significant decrease at age 17. The mean age of onset is 14.4 years. At age interval 16–17 a member of our cohort has the highest probability of committing an offense if he has not yet committed one (almost a 10 percent probability). As indicated earlier, the majority of these first arrests are for curfew or other minor violations.

Figure 8.1 shows graphically the probability distribution of committing a first offense per age category. When we applied regression equations to these observed probabilities, the decline at age 16 for all offenses and the variation in the relationship from age 7 to age 15.9 required that we utilize estimation procedures. We employed a second degree curve ($Y = a + bx + cx^2$) for the distribution from age 7 to age 16, and then a first degree curve ($Y = a + bx$) for ages 16 to 17. (The expected value for age 16 was utilized from the second degree curve as the observed value in the second degree regression equation.)[1]

Specifying rates first by race then by SES helps to clarify the general patterns. The probability of whites' committing an offense increases gradually to age 12, then increases rapidly to age 16, and drops sharply by age 17. The nonwhite rates begin to increase sharply by age 9 and continue a steep pattern of increase through age 16, then decrease sharply at age 17. The difference between white and nonwhite rates consistently increases over age-of-onset categories, except for age 17.

First offender rates by SES indicate that low income boys have a sharply rising probability distribution with a peak at age 16. The higher income boys also have an increasing probability of committing a first offense with age, but their distribution is much lower on the probability scale. In fact, the difference between lower SES and higher SES offenders generally increases over age-of-onset categories.

In combining race and SES we observe that the white higher SES boys have the least probability of committing a first delinquent act at every age of onset group but age 16. The difference for age 16 is most likely due to the many minor offenses (like curfew) they commit at this age.

The white lower SES boys have a consistent pattern of increasing probability of first offense from ages 7 to 16, with a drop at age 17. This rate of increasing probability of committing a first offense with age is similar to the higher SES nonwhites up to age 11. Then the lower SES whites continue to increase steadily to a peak rate of 98.3 per 1,000 population, while the higher SES nonwhites jump sharply from age 11 to age 12, level off to age 14, jump again to age 15 with a leveling through age 16, and finally, slightly decrease at age 17. Interestingly, the higher income nonwhites have the least probability of committing a first offense at age 16, but the highest at age 17.

1. See appendix F for a discussion and elaboration of age and offense probability.

TABLE 8.1

Offenses and Offenders by Age of Onset, Race, and SES

Offenses and Offenders	7	8	9	10	11	12	13	14	15	16	17
A. *All Offenders*											
Total offenses	185	353	783	944	1081	1261	1406	1284	1374	1133	410
Total offenders	25	56	124	179	234	301	412	484	596	718	346
$\bar{X}$[a]	7.4	6.3	6.3	5.3	4.6	4.2	3.4	2.6	2.3	1.6	1.2
Offender rate[b]	2.5	5.6	12.6	18.4	24.5	32.3	45.6	56.2	73.3	95.3	50.8
B. *Offenders by Race*											
White:											
Total offenses	33	113	261	319	361	398	548	648	752	738	287
Total offenders	10	29	54	80	106	131	212	288	368	496	245
$\bar{X}$	3.3	3.9	4.8	4.0	3.4	3.0	2.6	2.2	2.0	1.5	1.2
Offender rate	1.4	4.1	7.1	11.5	15.4	19.4	32.0	44.8	60.0	86.0	46.4
Nonwhite:											
Total offenses	152	240	522	625	720	863	858	636	622	895	123
Total offenders	15	27	70	99	128	170	200	196	228	222	101
$\bar{X}$	10.1	8.9	7.4	6.3	5.6	5.1	4.3	3.2	2.7	1.8	1.2
Offender rate	5.2	9.4	24.5	35.5	47.6	66.3	83.6	89.4	114.2	125.5	65.3
C. *Offenders by SES*											
Lower:											
Total offenses	162	242	697	753	868	950	1016	827	815	605	196
Total offenders	19	35	92	132	169	211	278	275	325	356	164
$\bar{X}$	8.5	6.9	7.6	5.7	5.1	4.5	3.6	3.0	2.5	1.7	1.2
Offender rate	4.1	7.7	20.3	29.7	39.2	51.0	70.8	75.4	96.4	116.8	60.9

Higher:											
Total offenses	23	111	86	191	213	311	390	457	559	528	214
Total offenders	6	21	32	47	65	90	134	209	271	362	182
$\bar{X}$	3.8	5.3	2.7	4.1	3.3	3.4	2.9	2.2	2.1	1.4	1.2
Offender rate	1.1	3.9	6.0	8.9	12.4	17.3	26.3	42.1	57.0	80.7	44.1
D. *Offenders by Race and SES*											
White lower SES:											
Total offenses	162	242	697	753	868	950	1016	827	815	605	196
Total offenders	19	35	92	132	169	211	278	275	325	356	164
$\bar{X}$	8.5	6.9	7.6	5.7	5.1	4.5	3.6	3.0	2.5	1.7	1.2
Offender rate	2.8	5.1	13.6	19.5	26.3	31.0	50.5	53.8	71.2	98.3	57.6
White higher SES:											
Total offenses	23	111	86	191	213	311	390	457	559	528	214
Total offenders	6	21	32	47	65	90	134	209	271	362	182
$\bar{X}$	3.8	5.3	2.7	4.1	3.3	3.4	2.9	2.2	2.1	1.4	1.2
Offender rate	.8	3.6	5.1	8.0	10.7	14.4	24.2	41.2	55.5	81.1	42.2
Nonwhite lower SES:											
Total offenses	141	193	510	587	650	752	767	589	556	352	97
Total offenders	13	24	63	91	115	149	180	176	201	197	80
$\bar{X}$	10.8	8.0	8.1	6.4	5.6	5.0	4.3	3.3	2.8	1.8	1.2
Offender rate	5.3	9.9	26.2	38.8	51.0	69.7	90.5	97.3	123.1	137.6	64.8
Nonwhite higher SES:											
Total offenses	11	47	12	38	70	111	91	47	66	43	26
Total offenders	2	3	7	8	13	21	20	20	27	25	21
$\bar{X}$	5.5	15.7	1.7	4.8	5.4	5.3	4.5	2.4	2.4	1.7	1.2
Offender rate	4.4	6.5	15.4	17.9	29.7	49.4	49.5	52.1	74.2	74.2	67.3

[a] $\bar{X}$ = Mean number of offenses per specified age of onset group; i.e., the number of offenses per specified age of onset group divided by the number of offenders in that age group.

[b] Offender rate = The number of offenders in each age of onset per 1,000 eligible cohort members. This is a "real" rate of onset. Any offender committing a crime prior to a specific age of onset group is not considered as a member of the eligible cohort population for that age of onset group. Thus, with increasing age the cohort population decreases.

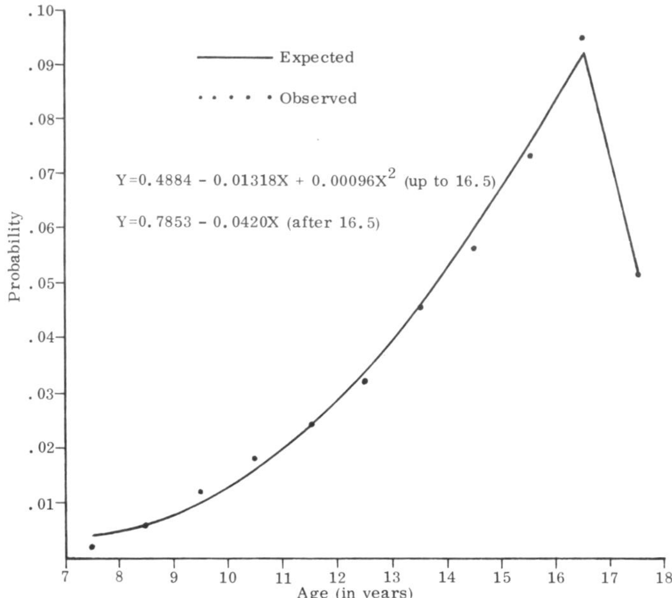

FIGURE 8.1
Yearly Probability of First Offense Commission (All Offense Types)

This seems to represent the very stable form of increasing probabilities of committing a first offense, as well as the fact that higher SES nonwhites commit other than minor crimes compared to the higher and lower SES whites.

The lower SES nonwhites are the boys most likely to commit a first offense at all ages but age 17. Their probability distribution is one of continuing increase, with a peak rate of 137.57 first offenses per 1,000 population at age 16. These are the boys most likely by far to commit an offense, but they also commit a large proportion of minor offenses. This is witnessed by the sharp drop in the offender rate from age 16 to age 17 (72.79 per 1,000 population or a 53 percent decrease over time).

Mean Age of Onset, Number of Offenses, Race, and SES

Boys who began their delinquency at age 13 (mean and mode) committed more offenses from the onset years through age 17 than boys who began at any other year. Thus, age 13 onset boys committed 1,406 of the 10,214 offenses in the cohort. In general, the pattern generated by age of onset and the number of offenses represents a unimodal, leptokurtic curve with the peak at age 13. However, it is obvious that this pattern is dependent upon the delinquent distribution; therefore, our emphasis will be on the mean number of offenses associated with different age of onset groups.

Most delinquents are initially contacted by police between the ages of 12 and 16 (72.3%). Few contacts are incurred at 10 or 11 (11.9%), and only 205 or 5.9 percent of the offenders initiate their delinquent careers before age 10. The modal age of onset for offenders is 16, at which age 20.6 percent of juvenile offenders are initially taken into custody, while the next highest age-of-onset category (15) comprises 17.2 percent.

The distribution of all offenders by age of onset of delinquency is similar to the patterns observed when all delinquent offenders (regardless of age of onset) were examined by age. In each distribution the proportion of offenders increases with age up to and including 16 years but then declines at age 17. The data on age of onset show that only 25, or 0.72 percent, of the youths incur their first police contact at age 7, while the number of offenders in subsequent age categories systematically increases through age 16 to a high of 20.6 percent. At 17 years of age the proportion of contacts (9.96%) drops to less than half the value observed for the 16-year-olds.

Meaningful patterns regarding onset of delinquency are also observed for the two races (table 8.1, section B). Nonwhites generally incur their first police contact at an earlier age than whites. The respective mean ages of onset are 13.4 for nonwhites and 14.3 for whites. Moreover, the percentage of nonwhite youth arrested for the first time is higher than the corresponding percentage of white youth in each age of onset category between 7 and 13 years, whereas a higher proportion of white than nonwhite youth fall into the 14–17 age categories. Thus, up to and including age 13, 48.7 percent of the nonwhite youth, compared to 30.8 percent of the white youth, have their initial police contact. The trend is reversed between 14 and 17 years: 69.2 percent of the white youth, but 51.3 percent of the nonwhite youth are arrested for the first time.

Meaningful patterns also appear for the two SES categories. Lower SES boys incur their first police contact earlier than higher SES boys. The mean ages of onset are, respectively, 12.3 for lower SES offenders and 13.5 for higher SES offenders. Moreover, the proportion of lower SES boys arrested for the first time is higher than the corresponding proportion of higher SES boys in each age-of-onset category between 7 and 14 years, whereas a greater proportion of higher SES youth than lower SES boys fall into the 15–17 categories. Thus, up to and including age 14, 54.2 percent of the lower SES offenders, compared to 42.6 percent of the higher SES boys, have their initial police contact. Obviously the trend reverses between ages 15 and 17, when 57.4 percent of the higher SES boys and 45.8 percent of the lower SES youth have their first police contact.

We have also analyzed offenders within onset categories by race and income group. The lower SES nonwhite boys have their first police contact earlier than all other categories, with 61.9 percent of such contacts between ages 7 and 14. The higher SES nonwhites and the lower SES whites are similar, with 56.3 percent of the higher SES nonwhites and 52.1 percent of the lower SES whites having their first contact before age 15. Finally, the higher SES whites are the group with the least proportion of contacts before age 15 (40.7%). Although this analysis emphasizes the variable of race, it also shows the relative importance of SES.

We are in a position now to consider the patterns that are exhibited when the number of offenses and offenders by age of onset are used to compute an average number of offenses per onset group. These figures appear in section A of table 8.1. As expected, the earlier the age of onset, the larger is the mean number of offenses. This fact indicates a direct negative relationship between length of exposure to arrests after the initial arrest and the average number of arrests per age-of-onset category. That is, there is a linearly descending mean number of offenses per age of onset from age 7 ($\bar{X}$ = 7.4) to age 17 ($\bar{X}$ = 1.2). The rank order correlation is -0.994, emphasizing this association.

When the delinquent group is divided into nonwhite and white categories, as in section B of table 8.1, we observe the same pattern for nonwhites, only further emphasized, with means ranging from 10.1 at age 7 to 1.2 at age 17. The rank order correlation is now a perfect -1.000. The white group does not follow the general pattern but rather peaks at age nine and then gradually declines to age 17. The rank order correlation is .882.[2]

2. Due to a tie at ages 8 and 10, the rank-order correlation coefficient is not a perfect -1.000.

If the delinquent group is divided into higher and lower SES categories, we find the lower SES boys more closely fitting the general pattern than the higher SES boys, but neither fits it perfectly. The rank order correlation coefficient for these respective groups is 0.991 for the lower SES boys and 0.863 for the higher SES boys.

Following through with the analysis, we shall now divide our socioeconomic groups into white and nonwhite categories so that the interaction effects of socioeconomic and racial patterns can be considered (table 8.1, section D). The rank order correlations for these data appear in table 8.2.

TABLE 8.2

Rank Order Correlations between Age of Onset by Race, SES, and Mean Number of Offenses

Race	Lower SES	Higher SES
White	.898	.920
Nonwhite	.991	.743

The overall impression generated by these data is the similarity between the white higher and lower SES categories and the difference between the nonwhite higher and lower SES categories. The nonwhite lower SES group has the highest rank order correlation, while the nonwhite higher SES has the lowest correlation. Of course, one reason for the sharp deviation in the higher SES nonwhites is the small size of the cells on which the correlation is based.

Table 8.3 permits us to examine weighted offender rates by age of onset. The general pattern is one of increasing rates with age of onset except for age 17, which is a decrease from age 16. Thus, offenders who start their career at age 16 do the most harm to the community. Among whites the weighted offender rate increases from age of onset to age 15, then decreases. Rates increase from age seven to age 16 among nonwhites, with minor inconsistencies at ages 13 and 15. At age 16, where the rates peak for nonwhites, the nonwhite rate is almost three times the white rate. Overall, both racial groups show increase with age, but the nonwhites consistently have higher rates than the whites across all age-of-onset categories.

The lower SES boys also display increasing rates between ages 7 and 16, then the rate decreases at age 17. Although the higher SES

TABLE 8.3

Mean Offense Seriousness Scores and Weighted Offender Rate for Specified Age-of-Onset Groups

Scores and Rates	7	8	9	10	11	12	13	14	15	16	17
A. *All Offenders*											
Mean offense score	119.22	118.59	122.00	122.60	120.04	128.89	111.56	109.27	107.16	93.14	118.43
Weighted offender rate[a]	313.52	530.52	1,397.61	1,537.37	2,343.27	3,643.50	3,788.83	5,264.22	6,991.88	7,453.01	6,150.67
B. *Race*											
White:											
Mean offense score	91.85	107.72	108.81	104.12	97.52	92.36	97.74	85.75	93.60	77.07	96.04
Weighted offender rate	154.90	362.72	889.34	1,019.86	1,144.69	1,932.93	2,250.26	3,371.59	5,847.38	5,252.38	4,774.72
Nonwhite:											
Mean offense score	125.16	123.70	126.60	132.03	131.33	145.74	120.39	133.25	123.55	123.17	170.66
Weighted offender rate	698.48	943.89	2,642.31	2,822.94	5,403.20	8,087.40	8,053.49	10.805.74	10.506.76	14.624.64	10,837.10
C. *SES*											
I-III:											
Mean offense score	126.61	126.00	125.22	130.58	122.73	133.82	114.61	122.91	123.80	103.67	125.33
Weighted offender rate	606.02	649.50	2,290.94	2,691.08	3,912.68	5,996.13	6,006.11	8,177.35	10.326.41	11,180.11	7,968.80
IV-V:											
Mean offense score	67.17	102.42	95.88	91.15	103.28	113.83	103.61	84.60	82.90	81.08	112.11
Weighted offender rate	63.42	431.56	638.92	571.67	1,057.29	1,729.67	2,100.08	3,152.17	4,670.70	4,969.38	5,017.40

D. *Race and SES*											
White I-III:											
Mean offense score	108.67	121.90	112.84	115.94	105.89	83.23	102.38	93.85	120.29	87.41	103.30
Weighted offender rate	386.92	345.36	1,750.35	2,106.97	1,972.72	202.01	3,105.32	4,282.32	9,070.11	8,206.68	6,672.61
White IV-V:											
Mean offense score	62.42	96.88	98.64	91.30	84.74	101.41	93.87	81.04	79.53	71.67	92.22
Weighted offender rate	53.64	370.28	514.85	553.13	791.78	1,577.12	1,897.57	3,006.11	4,570.91	4,101.71	4,049.32
Nonwhite I-III:											
Mean offense score	129.28	127.04	129.76	134.72	130.27	147.14	118.58	134.65	125.39	115.36	147.80
Weighted offender rate	797.87	916.50	2,767.76	3,212.88	5,680.42	9,011.22	8,831.07	12,137.09	11,665.03	14,535.61	9,497.97
Nonwhite IV-V:											
Mean offense score	72.36	109.98	78.92	90.53	141.16	136.21	135.62	115.62	108.09	187.16	255.92
Weighted offender rate	168.12	1,089.91	1,975.71	773.54	3,977.17	3,440.00	4,225.24	4,533.85	5,310.44	15,002.97	17,302.40

[a]Weighted offender rate – this is the total seriousness score of the first offense of offenders at a specific age divided by the eligible population at risk (per 1,000 individuals) at that age.

boys follow the same pattern, the lower SES boys have higher rates at all age-of-onset categories. For instance, at age 7 the rate for lower SES boys is over nine times as high as the rate for higher SES boys. This large difference tends to decrease in older age-of-onset categories.

The combination of race and income helps to clarify further the weighted rates over age-of-onset categories. Among the white lower SES boys there is a slightly inconsistent pattern of increasing weighted rates from age 7 to 15, and decreasing rates at ages 16 and 17. The higher SES boys' rates have a totally consistent pattern of increase between ages 7 and 15, then decrease at ages 16 and 17. However, the lower SES boys have a consistently higher rate across age-of-onset categories than higher SES boys, except for age 8.

Lower SES nonwhites generally have the highest rates for the combined race-SES categories. There is a consistent increase in the rates from ages 7 to 12, then some inconsistency to age 16, and a decrease at age 17. The nonwhite higher SES boys show an increasing pattern from ages 7 to 17, with the exception of age 10. Although the higher SES nonwhites initially have lower rates than the lower SES nonwhites, this changes at age 16, and the rate at age 17 is the highest rate of all race-SES age-of-onset categories. Generally, nonwhites tend to have higher rates than whites across SES categories. Only at ages 7, 10, and 15 do the lower SES whites have higher rates than the higher SES nonwhites.

The influence of race still stands as the foremost variable in this analysis. SES also shows distinct distributions of mean offense seriousness scores and weighted rates across age-of-onset categories, but the relative importance of SES is subordinate to that of race.

Age of Onset and the Quality of Offenses

An important relationship is that between age of onset and the mean seriousness score for all offenses committed by a specific onset group. Table 8.3 contains the offense seriousness scores for specified offender groups by age of onset. Several general findings emerge for all offenders analyzed together: (1) the 12-year-old onset group has the highest mean offense seriousness score; (2) the mean offense seriousness score for the first year of delinquency is lower than the overall mean offense seriousness score for each onset category; (3) the range of scores is only 35.8 points (if age 16 is excluded, the range is reduced to 21.7 points); (4) there is a moderately high negative relationship between age of onset and the total mean offense seriousness score (with a zero-order correlation = -.574).[3]

Table 8.3, section B, shows the onset offense seriousness means for whites and nonwhites. The nonwhites have their highest onset offense mean at age 17 with a range of 50.3. They also exhibit higher offense means in all categories than the total offense means. The relationship between age of onset and the nonwhite offense mean is moderately positive with a zero-order correlation of .431, indicating some relationship between the first delinquency and the seriousness of offenses committed for the nonwhite onset categories.

The white offense mean seriousness scores have their highest value at age 9, with a range of 31.74. The whites consistently have mean offense seriousness scores which are lower than that for the total cohort and, therefore, lower than for the nonwhites. The correlation between age of onset and the whites' mean seriousness scores is -.594.

Section C of table 8.3 contains the data on the offense seriousness means by SES onset groups. The lower SES groups have consistently higher means than both the higher SES groups and the total cohort across age-of-onset categories. The zero order correlation is -.461 for this lower SES group compared to .183 for the higher SES group. The range of means for the lower SES boys is 30.15, while for the higher SES boys it is 46.66. Overall, these two categories are dissimilar from each other as well as from the total cohort. Thus, SES, as does race, makes a difference in our evaluation of mean seriousness scores and age of onset at this stage of our analysis.

Finally, in section D of table 8.3 we have data which allow us to focus on the relationship of the mean offense seriousness score with age of onset by race and SES. The most striking pattern in the table is the strong positive relationship between age of onset and mean seriousness score for the nonwhite higher SES boys. The zero-order correlation for this group is .776, indicating that a boy who first becomes delinquent at an older age most probably will have a higher seriousness score than a boy who became delinquent at a younger age. (This correlation says nothing about the extent of difference in the magnitude of the scores over time; only that the difference is consistent.) The correlation is unlike the general trend of the entire cohort (as seen in section A of table 8.3).

3. Since the mean seriousness score is an interval datum, we have utilized a zero-order correlation rather than rank order as previously used.

The nonwhite lower SES boys follow the general pattern for nonwhites discussed earlier, with relatively high mean offense seriousness scores across all age-of-onset categories. This fact helps to explain why they have a very low correlation coefficient of .062.

The white lower SES boys generally have higher mean seriousness scores than the white higher SES boys, across all age-of-onset categories. Of all groups, the white higher SES youths generally have the lowest mean scores (with three exceptions at ages 9, 10, and 12). More interestingly, nonwhites, when holding SES constant, generally have higher mean scores across all ages, with one major exception. White lower SES boys consistently have higher mean seriousness scores between ages 7 and 10 than nonwhite higher SES boys. From ages 11 to 17 this reverses itself (except for age 15), and the nonwhite higher SES boys have higher mean seriousness scores. In fact, for ages 11, 13, 16, and 17, this group has the highest means of all the race-SES categories.

The zero-order correlation for white lower SES boys is -.449 and for white higher SES boys it is -.051. These correlations are in keeping with the correlation discussed earlier for SES groups across age-of-onset categories (-.461 and .183), but not for the racial breakdown which would predict both scores to be -.594 across SES. Thus, SES does play a role in interpreting the data.

Age of Onset and Type of Offense

Tables 8.4 and 8.5 present data on the number of offenses and the mean seriousness score by offense type (nonindex, injury, theft, damage, or combination) for the eleven age-of-onset categories.

Considering the distribution of nonindex offenses within onset categories, we note that, generally, the earlier the age of onset the lower the proportion of nonindex offenses. Thus, the percentages of nonindex offenses committed by whites in age-of-onset categories 7–17 are 51.5, 57.5, 52.9, 58.3, 63.0, 63.7, 67.4, 70.2, 71.8, 80.0, and 75.7, respectively. There is only one variation in the pattern, the drop to 75.7 at age of onset 17, which is relatively small when compared to the entire range and does not distort the overall pattern of an increasing proportion of nonindex offenses in the later age-of-onset categories. The nonwhite age-of-onset categories reflect the same pattern, though there are differences in the percentages. Thus, the percentages of nonindex offenses committed by nonwhites in age-of-onset categories 7–17 are respectively 46.7, 50.8, 50.3, 53.0,

55.5, 57.5, 61.4, 62.7, 64.3, 66.4, and 58.4. The difference between the proportions of whites and nonwhites at corresponding age-of-onset categories increases with age from 4.8 at age 7, to 6.2 at age 12, to 17.3 at age 17.

For index offenses (injury, theft, damage, and combination) theft offenses account for the largest proportion within all age-of-onset groups, but the proportion of theft offenses generally decreases as age of onset increases. This decrease is not reflected in an increase in the proportion of injury offenses. On the contrary, the proportion of injury offenses is remarkably stable. Injury offenses account for 3.0 percent of the offenses committed by whites beginning at age 7, for 7.2 percent (the peak) at ages 10 and 14, and for 5.9 percent at age 17. The range (excluding age 8, which had only two offenses) is only 4.2 percent from ages 7 to 17. Similarly, the range in percentages of injury offenses for nonwhites is only 4.9 percent over the entire eleven-year span of time with a low of 7.9 percent at age 8 and 12.8 percent at age 17.

The mean seriousness score for nonindex offenses is higher for nonwhites than for whites at all ages of onset. The average range of these differences is 5.12 points. We might also note the flatness of the distributions for nonindex offenses, indicating little relationship between age of onset and mean seriousness score for this offense type. (The zero-order correlations are -.174 for whites and .472 for nonwhites.)

The relationship of the mean seriousness score for injury and age of onset appears to be a strong, positive one. Nonwhites have higher mean seriousness scores than whites in eight of the eleven age-of-onset categories (7 to 14). The mean difference between mean seriousness scores for those eight categories where nonwhites have higher scores than whites is 203.8. For age-of-onset categories in which whites have higher injury scores than nonwhites, the mean difference is only 22.7. However, white scores tend to increase more steadily with age (relative to their distributions) than do nonwhite scores. This fact is reflected in the zero-order correlations between injury score and age of onset, which for whites is .922 and for nonwhites is .660.

This finding offers an explanation for the positive relationship between the nonwhite seriousness score for all offenses and age of onset. The positive relationship – compared to the negative one for whites – may be due to the difference in the magnitude of the mean

TABLE 8.4

Mean Number of Offenses and Mean Seriousness Score for Offense Types by Race and Age of Onset

Age and Offense	White N	White %	White $\bar{X}$	Nonwhite N	Nonwhite %	Nonwhite $\bar{X}$
Age 7:						
Nonindex	17	51.5	31.9	71	46.7	40.5
Injury	1	3.0	207.0	13	8.6	246.5
Theft	7	21.2	164.9	33	21.7	158.9
Damage	6	18.2	99.3	6	3.9	103.7
Combination	2	6.1	266.0	29	19.1	244.0
Total	33			152		
Age 8:						
Nonindex	65	57.5	25.7	122	50.8	33.1
Injury	2	1.8	150.0	19	7.9	313.4
Theft	26	23.0	209.5	48	20.0	155.9
Damage	8	7.1	159.3	14	5.8	56.9
Combination	12	10.6	289.8	37	15.4	270.8
Total	113			240		
Age 9:						
Nonindex	138	52.9	25.2	260	50.3	29.1
Injury	15	5.7	228.9	60	11.6	395.3
Theft	67	25.7	188.2	101	19.5	155.6
Damage	25	9.6	176.6	37	7.2	135.3
Combination	16	6.1	278.3	59	11.4	253.5
Total	261			517		
Age 10:						
Nonindex	186	58.3	23.1	33	53.0	26.8
Injury	23	7.2	313.7	74	11.9	441.1
Theft	49	15.4	183.7	125	20.0	161.7
Damage	30	9.4	141.9	35	5.6	150.1
Combination	31	9.7	272.7	60	9.6	259.1
Total	319			327		
Age 11:						
Nonindex	226	63.0	23.8	400	55.5	33.2
Injury	15	4.2	280.0	68	9.4	420.9
Theft	60	16.7	222.8	130	18.1	161.8
Damage	31	8.6	152.2	27	3.8	161.7
Combination	27	7.5	279.4	95	13.2	295.3
Total	359			720		
Age 12:						
Nonindex	254	63.7	28.5	494	57.5	35.9
Injury	22	5.5	283.1	101	11.8	409.4
Theft	68	17.0	171.2	142	16.5	188.7
Damage	27	6.8	160.6	40	4.7	167.2
Combination	28	7.0	268.5	82	9.5	397.0
Total	399			859		

TABLE 8.4 continued

Age and Offense	White N	White %	White $\bar{X}$	Nonwhite N	Nonwhite %	Nonwhite $\bar{X}$
Age 13:						
Nonindex	370	67.4	22.8	529	61.4	31.0
Injury	36	6.6	355.8	85	9.8	381.2
Theft	81	14.8	203.0	146	16.9	180.5
Damage	30	5.5	187.3	23	2.7	182.0
Combination	32	5.8	326.8	79	9.2	307.9
Total	549			862		
Age 14:						
Nonindex	456	70.2	24.8	398	62.7	34.7
Injury	47	7.2	297.3	79	12.9	443.1
Theft	91	14.0	204.8	98	15.4	191.6
Damage	36	5.5	179.0	20	3.2	165.0
Combination	20	3.1	274.3	40	6.3	340.5
Total	650			635		
Age 15:						
Nonindex	540	71.8	22.1	402	64.3	36.5
Injury	43	6.4	437.1	66	10.5	413.3
Theft	107	14.2	204.1	81	13.0	201.4
Damage	23	3.1	193.4	23	3.7	154.3
Combination	34	4.5	329.5	53	8.5	293.0
Total	752			625		
Age 16:						
Nonindex	588	80.0	21.0	263	66.4	32.8
Injury	35	4.8	427.9	37	9.3	392.3
Theft	77	10.5	188.0	55	13.9	213.1
Damage	17	2.3	205.9	13	3.3	154.2
Combination	18	2.4	626.6	28	7.1	428.1
Total	735			396		
Age 17:						
Nonindex	218	75.7	32.6	73	58.4	70.1
Injury	17	5.9	470.6	16	12.8	446.3
Theft	34	11.8	243.9	22	17.6	207.0
Damage	9	3.1	111.1	5	4.0	160.0
Combination	10	3.5	320.0	9	7.2	344.4
Total	288			125		

injury seriousness scores for whites and for nonwhites. That is to say, although both whites and nonwhites show an increase with age of onset in the mean seriousness scores for injury offenses, the magnitude of the difference of these scores between races can account for the overall finding of a positive association between the mean seri-

TABLE 8.5

Mean Number of Offenses and Mean Seriousness Score for Offense Type by SES and Age of Onset

	Lower SES			Higher SES		
Age and Offense	*N*	%	$\bar{X}$	*N*	%	$\bar{X}$
Age 7:						
Nonindex	71	43.8	39.6	17	73.9	36.0
Injury	12	7.4	247.8	1	4.6	220.0
Theft	38	23.5	159.9	3	13.0	179.7
Damage	10	6.2	104.4	2	8.7	87.0
Combination	31	19.1	245.4	0	0.0	0.0
Total	162			23		
Age 8:						
Nonindex	120	49.6	32.5	67	60.3	26.9
Injury	14	5.8	324.8	7	6.3	243.9
Theft	62	25.6	178.8	12	10.8	157.8
Damage	14	5.8	149.7	8	7.2	171.8
Combination	32	13.2	276.8	17	15.3	273.1
Total	242			111		
Age 9:						
Nonindex	351	50.4	28.9	51	59.3	18.0
Injury	67	9.6	375.3	8	9.3	250.9
Theft	156	22.4	166.0	13	15.1	198.1
Damage	50	7.2	147.5	12	14.0	170.7
Combination	73	10.5	256.3	2	2.3	350.0
Total	697			86		
Age 10:						
Nonindex	407	5.1	26.4	110	57.6	21.9
Injury	85	11.3	452.0	12	6.3	117.8
Theft	133	17.7	161.5	41	21.5	188.6
Damage	49	6.5	142.1	16	8.4	159.2
Combination	79	10.5	262.2	12	6.3	276.1
Total	753			191		
Age 11:						
Nonindex	490	56.4	30.2	138	64.7	28.0
Injury	69	8.0	401.5	14	6.7	307.6
Theft	161	18.6	178.5	29	13.6	195.3
Damage	46	5.3	148.0	13	6.1	190.3
Combination	102	11.8	291.3	19	8.9	299.4
Total	868			213		
Age 12:						
Nonindex	560	59.0	31.6	191	61.4	38.2
Injury	101	10.6	401.6	22	7.1	318.6
Theft	151	15.9	185.5	59	19.0	180.8
Damage	48	5.0	169.7	18	5.2	150.7
Combination	90	9.5	363.3	21	6.8	367.9
Total	950			311		

TABLE 8.5 continued

Age and Offense	Lower SES *N*	Lower SES %	Lower SES $\bar{X}$	Higher SES *N*	Higher SES %	Higher SES $\bar{X}$
Age 13:						
Nonindex	630	62.0	26.4	264	67.7	29.6
Injury	93	9.2	484.3	28	7.2	338.4
Theft	173	17.1	181.5	54	13.0	207.4
Damage	32	3.2	176.8	21	5.4	197.3
Combination	88	8.7	306.8	23	5.9	338.2
Total	1016			390		
Age 14:						
Nonindex	542	65.5	33.8	313	68.5	22.0
Injury	95	11.5	425.3	30	6.6	282.5
Theft	118	14.3	198.4	69	15.4	199.3
Damage	31	3.8	175.8	25	5.5	171.8
Combination	41	5.0	342.4	20	4.4	263.4
Total	827			457		
Age 15:						
Nonindex	524	64.3	33.4	415	74.2	20.7
Injury	85	10.4	444.4	29	5.2	361.4
Theft	113	13.9	200.9	75	13.4	205.9
Damage	29	3.6	155.9	17	3.0	204.4
Combination	64	7.8	287.2	23	4.1	363.4
Total	815			559		
Age 16:						
Nonindex	432	71.4	29.8	420	79.6	19.5
Injury	47	7.8	418.5	26	4.9	381.5
Theft	78	12.9	210.2	55	10.1	180.1
Damage	20	3.3	170.2	10	1.5	210.0
Combination	28	4.6	370.1	17	3.2	747.1
Total	605			528		
Age 17:						
Nonindex	127	64.8	54.9	161	75.2	32.1
Injury	18	9.2	353.3	15	7.0	606.7
Theft	34	17.4	215.5	22	10.3	250.9
Damage	9	4.6	144.4	5	2.3	100.0
Combination	8	4.1	325.4	11	5.1	336.4
Total	196			214		

ousness score for all offenses and age of onset for nonwhites, but not for whites.

The mean seriousness scores for theft and damage offenses for whites and nonwhites exhibit varying degrees of relationship to age of onset. The zero-order correlation between age of onset and mean seriousness score for theft offenses is .502 for whites and .945 for nonwhites, while for damage offenses it is .367 for whites and .663 for nonwhites. These correlations indicate a stronger general pattern of relationship for nonwhites than for whites in both of these offense types and age of onset.

The relative magnitudes of white and nonwhite seriousness scores are also enlightening. In theft offenses the mean seriousness scores are higher for whites than for nonwhites in eight of the eleven onset categories (7–11, 13–15, and 17). In six of the eleven onset categories (8, 9, and 13–16) the white means are higher than the nonwhite means for damage offenses. (It should be remembered, however, that the magnitude of means is independent of their consistency over time as reflected in the correlation analysis.) The mean difference between white and nonwhite seriousness scores for theft is 25.1, and for damage offenses, 8.32. Although once again the range in differences is narrow, the trend is for whites to have higher mean seriousness scores within age-of-onset categories for theft and for damage.

The significance of the mean seriousness scores for combination offenses is similar to those for both damage and theft. The white mean scores are greater than the nonwhite in seven of the eleven categories (7–10, 13, 15, and 16) with a relatively wide range (mean difference = 128.75 for all onset categories). The trend is toward a positive relationship between age of onset and mean seriousness score for combination offenses – a relationship we observed in other instances where whites exhibited the larger number of highest means over the eleven age-of-onset categories. (The correlation for whites is .530, and for nonwhites, .718.)

In sum, analysis of the relationship between number of offenses and mean seriousness score by type of offense within age-of-onset categories, divided on the basis of race, has indicated the following trends: (1) an increasing proportion of nonindex offenses occurs with each consecutive age of onset; (2) white offenders within age-of-onset categories consistently exhibit higher means in the damage, theft, and combination categories; (3) nonwhite offenders have higher mean seriousness scores on nonindex offenses and injury offenses; (4) the positive relationship between the nonwhite mean seriousness score for all offenses and the age of onset is in part due to the impact of the higher proportion and degree of seriousness of injury offenses committed by nonwhites.

Turning to the mean seriousness scores of age-of-onset categories broken into our five offense types, we are able to see that the lower SES boys had higher mean seriousness scores in all age-of-onset categories. For nonindex offenses (with the exception of ages of onset 12 and 13) the lower SES boys have higher mean seriousness scores than the higher SES boys. The mean range of these differences is 12.32, a relatively small dispersion. Zero-order correlations show that neither high nor low SES boys show a strong correlation between age of onset and mean nonindex seriousness score (-.173 and .339, respectively for high and low SES boys).

The mean seriousness injury score demonstrates a positive relationship with age of onset for both SES groups. The higher SES boys have a correlation coefficient of .781 for age of onset and injury score, and the lower SES boys have a correlation of .520. The lower SES boys have higher mean seriousness scores for injury at all ages of onset.[4] The average range of the differences between SES groups over age-of-onset categories is 255.68, which is a relatively wide dispersion.

The mean seriousness score for theft is also positively related to age of onset for both SES groups. The zero-order correlation for the lower SES boys is a surprising .925, while the correlation coefficient is .645 for the higher SES boys. In eight of the eleven age-of-onset categories (7, 9–11, 13–15, and 17) the higher SES boys have larger mean seriousness scores than the lower SES boys, with an average mean difference between theft scores of 83.46. Although the magnitude of the mean theft seriousness scores for higher SES boys is substantially greater than for lower SES boys, there is not a consistent increase in seriousness over onset categories.

In damage offenses, lower SES boys show a more positive relationship between age of onset and mean seriousness score ($r = .587$) than do higher SES boys ($r = .265$), but neither group shows a strong association. The mean difference between SES groups for the mean damage seriousness score is 55.50. The relationship of the mean seriousness score for combination offenses and age of onset is moderately positive for both SES groups: zero-order correlations are .801 and .635 for the lower and higher SES groups respectively. As for

4. Except at age 17, for which higher SES boys have an extremely high score of 606.7. This score, however, is based on a cell size of only fifteen and is probably not very stable.

damage and theft, the large majority of onset categories (eight) have high mean seriousness scores for the higher SES boys compared to the lower SES boys. The mean difference between high and low SES mean seriousness scores is 163.30.

In general, the magnitude of the mean seriousness scores for nonindex and injury offenses tends to be greater for the lower SES boys across age-of-onset categories, while the magnitude of the mean seriousness score for theft, damage, and combination tends to be greater for the higher SES boys.

The final step in this analysis of offense type and age of onset would be to indicate their relationships to race and SES groups in combination. The problem with this particular analytical step is that the table representing the data contains 220 cells, with the majority of cells containing 20 or fewer cases. The only offense category that can properly be analyzed by race and SES is the nonindex type. For both whites and nonwhites in the lower SES group this proportion increases across age-of-onset categories. For nonwhites the increase is 30.47 percent from age 7 to age 17, and for whites it is 37.38 percent for the same age span. In addition, the magnitude of proportions for whites and for nonwhites is similar across age-of-onset categories, with exception of age 7. Thus, as lower SES boys of both races get older, their first offense is more likely to be a nonindex one.

For higher SES boys, both races show similar patterns for nonindex offenses according to age of onset. Offense proportions decrease from age 7 to ages 10 or 11 and then reflect an inconsistent increasing and decreasing pattern to age 17.

The nonindex mean seriousness scores show a general pattern of increase across age-of-onset categories, except for the white higher SES boys. The zero-order correlations are .412 for the nonwhite lower SES boys, .606 for the nonwhite higher SES boys, .677 for the white lower SES boys and –.437 for the white higher SES boys. In all race-SES categories (except higher SES white boys) the mean seriousness score at age of onset 17 is at its highest.

In summary, nonindex offenses consistently constitute the largest number of offenses per age-of-onset category. Nonwhites and lower SES boys have higher mean seriousness scores for nonindex and injury offenses; whites and higher SES boys have higher mean seriousness scores for damage, theft, and combination offenses. Thus, the relationship of age of onset to offense type is influenced by both race and SES, but more clearly by the former.

9 Static and Contingent Probabilities: Introduction

We are now ready to consider the dynamics of delinquency in our cohort. That is, we shall investigate the patterns of offensivity for the delinquents in our cohort as we follow them from the first through subsequent offenses. The substantive issues we shall consider will involve questions of specialization in delinquency, offense switching, and shifts in the qualitative dimensions of offensivity, as the individual boys in our study and the cohort delinquents as a whole proceed from their first to their last offense in their delinquency careers.

This concern initially raises four methodological problems: (1) the procedure to be followed in classifying offenses; (2) the procedure to be followed in comparing adjacent offenses (the k-1st and kth offenses); (3) the procedure to be followed to compare adjacent comparisons (all k-1st and kth comparisons); and (4) the empirical transitions between offense types for the first to kth offense. As noted earlier,[1] offenses may be classified either by reference to their crime code (the legal label) or by reference to the type of harm the offense involves (injury, theft, damage, combination, and nonindex in the

1. See chapter 1, pp. 3–26, and chapter 3, pp. 39–52.

Sellin-Wolfgang scoring procedure). We have chosen the latter procedure because it reduces the number of potential cells in the offense classification scale from some 26 to 5, and because it allows consideration of patterns of offenses that are similar in behavioral form while differing in their legal classification (for example, burglary, larceny, fraud, etc., are all theft offenses). The Sellin-Wolfgang classification provides a precise characterization of the relevant behavioral content of the offense and therefore produces a more meaningful base from which to assess patterns of delinquent behavior. Our consideration of the dynamics of delinquent careers begins with the classification of each offense into one of the five types committed by the cohort.

Assessment of k–1st and kth offense distributions and all k–1st and kth offense distributions classified into the five offense types presents problems of distribution and trend analysis. In chapter 10 we shall primarily utilize regression analysis to consider the independent offense distributions (i.e., the first through kth offense distributions for the cohort). We shall be concerned with shifts in the offense distributions of the cohort as offenders proceed from the first offense to the fifteenth offense. This analysis does not involve transitions between offenses but rather approaches each offense number as an independent distribution.

The other relevant problem, pursued in chapter 11, involves the transitions between offenses – the aspect of the dynamics of delinquency most pertinent to the issues noted above. The problem is to analyze the paths followed from the k–1st to the kth offense for all offenses in the manner displayed in tabular form in table 9.1.

We can imagine a similar table for the second-to-third transition, etc., to the k–1st-to-kth transition. The data in the cells are probabilities (e.g., p_{22} is the probability of committing a second injury offense following a first injury offense). In chapter 11 our primary focus will be on the probabilities associated with each cross-classification (i.e., "path"). We can compare each adjacent offense transition or we can compare transitions given previous offense histories (the second to the third transition, given a first injury offense, etc.). The investigation of successive matrices as presented in table 9.1 has proven most amenable to Markovian analysis – a technique that has only recently been introduced into sociological literature. We have utilized this procedure and shall review the technique and its uses in sociology in order to furnish the background for this aspect of our investigation.

TABLE 9.1

Model of Transition from First to Second Offense

First to Second Offense	Nonindex	Injury	Theft	Damage	Combination	Desist
Nonindex	p_{11}					
Injury		p_{22}				
Theft			p_{33}			
Damage				p_{44}		
Combination					p_{55}	
Desist	p_{61}					p_{66}

In chapter 11 we shall attempt to model the transition probabilities of the cohort offenders' delinquent careers in a tentative way as a finite homogeneous Markov chain.[2] The characteristics of this process are as follows:

(a) A set of states E_1 E_2 $E_3 \ldots E_n$. In this case the states are the offense types of nonindex, injury, theft, damage, combination, and desistance.

(b) A conditional probability $[P_{ij}(k)]$ associated with being in state j at time k, having been in state i at time period k-1 subject to $0 \leqslant P_{ij} \leqslant 1$ and $\Sigma_{j=1}^{N} P_{ij} = 1$, for any $i = 1$ to N (the elements of the rows of the transition matrix must lie between 0 and 1 while summing to 1). We shall define our time periods here as offense numbers rather than as continuous time. Thus time period 1 will be defined as the first offense, time period 2 as the second offense, and so on.

(c) A square matrix of the probabilities called a stochastic matrix as described above.

(d) Independence of the process from time period (k). That is, the transition probabilities $P_{ij}(k)$ do not depend on k. The transition matrix $P(k) = P$ for all k and is thus constant and unchanging over time.

This last quality of a homogeneous or time-independent Markov chain may seem to be a rather difficult one to meet, particularly for sociological data, for it appears to be essentially a denial of the influence of time or history on the (in this case) choice of offenses as one

2. We present here a rather informal discussion of the concept of a Markov chain. The reader is referred to the standard text on this subject: John G. Kemeny and J. Laurie Snell, *Finite Markov Chains* (Princeton: D. Van Nostrand Co., 1960).

progresses from one offense to the next. Such need not be the case, for we do not necessarily have to assert that the content of the *histories* of the subjects be the same simply because the probabilities of committing the next offense appear to depend only on the type of the last offense. On the contrary, we need only to realize that the aggregate effect is the generation of probability matrices which appear constant over time. Offense switching may occur in such a way that the independence from time is the observable result, even though the actual behavior is not probabilistic. Nonetheless, for our purposes we need only be concerned with the problem of whether or not the behavior *appears* to be probabilistic and time-independent.

It will become apparent in chapter 11 that a complete assessment of this model is not possible for two reasons: (1) in spite of the large number of offenders and offenses analyzed in the cohort study, additional cases would still be needed to fill the branch probabilities to the extent that a complete test of order of the chain would be possible; and (2) the sample is truncated at age 18 so that the model has an artificial boundary placed upon it.

We may visualize the progression from birth to the first offense, then to the second, to the third, and so on as pathways along the branch of a tree which has six alternative paths at each juncture (see figure 9.1). Each point of departure is the probability of arriving at that location, having come from the offense type at the origin point along the path. Of course, after any offense, or from birth, one may desist from delinquency and thus become "absorbed" into the state of desistance.

Thus, one may follow any one of a multitude of discrete pathways which follow the expansion of 6^k.

This tree, or "snowflake," of offensive diversity, which we have only partially diagramed, becomes extraordinarily large quite rapidly and exhausts the supply of offenders in the sheer number of available pathways. However, enough cases exist to test the dependency of offense choices on the type or types of offenses committed *before* the last for the first three offenses. This data limitation becomes an unpleasant fact of research life in several areas.

The problem of truncation need not bother us at this time, for we shall attempt to model the offense histories associated with that limited age span of maximum delinquency proneness from roughly 13 to 17 years of age.

We shall attempt to use this model to describe offense transitions so that such an elaborate representation will not be necessary. If the

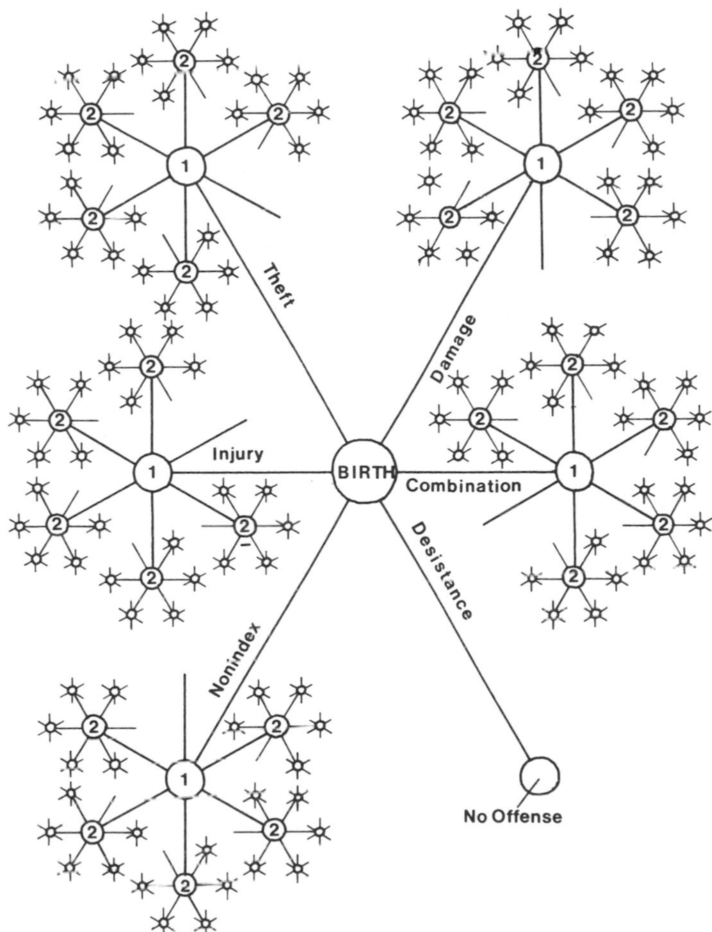

FIGURE 9.1
Branch Probability Model of Offensive Diversity

process can be represented as a simple one-step chain, the detailing of extensive careers will not be necessary in order to predict the type of the next offense.

Let us now briefly look at a couple of studies which have attempted to use this model in sociological investigation. Markov chain analysis has been used in a variety of substantive areas but most extensively in the study of mobility (industrial and social), small groups' decision-making processes, and demographic characteristics. Although it is not particularly instructive for our purposes to review this material in any depth, we shall consider work in each of these areas to illustrate further the Markov chain procedure.

A major impetus to the application of the procedure in the social sciences came from the study of industrial mobility by Blumen, Kogan, and McCarthy.[3] They attempted to develop a model that would describe the flow of workers through the industrial structure of the United States. Utilizing data from the continuous work history samples from the Bureau of Old-Age and Survivors' Insurance for quarters during the period 1947–49, they tested the adequacy of a Markov chain model in characterizing the transitions of workers between industries from quarter to quarter, and summarized their observations as follows:

> In practically every instance, it was found that the expectation under the model showed fewer workers remaining in an industry of origin than were actually observed to be in that industry. This suggests that one might consider an industry at a particular time as containing a mixture of workers whose amount of movements will differ.[4]

Time in an industry was found to have a cumulative effect in the sense that some workers were disproportionately "stayers" – that is, there was a tendency toward lumping on the diagonals of the transition matrices. The mover-stayer model of transition has become a generally accepted feature of Markov chains in the social sciences.[5] Although this model was found to be of only limited usefulness by Blumen, et al., it identified a mode of analysis that has proved quite useful in adapting Markov chain models to observed data, namely the partitioning of transition matrices in some way so as to allow for cumulative effects.

The most developed model of social mobility has incorporated the stayer condition as a variable component of a Markov chain model.

3. I. Blumen, M. Kogan, and P.J. McCarthy, *The Industrial Mobility of Labor as a Probability Process* (Ithaca: Cornell University, 1955).

4. Ibid., p. 66.

5. For a detailed discussion of this model, see Leo A. Goodman, "Statistical Methods for the Mover-Stayer Model," *Journal of the American Statistical Association* 56 (December 1961): 841–68. For an alternative approach to this problem, which combines the Markov process with the notion of unreliability of responses to account for instabilities in the transition matrices, see J. Coleman, *Models of Change and Response Uncertainty* (Englewood Cliffs: Prentice-Hall, 1964).

This is the Cornell Mobility Model (CMM) constructed by Robert McGinnis.[6] This model accounts for shifts between social class positions by reference to positions at times t and $t + 1$ and to the factor of "cumulative inertia," which refers to the following axiom: "The probability of remaining in any state of nature increases as a strict monotone function of duration of prior residence in that state."[7] Thus, the stayer condition is expanded from the notion of lumping in the diagonal from t to $t + 1$ to include the increased probability of lumping, given the passage of differing lengths of t. The model becomes far more complex than the simple Markov chain as it becomes readily apparent that the probabilities are not constant through time. The mobility studies, in not achieving adequate fits between models and observed data, have demonstrated that "few applications of the temporal functions (Markov chains) worked especially well when tested against data and some of them were howling failures."[8] The increasing complexity of models is dictated by the failure of the simple form.

Bernard Cohen's analysis of the process of conformity as a probability process represents the most frequently cited effort to apply Markov process analysis to the area of small groups.[9] The work is based on a variation of the Asch experiments on conformity and has been extended by recent work at the Laboratory for Social Research at Stanford University.[10] The effort in these works is to generate a model containing the smallest number of parameters necessary to account for the process of conformity in experimental conditions. The trial-to-trial change in conformity is expressed, in the general model developed by Cohen (the "conflict model"), in terms of a four-state Markov process of considerable complexity. In general, Cohen concludes that the Markov model is a good fit to the observed data. The Markov process employed by Cohen is far more complex than the Markov chain (as discussed earlier), but group processes are

6. Robert McGinnis, "A Stochastic Model of Mobility," *American Sociological Review* 33 (October 1968): 711–22.

7. Ibid., p. 716.

8. Ibid., p. 713.

9. Bernard P. Cohen, *Conflict and Conformity* (Cambridge: M.I.T. Press, 1963).

10. The most recent report available on these studies is J. Bergen, T.L. Conner, and W.L. McKeown, *Evaluations and the Formation and Maintenance of Performance Expectations* (Stanford: Laboratory for Social Research, Technical Report #22, 1968).

usually so complex that the more sophisticated model is necessary. In fact the work that Cohen stimulated has led to even more complex models (i.e., higher order parameter models).

The application of stochastic models in the area of demographic and economic analysis includes a variety of substantive issues. For example, brand choice,[11] fertility,[12] mental health,[13] the distribution and size of firms,[14] and the patterns of growth and decline of small towns[15] have been treated as probability processes.

Among the more recent of these studies is Fuguitt's analysis of the patterns of small town distribution in Wisconsin.[16] Fuguitt attempted to characterize the distribution of small towns at the beginning and the end of each decade from 1880–90 to 1950–60 as a Markov chain. As expected, the model was not adequate. Fuguitt concluded that "the mover-stayer model might better describe the patterns of shifts between decades and increase understanding of the process of urbanization."[17] Again, the simple model was found not adequate to characterize the process.

Our review indicates this lack of fit to be the general condition of attempts to utilize the Markov chain model in the analysis of demographic characteristics, and reflects the general lack of congruence between first-order Markov chain models and data in the social sciences. However, inspection of the data in the next two chapters indicates that such may not be the case for juvenile offense histories at least as reflected in official recordings.

11. F. Harary, and B. Lipstein, "The Dynamics of Brand Loyalty: A Markovian Approach," *Operations Research* 10 (January 1962): 19–40.

12. E.B. Perrin, and M.C. Sheps, "Human Reproduction: A Stochastic Process," *Biometrica,* March 1964, pp. 28–45.

13. A.W. Marshall, and H. Goldhamer, "An Application of Markov Processes to the Study of the Epidemiology of Mental Disease," *Journal of the American Statistical Association* 50 (March 1955): 99–129.

14. G. Adelman, "A Stochastic Analysis of the Size Distribution of Firms," *Journal of the American Statistical Association* 53 (December 1958): 893–904.

15. G.V. Fuguitt, "The Growth and Decline of Small Towns as a Probability Process," *American Sociological Review* 30 (1965): 403–11.

16. Ibid.

17. Ibid., p. 410.

10 Static Offense Probabilities

In this chapter we shall develop and assess the probability of committing offenses classified by type of offense, the distribution of seriousness scores, and the distribution of mean time intervals between offenses for the first fifteen offenses.[1] There is some repetition of findings reported in earlier chapters in order to put the offense tracking in its proper context. We have tried to keep such repetition to the minimum necessary for displaying the probabilities involved in committing from one to fifteen offenses.

The First Offense

Of the total cohort population (9,945), 2,275 of the boys encountered the police in a first offense that was in the nonindex category (22.9%), 264 for an injury (2.6%), 484 for a theft (4.9%), 282 for damage (2.5%), and 200 for a combination (2.0%). The total number of first offenders is 3,475, or about one-third of the cohort (34.9%). Among these offenders, 65 percent committed a nonindex

1. It should be noted that only 40 boys in the delinquent group committed more than 15 offenses and that the numbers in each category became too small to permit meaningful discussion. Thus in this section we shall not treat those offenses beyond the fifteenth.

TABLE 10.1
Probability of Committing a First Offense by Type of Offense

Type of Offense	Proportion (of total cohort)	Proportion (of offenders)	Mean Seriousness Score	Mean Time (months from birth)
Nonindex	.2288	.6547	23.7	175.9 (14.6 years)
Injury	.0265	.0760	331.0	171.4 (14.3 years)
Theft	.0487	.1393	183.0	169.4 (14.1 years)
Damage	.0253	.0725	157.0	153.3 (12.8 years)
Combination	.0201	.0576	291.2	164.3 (13.7 years)

offense in their first encounter with the police while eight percent committed an injury offense, 14 percent theft, seven percent damage, and six percent some combination of injury, theft, or damage (see table 10.1).

As table 10.1 also indicates, the mean time in months from birth to commission of the first offense was greatest for nonindex (175.9 months or 14.6 years), followed by injury (171.4 months or 14.3 years), theft (169.4 months or 14.1 years), combination (164.3 months or 13.7 years), and damage (153.3 months or 12.8 years).

With regard to mean seriousness scores, as expected, injury offenses exhibited the largest value (331.0), followed by combination (which may have components of injury, 291.2), theft (183.0), damage (157.4), and nonindex (23.7).

In table 10.2 we see that 46.4 percent (1,613) of the offender group had only one police contact and then desisted – that is, they committed no further delinquencies through age 17. Of the one-time offenders, 72 percent committed a nonindex offense, 7 percent injury, 11 percent theft, 6 percent damage, and 4 percent combination. Thus the one-time offender, like the repeater on his first offense, is overwhelmingly a nonindex offender.

Looking at the same data from a different perspective, slightly over one-half (51%) of all those who committed a nonindex first offense committed no further violations, while 43 percent of the injury first offenders, 37 percent of the theft first offenders, 38 percent of the damage first offenders, and 32 percent of the combination first offenders desisted. Depending on the type of first offense, then, one-third to one-half of the offenders committed no further violations. Although nonindex offenders are most likely to stop after

TABLE 10.2

Proportion of One-time, Recidivist, and Desisted Offenders by Type of First Offense

Type of Offense	One-Time (N = 1613)	Desisted (N = 1613)	Recidivist (N = 1862)
Nonindex	.7204	.5108	.5977
Injury	.0700	.4280	.0810
Theft	.1110	.3698	.1638
Damage	.0589	.3770	.0843
Combination	.0397	.3200	.0730

the first police encounter, substantial numbers of all first offender types never commit a second offense.

It is also evident from table 10.2 that those boys who went on to a second encounter with the police (recidivist column) were somewhat more likely to have been involved in a violation involving components of injury, theft, or damage in the first offense than those who stopped. Thus, 8 percent of the recidivists had committed an injury as their first violation, 16 percent a theft, 8 percent damage, 7 percent a combination, and 60 percent a nonindex offense. In short, some 40 percent of the recidivists and 28 percent of the one-timers had committed a first offense involving index components. These differences in first-offense probabilities between the one-time and the recidivist groups are not impressively large. In the choice of an offense involving bodily injury only, the proportions are nearly identical (7% for one-timers, 8% for recidivists).

In summary, about one-third of the cohort experienced at least one police contact, primarily for a nonindex offense. Boys who committed nonindex first offenses were somewhat more likely to stop after the first offense than were boys who inflicted some bodily or property harm.

The Fifteen Offenses, Static Presentation

In table 10.3, the static probabilities (the probability of committing another offense regardless of type of prior offense) from the first to the fifteenth offense are presented by type of offense.[2]

2. The static probability $P_{(\text{static})}$ is defined as: $P_{(\text{static})} = N_k \div N_{k-1}$ where N_k is the number of boys who commit the kth (rank number) offense and N_{k-1} is the number of boys who committed the prior offense and are thus defined as the population at risk of committing a further offense. For example,

TABLE 10.3

Probability of Committing kth *Offense by Type of Offense, All Offenders*

k (Number of Offense)	Probability						
	All Types (Σ of N, I, T, D, C)	Nonindex	Injury	Theft	Damage	Combination	Desisted (after kth offense)
1	1.0000	.6547	.0760	.1393	.0725	.0576	.4641
2	.5358	.3430	.0455	.0794	.0222	.0458	.3492
3	.6509	.4044	.0483	.1246	.0236	.0499	.2838
4	.7161	.4439	.0736	.1238	.0248	.0503	.2778
5	.7223	.4320	.0657	.1313	.0264	.0668	.2584
6	.7416	.4705	.0526	.1435	.0128	.0622	.2085
7	.7913	.4409	.0925	.1398	.0387	.0796	.2337
8	.7663	.4511	.0815	.1440	.0163	.0734	.2021
9	.7978	.4787	.0887	.1241	.0177	.0887	.1733
10	.8266	.4489	.1111	.1956	.0089	.0622	.2096
11	.7903	.4624	.0645	.1559	.0054	.1022	.1974
12	.8027	.4830	.0816	.0884	.0544	.0952	.2712
13	.7288	.4068	.0593	.1441	.0254	.0932	.1162
14	.8837	.5233	.1163	.0814	.0349	.1279	.3026
15	.6973	.4474	.0263	.1316	.0000	.0921	.2453

In looking at the probabilities of committing all types of offenses – that is, the probability of committing any kind of offense regardless of type – it appears that the likelihood of committing a second offense is the least of the array (.5358). However, if a second offense is committed, the probability of committing a third offense of any type is greater (.6509). Beyond the third offense the likelihood of committing any further offense ranges from about .70 to .80.[3]

This characteristic is reflected in another way in the "desisted" column, namely, the proportion of boys who, during the time period under study, were never involved after the kth police encounter in a law violation which resulted in an official recording of the event. Forty-six percent desisted after the first police contact, 35 percent after the second, and 20 to 30 percent at each remaining step.

Because the relationships appear to be essentially linear, we have plotted the least squares estimates of the regression lines through these data in figure 10.1. Two qualities are immediately apparent in figure 10.1: first, the relatively low probability of index offense commission, for all types of index offenses, and second, the very small value of the slopes for all of the regression lines. Thus, the likelihood of committing a damage offense remains at about .02 from the second to the fifteenth offense, for combination from about .05 to .11, for injury from about .06 to .08, and for theft from about .12 to .13 across the offenses from the second to the fifteenth. The probability of a nonindex offense is considerably higher, ranging between .41 and .48.

Of importance for our purposes is the finding that the slopes of the various offense probabilities are very small. For the offenses of injury, theft, and damage they are essentially nonexistent or almost equal to zero. The inference that can be made on the acceptance of the near-zero regression coefficients is that the probability of committing these various offense types is virtually unchanging from the second to the fifteenth offense.

---

if $k = 2$, that is, the second offense, and 1,862 boys committed a second offense, while 3,475 boys committed a first offense and are at risk of committing a second, then $N_k = N_2 = 1{,}862$ and $N_{k-1} = N_1 = 3{,}475$, and $P_{(\text{static})} = 0.5358$ (entered in cell [2,1] in table 10.3 as the probability of committing any kind of second offense).

3. For an interesting and similar analysis, see Alan Little, "The Increase in Crime 1952–62: An Empirical Analysis on Adolescent Offenders," *The British Journal of Criminology* 5, no. 1 (1965): 77–82.

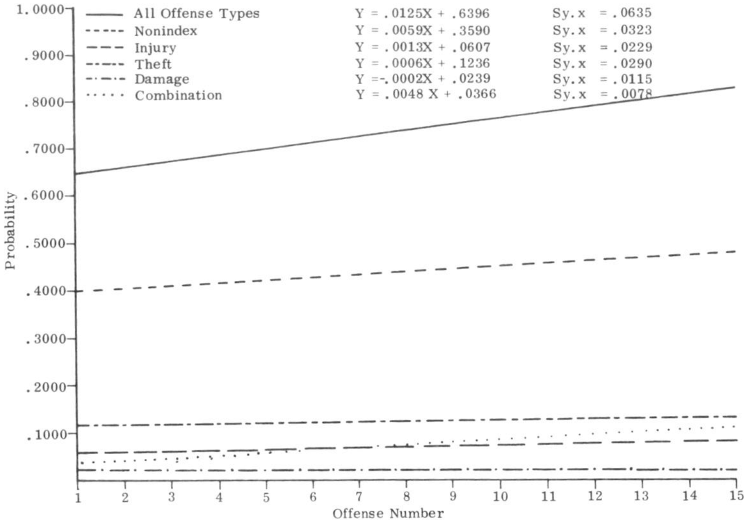

FIGURE 10.1
Regression Estimate of Probability of Committing First to Fifteenth Offense by Type of Offense (All Offenders)

The increment per offense number which is observed in the "all types" plot is explained primarily by the increments observed in the nonindex and combination categories. However, it must be stressed that the magnitude of these increments by offense number – although larger than those noted for injury, theft, and damage – is nonetheless quite small, amounting to an increase of .0059 in the likelihood of committing a nonindex offense per rank number, and of .0048 for a combination offense. The total effect of all offense types summed, in contributing to the "all types" category coefficient of regression, is .0125 per offense number. That is to say, if the estimated probability of committing a fourth offense is .6896, then on the average the probability of committing a fifth offense, regardless of type, will be only .0125 greater, or .7021, and so on out to the fifteenth offense.

That the clustering of the data around the regression lines is quite tight can be inferred from an inspection of the data in table 10.3 and is substantiated by the small standard errors of estimate which appear in figure 10.1.[4] Thus, the least squares equations in figure 10.1 are fairly good representations of the progression of offense probability by offense numbers. The most striking finding, then, to be drawn from these data is that the increment in offense probability by type and rank is quite small. For the offenses of injury, theft, and damage, the change by offense number is almost unobservable, while for nonindex and combination it is noticeable but still quite small.

Our conclusions from this analysis of the static probabilities are that: (1) the probabilities of committing various index offenses by type are small when compared to the probability of a nonindex commission – an entirely expected finding; and (2) the probability of committing an offense type is almost unchanged across offense number – an unexpected finding.

Although at this stage of the data analysis we know nothing of the likelihood of one type of offense following another – say of injury following injury, theft following theft, and so on – it would seem that the trend toward channeling from one type of offense to another or toward unique pathways is not strong; otherwise, the static offense probabilities when broken by type of offense would not be so uniformly distributed over rank. An investigation of the probabilities of these discrete pathways will follow the discussion of mean seriousness scores and mean time intervals for the static probabilities (chapter 11).

Mean Seriousness Score

The mean seriousness scores for all offense types exhibit a small upward trend as the offense rank number increases. This is clear from the data in table 10.4. These data, as in the previous section, again appear to be essentially linear although rather large swings develop past the tenth offense (probably because so few boys committed that many offenses). With this caution in mind, we have also presented the least squares estimates of the regression of seriousness score on rank number in figure 10.2.

4. For a discussion of the computation and interpretation of the coefficient of regression and of the standard error of estimate, see Mordecai Ezekiel and Karl A. Fox, *Methods of Correlation and Regression Analysis* (New York: John Wiley and Sons, 1959), chapters 5–9.

TABLE 10.4

Mean Seriousness Score, First to Fifteenth Offense by Offense Type

Offense Number	All Offenses	Nonindex	Injury	Theft	Damage	Combi-nation
1	94.3311	23.71	330.95	183.04	157.39	291.18
2	108.3156	26.44	346.07	185.37	164.96	324.68
3	111.8579	30.39	371.48	192.85	160.86	295.01
4	126.3774	33.57	438.67	189.02	164.97	316.25
5	131.1587	35.60	417.11	187.88	157.91	345.88
6	113.1047	27.28	414.61	192.21	250.00	296.54
7	146.8272	32.76	453.53	175.46	170.78	360.43
8	147.4677	37.86	560.47	176.02	200.00	294.74
9	141.7353	37.21	478.72	217.46	193.00	252.92
10	150.2412	30.91	494.72	176.25	200.00	307.14
11	120.4559	33.43	300.00	194.97	74.00	289.68
12	150.1371	44.44	392.25	200.46	184.25	498.14
13	139.9750	47.10	329.57	222.00	166.67	290.55
14	180.5775	59.73	606.70	205.00	116.00	289.64
15	166.0907	45.26	900.00	173.50	0.0	532.71

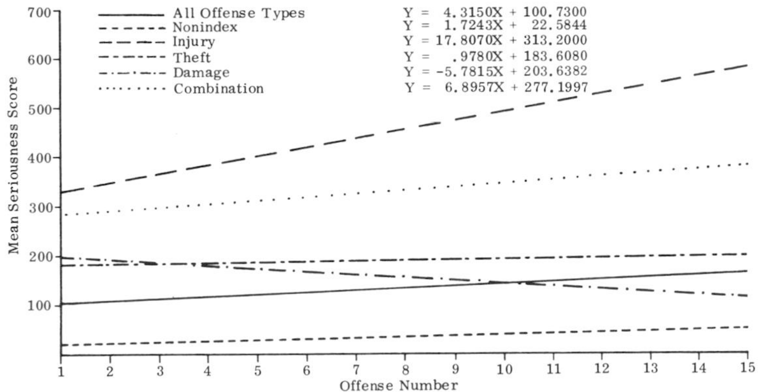

FIGURE 10.2
Regression Estimate of Mean Seriousness Score of First to Fifteenth Offense by Type of Offense (All Offenders)

On the average, and disregarding type (the "all offense" plot), each offense will be 4.3 seriousness score points greater than the one that preceded it. The least squares estimate of the mean seriousness score for all offenses increases from about 105 for the first offense to about 165 for the fifteenth offense.

The notion that offense severity is positively related to the number of offenses that one commits is not strongly substantiated by these data. In fact, if we look at the slopes for the mean seriousness score plots for nonindex, theft, and damage offense types, it is clear that the net effect of these three offense types is a negative slope ($b_{\text{nonindex}} = 1.7243$, $b_{\text{theft}} = 0.9780$, and $b_{\text{damage}} = -5.7815$, or, together, $b_{n,t,d} = -3.0792$). The increment in offense severity by offense number, for nonindex and theft offenses, is almost nonexistent, while the seriousness score for damage offenses is negatively related to rank number. As a result, the least squares estimates of offense seriousness range from 184 to 198 for theft, 24 to 48 for nonindex, and 198 to 117 for damage, over the fifteen offenses.

Of concern in this evaluation of offense severity is the plot for offenses involving bodily injury. Here we observe a strong upward trend from about 330 to 500 for the first ten offenses. After the tenth offense, the data are rather choppy, and it is difficult to draw any conclusions from the points, but the upward trend still exists if the end points are accepted as meaningful. For offenses involving injury only, the seriousness score rises sharply in comparison to the other offense types and yields least squares estimates of 331 to 580 for the fifteen offenses.

It will be remembered that the category "combination" includes any combination of injury, theft, or damage. It is reasonable, then, that the plot for combination offenses should have a positive slope greater than theft, damage, and nonindex but less than that for injury. Indeed, it does, for, as indicated, the slope for combination offenses is 6.9, yielding estimates of 284.1 to 380.6. The acceptance of this slope must be guarded, however, for its positive magnitude is determined exclusively by the seriousness scores associated with the twelfth and fifteenth offenses. If these two points were eliminated (they do seem to be artifacts of the small number of cases at these points [7]) the regression equation becomes $Y = -2.1127 + 319.4445$, which indicates a small decline in the average seriousness score over time for combination offenses.

If we bear in mind this possible explanation for the seriousness score increment of the combination category, it seems that the increase in seriousness for injury offenses is the finding worthy of concern in this set of data. Overall, the effect of repetitions on the seriousness scores of the categories of nonindex, theft, damage, and combination is nil. In comparison, the increase in seriousness score with each injury event clearly stands out.

Mean Time between Offenses

In table 10.5 and figure 10.3 the mean time in months between the kth and k + 1st offense is seen to be logarithmically related to offense number. The differences in mean times among the various offense types at each rank number are so slight as to be insignificant. Therefore, the nonindex data set has been used as the base for the curve-fitting process because the largest number of entries are in this category, and, as a result, the smoothest trace follows. At least until the tenth offense the data for each of the offense type plots are fairly smooth; beyond that point, as with the mean seriousness scores, the fluctuations increase rapidly.

TABLE 10.5

Cohort Mean Time in Months between Offenses through First Fifteen Offenses by Offense Type

Offense Sequence	Nonindex	Injury	Theft	Damage	Combination
1 - 2	18.57	18.13	16.60	16.81	16.96
2 - 3	10.62	11.83	10.39	7.31	8.79
3 - 4	8.06	8.29	7.94	8.36	6.47
4 - 5	7.10	7.26	6.27	5.20	6.51
5 - 6	5.38	8.30	6.30	6.30	6.28
6 - 7	5.22	5.81	5.48	6.59	5.95
7 - 8	5.23	5.84	4.38	7.12	5.93
8 - 9	4.59	5.04	2.39	6.36	5.04
9 - 10	4.09	4.38	6.26	6.10	4.51
10 - 11	3.96	4.77	4.22	0.20	3.21
11 - 12	3.35	5.42	5.47	4.85	9.28
12 - 13	4.17	5.56	5.35	8.63	5.08
13 - 14	3.15	4.15	1.93	7.37	2.38
14 - 15	2.98	12.30	4.32	0.0	5.29

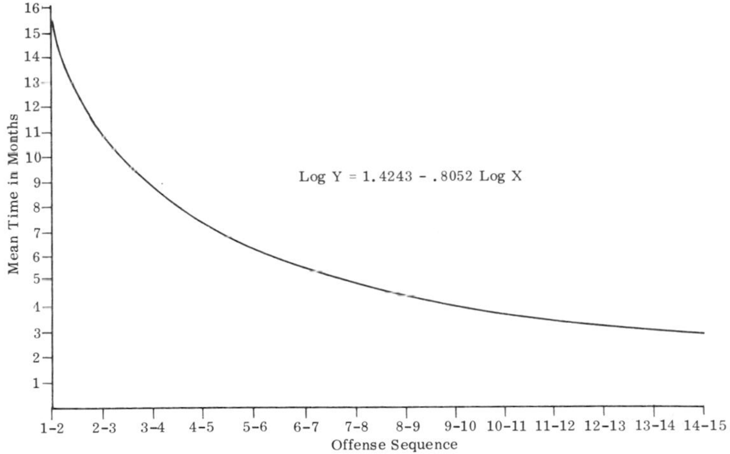

FIGURE 10.3

Regression Estimate of Mean Time between Offenses, Nonindex Offense Type

The time between the first and second offense on the average is about 16 to 18 months regardless of the type of offense. Between the second and third offense the time drops to approximately 10 months and then to 8 months for the interval between the third and fourth offenses. The interval continues to diminish at a declining rate at each offense number, ranging from about 5 months at the seventh to eighth transition and 3 months from the twelfth and following transitions.

This progression in mean time intervals can be represented fairly closely by the expression: $\log Y = 1.4243 - 0.8052 \log X$. This formula is easily recognized as the familiar linear regression expression where the X and Y variables have been compressed logarithmically.

The form of the relationship between the number of the offense and the mean transition time will be shown to be the usual configuration of this relationship even when other classifications are utilized in the analysis of transition times. The relationship is a result of the cumulative sums which are generated when the probability of committing an offense is computed on a yearly basis. Thus, in table 10.6 it is clear that the age spread over the fifteen offenses is not great. On the average, the cohort members were 14.4 years old at the commission of the first offense and 16.0 years old at the fifteenth offense. Those boys committing nonindex and injury offenses were on the average about one year older at each offense number than those who committed damage, theft, and combination offenses.

Generally speaking, the offense histories are compressed over a rather short period, regardless of the type of offense. This finding is reflected both in the average age at commission of each offense and in the mean time between offenses.

TABLE 10.6

Mean Age in Years at Commission of First and Fifteenth Offense by Offense Type

	1st Offense	15th Offense
Nonindex	14.6	16.0
Injury	14.3	17.4
Theft	14.1	15.8
Damage	12.8	16.1 (14th offense)
Combination	13.7	16.1
All Offenses	14.4	16.0

Race and SES

In analyzing offense probabilities from the first to the fifteenth offense, seriousness scores, and mean times between offenses, all by type of offense, we again followed the mode of considering race and socioeconomic status. When the five types of offenses, plus desistance, are displayed by whites and nonwhites from high and low SES levels, the text and tables become increasingly complex. For the research scholars who will be interested in them we have placed the details of these discussions in appendixes G.1 and G.2. We have preserved so much of these specific materials because of their rare quality as cohort, longitudinal data. In general, the lower SES nonwhite boys start their delinquency earlier than any other SES-race group, commit more serious offenses (especially in the injury category), have shorter periods of time between offenses, and are less likely to desist after each offense rank. We briefly summarize this chapter and some of the appendix materials below.

Summary

We have observed that about one-third of the cohort experienced at least one police contact, primarily for a nonindex offense, and that those boys who committed a nonindex first offense are somewhat more likely to desist from further delinquency.

A remarkable uniformity in the probability of committing an offense exists when the data for the fifteen offense numbers for all offenders are examined by type of offense (nonindex, injury, theft, damage, and combination). The increment in offense probability per rank number is nil for the offenses of injury, theft, and damage; it is quite small for nonindex and combination offenses. The most common offense type at each rank is nonindex, followed (respectively) by theft, combination, injury, and damage.

With the commission of each additional offense, the seriousness scores for nonindex, theft, damage, and combination offenses change negligibly, while injury seriousness scores advance dramatically at each offense rank number.

The mean time intervals follow the general expression, $\log Y = a + b \log X$, for all offense types. In addition, the mean times between offenses are similar enough for all offense types that one function, $\log Y = 1.4243 - 0.8052 \log X$, suffices to represent any type. We have also shown that the offense histories are compressed over a rather short period, regardless of offense type. Thus, the cohort members were on the average 14.4 years old at the commission of the first offense and 16.0 years old at the fifteenth.

When we divided the cohort into whites and nonwhites, we found that 50 percent of all nonwhites and 29 percent of all whites were classified as delinquent by the police, and that only 34 percent of nonwhites stopped after the first offense, compared to 55 percent of whites. Nonwhites were more likely than whites to commit all types of offenses, particularly violent attacks against the person.

This tendency toward elevated offensivity among nonwhites persists from the first to the fifteenth offense. Between 30 and 45 percent of the whites desist from further delinquency at each offense rank, while only 18 to 25 percent of the nonwhites cease their delinquencies at each rank. The uniformity in offense probability still obtains within each racial group as it does for all offenders regardless of race. The seriousness scores for theft offenses are higher for whites than for nonwhites, while injuries inflicted by nonwhites are more serious than those inflicted by whites.

The mean times between offenses for the various offense types still follow the same function when the data are divided by race. Whites tend to be older than nonwhites at age of onset and at subsequent offense ranks. Up to the fourth or fifth offense, the white mean transition times tend to be greater than the nonwhite, while the opposite holds true after the fourth or fifth offense.

Adding socioeconomic status to the racial dichotomy leads to the further conclusion that, regardless of income group, nonwhite boys are more likely to commit violent offenses, while white boys are slightly more likely to be involved in property offenses. At the same SES level, white boys are more likely to desist from further law violations than are nonwhite youths.

Regardless of SES level, nonwhite offenders commit more serious offenses against the person while white delinquents are involved with more serious property offenses. In many instances high SES boys commit more serious violations than do low SES boys.

In analyzing mean age at commission and mean time between offenses for the race-SES classification, we found that high SES boys are likely to be older at the first and ninth offense than low SES boys, and that within SES categories white offenders tend to be older than nonwhites. We also found that the mean times between offenses are approximately the same for whites and nonwhites belonging (a) to high and low SES levels for nonindex offenses, (b) to low SES for injury offenses, and (c) to low SES level for damage offenses. Conversely, the racial differentials override SES in the mean time estimates for theft and combination offenses.

We are prepared now to examine further the apparent unvarying quality of these offense probabilities which appear for each type of offense, regardless of the number of offenses committed.

11 Contingent Probabilities

In the last chapter we discussed the probability of committing an offense, by type of offense, for each offense number. We called this probability of committing a first, second, third, and so on out to the kth offense a "static" probability because in its computation the likelihood of each offense type was considered without regard to the type of prior offense; that is, we implied no link to previous offense type. Therefore, we were able to make no probabilistic statements about the sequences of types of offenses. One finding, however, was clear: the probability of committing an offense, when classified by type, changed very little over offense number. The variation in the probability distributions by offense type was surprisingly small.

This finding was unexpected, for one would think that, if more serious offenses (index offenses) are likely to appear among the later offenses in a delinquent career, the probability distributions of property and bodily offenses would shift noticeably as the number of offenses increases, thereby reflecting a propensity toward the commission of more serious offenses. In short, one might expect the probability of committing an index offense to increase more or less directly with offense number. Particularly for index offenses such was not the case. Thus, we may suggest that the process which generates these offense-specific (by type) probability distributions operates essentially in the same manner at each offense number. This suggestion is an important one, for, if it is true, we are implying that the probability of being involved in a particular type of offensive behavior is independent of the number of offenses that a juvenile may have committed. We may state simply, as an example, that a boy is no more likely at, say, the eleventh offense to be involved in a violent act than he was at the fifth.

We shall now take this analytical task further by considering those probabilities associated with offense type changes – the "dynamic" or transition probabilities. Our primary concern is with the development of inferential statements about switching from one type of offense to another or continuing with the same type as offense number advances. Two problems form the substance of this concern: (a) the determination of the transition probability, $P_{ij}(k)$, of committing the kth offense (where k is the number of the offense in a series of offenses) by the type j of the kth offense given the type i, of the k-1st offense; and (b) the comparison of the transition matrices which are generated by the determination of the P_{ij}'s mentioned in *a* above.

The questions we pose are: (a) Does the type of the offense that a cohort member committed at the k-1st offense number have any bearing on the probability that he will commit a certain type of offense at the kth number? and (b) Does the same process operate at each offense level (1st, 2d, 3d, etc.) so that similar transition matrices will be generated when the offenses are classified by type? In short, are the transition configurations such that a homogeneous or number-independent Markov chain can be said to exist?

The Data Matrices

In matrices 11.1 to 11.8 we present the transition probabilities of committing each of the five types of offense delineated earlier, given the type of prior offense. We may now define as "states" the categories of offenses heretofore denoted as "types." Thus, for each offense number, k, one must be in one of the six possible states of nonindex, injury, theft, damage, combination, or desistance. The entries in each matrix are the probabilities of being in the state j at offense number k (columns), having been in state i at offense number k-1 (rows) for the transitions from the first to second, second to third, third to fourth, and so on out to the eighth to ninth. There are eight matrices where the first transition is that switch from the first state to the second state, and the eighth transition is that switch from the eighth state to the ninth state. By comparing adjacent matrices we may ascertain whether any pattern of progression exists between pairs.

MATRIX 11.1

Transition Probabilities: All Offenders, First Transition

k–1/*k*	*N*	Non-index	Injury	Theft	Damage	Combi-nation	Desist
Nonindex	2275	.3349	.0378	.0646	.0163	.0356	.5107
Injury	264	.3750	.0795	.0568	.0265	.0265	.4280
Theft	484	.3264	.0537	.1508	.0310	.0310	.3698
Damage	252	.3968	.0397	.1032	.0357	.0357	.3769
Combination	200	.3650	.0750	.0750	.0450	.0450	.3200
Total	3475						

MATRIX 11.2

Transition Probabilities: All Offenders, Second Transition

k–1/*k*	*N*	Non-index	Injury	Theft	Damage	Combi-nation	Desist
Nonindex	1192	.4077	.0445	.0956	.0235	.0361	.3926
Injury	158	.3861	.0633	.1329	.0253	.0316	.3607
Theft	276	.3768	.0471	.1993	.0217	.0725	.2826
Damage	77	.5195	.0649	.1429	.0260	.0390	.2077
Combination	159	.3899	.0566	.1950	.0252	.1384	.1949
Total	1862						

MATRIX 11.3

Transition Probabilities: All Offenders, Third Transition

k–1/*k*	*N*	Non-index	Injury	Theft	Damage	Combi-nation	Desist
Nonindex	753	.4502	.0637	.1036	.0226	.0398	.3200
Injury	90	.4111	.1444	.1111	.0333	.0333	.2666
Theft	232	.4483	.0776	.1638	.0259	.0733	.2155
Damage	44	.3864	.1364	.1136	.0227	.0227	.3409
Combination	93	.4409	.0430	.2043	.0323	.1075	.1935
Total	1212						

MATRIX 11.4

Transition Probabilities: All Offenders, Fourth Transition

k–1/k	N	Non-index	Injury	Theft	Damage	Combi-nation	Desist
Nonindex	538	.4368	.0595	.1152	.0242	.0520	.3122
Injury	89	.4719	.0674	.0449	.0449	.0787	.2921
Theft	150	.3867	.0733	.2200	.0200	.0933	.2066
Damage	30	.5000	.1000	.1667	.0333	.0667	.1333
Combination	61	.4098	.0820	.1639	.0328	.1148	.1967
Total	868						

MATRIX 11.5

Transition Probabilities: All Offenders, Fifth Transition

k–1/k	N	Non-index	Injury	Theft	Damage	Combi-nation	Desist
Nonindex	375	.4747	.0560	.1307	.0133	.0453	.2800
Injury	57	.3860	.0877	.1404	.0175	.0351	.3333
Theft	114	.4561	.0263	.1842	.0175	.0877	.2280
Damage	23	.6522	.0870	.1304	.0000	.0435	.0869
Combination	58	.4828	.0345	.1552	.0000	.1552	.1724
Total	627						

MATRIX 11.6

Transition Probabilities: All Offenders, Sixth Transition

k–1/k	N	Non-index	Injury	Theft	Damage	Combi-nation	Desist
Nonindex	295	.2500	.1051	.1119	.0441	.0508	.2271
Injury	33	.3333	.1212	.0606	.0303	.1212	.3333
Theft	81	.4333	.0778	.2556	.0222	.1111	.1000
Damage	8	.5000	.0000	.1250	.2500	.0000	.1250
Combination	39	.3846	.0256	.1538	.0000	.2051	.2307
Total	456						

MATRIX 11.7

Transition Probabilities: All Offenders, Seventh Transition

k–1/k	N	Non-index	Injury	Theft	Damage	Combi-nation	Desist
Nonindex	205	.5073	.0732	.1073	.0146	.0683	.2292
Injury	43	.4419	.1395	.0698	.0000	.0465	.3023
Theft	65	.3231	.0308	.3231	.0308	.1231	.1692
Damage	18	.3889	.1111	.2222	.0556	.0556	.1666
Combination	37	.4054	.1351	.0811	.0000	.0541	.3243
Total	368						

MATRIX 11.8

Transition Probabilities: All Offenders, Eighth Transition

k–1/k	N	Non-index	Injury	Theft	Damage	Combi-nation	Desist
Nonindex	166	.5060	.1084	.1145	.0241	.0663	.1807
Injury	30	.4667	.0333	.0667	.0000	.1000	.3333
Theft	53	.4906	.0377	.2075	.0189	.1132	.1320
Damage	6	.6667	.1667	.1667	.0000	.0000	.0000
Combination	27	.2593	.1111	.0741	.0000	.1852	.3703
Total	282						

Matrix Tests and Estimate of the Generating Process

At the outset, we should like to test the eight[1] data matrices two at a time, according to the procedure outlined by Goodman,[2] to determine whether the same generating process exists which would enable us to model the process at least for each adjacent comparison.

1. We have assessed the matrices in this way out to the fourteenth transition; however, the sample sizes became too small to permit meaningful comparisons.

2. T. Anderson and L. Goodman, "Statistical Inference about Markov Chains," *Annals of Mathematical Statistics* 28 (1957): 89–110. Leo A. Goodman, "On the Statistical Analysis of Markov Chains," *Annals of Mathematical Statistics* 26 (1955): 771; "Statistical Methods for Analyzing Processes of Change," *American Journal of Sociology* 68 (1962): 57–78; "On the Statistical Analysis of Mobility Tables," *American Journal of Sociology* 70 (1964): 564–85.

In other words, we would like to determine whether the matrices are essentially the same within the limits of chance and to test the hypothesis that each of the data matrices was generated by one transition probability matrix; for if such were the case, we would then be able to suggest that, regardless of offense number, the likelihood that the next offense will be of a certain type depends only on the type of offense just committed. We would be saying that the configurations of offense histories, insofar as we are considering offense type, cannot be predicted from knowledge of the number of offenses that a group might have committed but only from knowledge of the type of offense committed just prior to the instant delinquent event. If this assertion is true, then the process may be defined as a simple (one-step) homogeneous Markov chain.

In table 11.1 we present the chi-square tests and probability values associated with obtaining these chi-squares under the null hypothesis that each matrix pair could have been generated by the same process.[3]

In each element of this sequence of matrix comparisons the chi-square values fall short of permitting rejection of the null hypothesis. Thus, we may with appropriate caution conclude that the two data matrices could have been generated by one process at least at each step. Because we are testing a chain of such matrices, we may hint

TABLE 11.1

Matrix Tests and Chi-square Values: All Offenders, First versus Second out to Seventh versus Eighth Transitions

Transition Comparison	Chi-square	Decision (.05 level)
1st vs. 2d	23.3171	Accept
2d vs. 3d	11.4340	Accept
3d vs. 4th	14.3239	Accept
4th vs. 5th	17.9578	Accept
5th vs. 6th	26.1788	Accept
6th vs. 7th	22.6536	Accept
7th vs. 8th	12.8252	Accept

3. See Goodman, 1962 (n. 2 above), p. 71, for details of this test. In order to perform the test we have partitioned out the state of desistance and based the test on that submatrix of offenders who "went on" at each step to commit another violation. The reason for this segmenting is discussed below.

that, in fact, they are *all* the same. This hypothesis may be tested by combining the raw frequencies for each prior offense type over all k's in the manner shown in tables 11.2 to 11.6.[4]

TABLE 11.2

Homogeneity Test, Prior Offense: Nonindex

		*k*th Type					
Transition Number	k–1 Type	Nonindex	Injury	Theft	Damage	Combination	Total
1st	Nonindex	762	86	147	37	81	1113
2d	Nonindex	486	53	114	28	43	724
3d	Nonindex	339	48	78	17	30	512
4th	Nonindex	235	32	62	13	28	370
5th	Nonindex	178	21	49	5	17	270
6th	Nonindex	136	31	33	13	15	228
7th	Nonindex	104	15	22	3	14	158
8th	Nonindex	84	18	19	4	11	136

$\chi^2 = 58.2701$, reject

TABLE 11.3

Homogeneity Test, Prior Offense: Injury

		*k*th Type					
Transition Number	k–1 Type	Nonindex	Index	Theft	Damage	Combination	Total
1st	Injury	99	21	15	7	9	151
2d	Injury	61	10	21	4	5	101
3d	Injury	37	13	10	3	3	66
4th	Injury	42	6	4	4	7	63
5th	Injury	22	5	8	1	2	38
6th	Injury	11	4	2	1	4	22
7th	Injury	19	6	3	0	2	30
8th	Injury	14	1	2	0	3	20

$\chi^2 = 30.1273$, accept

4. See Goodman, 1962 (n. 2 above), p. 42, for this test.

TABLE 11.4

Homogeneity Test, Prior Offense: Theft

		*k*th Type					
Transition Number	*k*–1 Type	Nonindex	Injury	Theft	Damage	Combi-nation	Total
1st	Theft	158	26	73	15	33	305
2d	Theft	104	13	55	6	20	198
3d	Theft	104	18	38	6	17	183
4th	Theft	58	11	33	3	14	119
5th	Theft	52	3	21	2	10	88
6th	Theft	39	7	23	2	10	81
7th	Theft	21	2	21	2	8	54
8th	Theft	26	2	11	1	6	46

$\chi^2 = 21.7377$, accept

TABLE 11.5

Homogeneity Test, Prior Offense: Damage

		*k*th Type					
Transition Number	*k*–1 Type	Nonindex	Injury	Theft	Damage	Combi-nation	Total
1st	Damage	100	10	26	9	12	157
2d	Damage	40	5	11	2	3	61
3d	Damage	17	6	5	1	1	30
4th	Damage	15	3	5	1	2	26
5th	Damage	15	2	3	0	1	21
6th	Damage	4	0	1	2	0	7
7th	Damage	7	2	4	1	1	15
8th	Damage	4	1	1	0	0	6

$\chi^2 = 21.3039$, accept

TABLE 11.6

Homogeneity Test, Prior Offense: Combination

Transition Number	k–1 Type	Nonindex	Injury	Theft	Damage	Combination	Total
		*k*th Type					
1st	Combination	73	15	15	9	24	136
2d	Combination	62	9	31	4	22	128
3d	Combination	41	4	19	3	10	77
4th	Combination	25	5	10	2	7	49
5th	Combination	28	2	9	0	9	48
6th	Combination	15	1	6	0	8	30
7th	Combination	15	5	3	0	2	25
8th	Combination	7	3	2	0	5	17

$\chi^2 = 33.8810$, accept

Thus, for the prior offenses of injury, theft, damage, and combination we may conclude that the probability distributions are essentially independent of offense rank, but such is not the case for the k–1st nonindex offense over offense number. However, in chapter 10 we showed that the proportion of boys who desisted from further violative behavior was greater after the first offense than after those that followed, particularly if that first offense was of a *nonindex* type. We would therefore expect that independence over offense number might exist if we considered the transitions from the *second* to the eighth, as has been done in table 11.7.

As a result of eliminating the one-time offender, the null hypothesis that the transition probabilities are the same for each category of prior offense type may be accepted. In addition, because the sum of the five chi-square values is nonsignificant, we may conclude that *all* the matrices in this test could have been generated by the same process, or parent matrix, of which each data matrix is a sample estimate.

If this process is amenable to modeling as a one-step homogeneous Markov chain, then some estimate of the "generating matrix" could be tested against each data matrix in the same manner as in table 11.1 above, with nonsignificant chi-squares the result. For such an estimate we suggest the average of the data matrices (matrix 11.9).

TABLE 11.7

Homogeneity Test by Prior Offense Type, Second to Eighth Transitions

k–1 Offense Type	Chi-square	Decision (.05 level)
Nonindex	25.0643	Accept
Injury	26.1889	Accept
Theft	18.2973	Accept
Damage	18.4061	Accept
Combination	23.8154	Accept

$\Sigma \chi^2 = 117.7592$, accept

MATRIX 11.9

Summary Transition Matrix: All Offenders, First to Eighth Transitions

k–1/*k*	Nonindex	Injury	Theft	Damage	Combi-nation	Desist
Nonindex	.4473	.0685	.1054	.0228	.0492	.3068
Injury	.4090	.0920	.0854	.0222	.0600	.3314
Theft	.4051	.0530	.2130	.0235	.0928	.2126
Damage	.5013	.0882	.1463	.0529	.0343	.1770
Combination	.3922	.0703	.1378	.0169	.1350	.2478
Desist	.0000	.0000	.0000	.0000	.0000	1.0000

We have expanded this matrix to 6 x 6 by adding the sixth row and column – the state of desistance. Of course, all the entries of the sixth row must be equal to 0 except that of "desist" to "desist," which must be equal to 1, since the state of desistance, once entered during the time period of this study, cannot be left.[5]

The null hypothesis now is that each data matrix is generated by the same parent matrix, the estimate of which is matrix 11.9. We perform this test by multiplying the P_{ij}'s of the summary matrix by the initial vector of first-offender counts by type of offense. The products of this multiplication are the "estimated" or expected frequen-

5. Such a state is defined as an "absorbing state."

TABLE 11.8

Matrix Tests and Chi-square Values: All Offenders, Summary Matrix versus First to Eighth Data Matrices

Summary Matrix vs.	Chi-square	Decision (.05 level)
1st data matrix	203.2340	Reject Null
2d data matrix	44.6411	Reject Null
3d data matrix	18.8566	Accept Null
4th data matrix	7.2019	Accept Null
5th data matrix	13.7588	Accept Null
6th data matrix	21.8759	Accept Null
7th data matrix	14.7685	Accept Null
8th data matrix	18.4616	Accept Null

cies for the first transition under the null hypothesis. We then apply the transition probabilities again to the remainder, which yields the expected frequencies for the second transition. This process is repeated until all eight sets of expected frequencies are generated. The chi-square test similar to that already described is then routinely performed between each data matrix of frequencies and the respective matrix of expected frequencies. The results of these calculations form the substance of table 11.8.

The summary matrix is an adequate fit for the six transitions following the second. The first two transition matrices are not adequately modeled. We know from chapter 10 (table 10.3) that the probability of desistance declines from .4641 after the first offense to .3492 after the second and then ranges from about .2000 to .3000 from then on. We also found in the matrix test of homogeneity earlier in the present chapter that the large proportion of one-time offenders, as reflected in the probability of desistance especially from nonindex first offenses, caused significant chi-square values to appear. We would expect, then, that the unpartitioned summary matrix – that is, the whole matrix including the absorbing state of desistance – would not be a good model for the first two transitions as such.

We may test this supposition in exactly the same manner as above. However, this time we shall test only those transitions *to offenses.*

In this instance the exclusion of the desistance state resulted in an adequate fit for all data transitions. Thus we may suggest that the

TABLE 11.9

Matrix Tests and Chi-square Values: All Offenders, Summary Matrix, Desistance Excluded, versus First to Eighth Data Matrices

Summary Matrix vs.	Chi-square	Decision (.05 level)
1st data matrix	22.5064	Accept Null
2d data matrix	16.4193	Accept Null
3d data matrix	12.3650	Accept Null
4th data matrix	5.8064	Accept Null
5th data matrix	10.8736	Accept Null
6th data matrix	13.3373	Accept Null
7th data matrix	10.0248	Accept Null
8th data matrix	7.4760	Accept Null

process is generated by one matrix and that the summary matrix is a reasonable estimate of that generating process. The fact that the fit is not adequate for the first and second transitions where the state of desistance is included need not be too damning if we realize that: (a) the fit is good for *all* transitions *to offenses* regardless of offense number, and (b) the fit is good for the primary recidivists having at least three police contacts. Thus, although the predictive power of the "expected generating matrix" is somewhat weakened by this inability to generate accurately the desistance counts for the first two transitions, it is by no means vitiated in the substantive areas of offense choice and multiple recidivism. The importance of this finding must be stressed, for if it is a viable one we may conclude that the data matrices relating the k and k–1st offenses are essentially the same and can be thought of as samples from a parent generating process which is *not* unique for the offense numbers under consideration.

Up to now we have shown that the data matrices are practically unchanging from the first to the eighth transition, that one matrix could have generated the observed transition matrices (with the above-mentioned restrictions on the early desistance probabilities), and that the average matrix is a good estimate of that parent generating process.

We may also try to assess the effect of knowing the types of the two prior offenses, that is, of knowing the k–2nd and the k–1st types

MATRIX 11.10

Transition Probabilities by Type of Prior Two Offenses: All Offenders

k-2	k-1	N	k Nonindex	k Injury	k Theft	k Damage	k Combination
N	N	452	.4199	.0367	.0827	.0197	.0341
N	I	52	.3488	.0698	.1512	.0233	.0116
N	T	95	.3810	.0544	.1156	.0204	.0748
N	D	29	.5676	.0270	.0811	.0541	.0541
N	C	61	.3827	.0864	.1728	.0247	.0864
I	N	58	.3535	.0505	.0808	.0404	.0606
I	I	13	.4762	.0952	.0000	.0000	.0476
I	T	12	.4000	.0667	.1333	.0000	.2000
I	D	5	.7143	.0000	.0000	.0000	.0000
I	C	9	.2222	.0000	.5556	.1111	.1111
T	N	101	.3544	.0696	.1456	.0316	.0380
T	I	19	.4281	.0385	.1538	.0385	.0769
T	T	56	.3151	.0274	.3699	.0137	.0411
T	D	12	.4667	.2000	.1333	.0000	.0000
T	C	28	.4242	.0303	.2121	.0000	.1818
D	N	61	.3800	.0600	.1200	.0200	.0300
D	I	8	.6000	.0000	.2000	.0000	.0000
D	T	24	.4615	.0769	.2692	.0000	.1154
D	D	9	.7778	.0000	.2222	.0000	.0000
D	C	11	.5833	.0833	.0833	.0000	.1667
C	N	52	.5068	.0411	.1096	.0274	.0274
C	I	9	.2667	.0667	.1333	.0667	.0667
C	T	13	.4667	.0000	.1333	.1333	.1333
C	D	6	.0000	.1111	.4444	.0000	.1111
C	C	19	.3333	.0000	.1667	.0417	.2500

$\chi^2 = 100.0250$, Accept (.05 level)

instead of having only the k-1st offense type to predict the type of the kth offense (matrix 11.10). In Markovian terminology, we should like to determine if the model is first or second order. We are hindered in achieving a full evaluation here because the sample sizes are too small in many of the transitions to permit reliable testing. Interpretation of these data must thus be called tentative. The problem of sample size is persistent throughout this chapter even though we have a comparatively large number of cases. We have to utilize enough categories to develop meaningful transitions, while maintaining an adequate number of cases to travel the pathways or "branches" to the various P_{ij} cells.

As a result, matrix 11.10 consists only of the first three offenses due to the large number of P_{ijk} cells which must be filled in order to permit testing.[6] Too few boys in the cohort went on to the various offense types beyond the third offense to fill the various positions at higher offense numbers. Nonetheless, our decision is to accept the null hypothesis of independence here and to conclude that the model is most likely first order; that is, our knowing the type of the k-2d offense does not materially aid us in predicting the type of the kth offense. However, we must again assert that this test is rather shaky for reasons already mentioned. Additional cases must be accumulated for meaningful testing under this five-way classification system.

The summary matrix, besides being the estimate of the generating process, exhibits several interesting substantive features. It does, after all, outline the contingent probabilities of offense commission. It is clear from looking at the cells that, as with the static probabilities, the most likely transition is to a nonindex offense regardless of the type of the prior offense. Injury, theft, and combination offenders are less likely to follow those particular offenses with a nonindex offense, .4090, .4051 and .3922 respectively, while damage offenders are the most likely, with a transition probability of .5013.

The next most likely transition is to the desistance state, with probabilities ranging from .1770 for damage to .3314 for injury.

The most likely index offense transitions are to theft, ranging from .0854 as the probability of committing a theft offense, having committed an injury, to .2130 from theft to theft. Combination and injury transitions follow, sharing the range of roughly .05 to .14, with a transition to damage being the least likely path followed for combination prior offense (.0345), and a transition to theft from injury prior offenses having a probability of .0530. Of course these values are essentially the same as the static probabilities when the prior offense type is not considered.

6. The method used for this test may be found in Goodman, 1962 (n. 2 above), pp. 74–75.

Of concern in the analysis of this type of data is the extent to which specialization may exist in the offense histories of cohort members as reflected in the transition matrices. By specialization we mean the likelihood that an offense of a certain type will be followed by another of the same type – injury following injury, theft following theft, and so on.

For each of the index offense categories in matrix 11.9, like offenses are more likely to follow one another. The probability of injury following injury is .0920, while the probability of injury following other types of offenses ranges from .0530 from theft to .0882 from damage. The probability of a theft following a theft is .2130, compared to .0854 (from injury to theft) and .1463 (from damage to theft). The difference between the value of .0529 for damage to damage and the remaining transition probabilities to damage is not great, ranging from .0169 from combination to .0235 from theft. Combination offenses are more likely to follow one another (.1350) compared to the low value of .0343 (from damage to combination) and the high figure of .0928 (from theft to combination).

As a general statement, it is possible to assert that some evidence for offense specialization exists, although the strength of that tendency is difficult to assess. Strong support for a hypothesis of specialization would be gained if substantial proportions of boys followed offense lines of the same type. For example, if the probability of transitioning to the same type of offense were of the magnitude of .50 instead of the values observed, we would have stronger grounds for a conclusion that distinct pathways are followed along a chain of like offenses. With the exception of this observed moderate diagonal "clustering" along like offense types, the row values are not very dispersed. Thus, it is possible to conclude that the transition probabilities to a particular offense type, with the exception of the likelihood of going to the same type of offense, are almost identical regardless of the type of the prior offense.

The probability of committing an injury offense, except where an injury offense has been committed in the prior offense rank, is .0530 to .0882, or practically independent of the type of the k–1st offense. The same statement can be made for the transitions to theft offenses, which range from .0854 to .1463 (except for theft to theft), and for the transitions to damage offenses (.0169 to .0235). The transitions to combination offenses do not fit this pattern quite so neatly since the transition probability between damage and combination is low (.0343); however, the remaining three switches are more tightly clustered (.0492 to .0928). Each index offense type is more likely to be followed by its own type than by any other, while the remaining transition probabilities are not widely different from one another.

To generalize the content of this matrix, then, it may be said that the typical offender is most likely to commit a *nonindex offense* next, *regardless* of what he did in the past. If he does not commit a nonindex type next, he is most likely to *desist from further delinquency*. If he were to commit an index offense next, it would most likely be the theft of property and least likely damage to property. With the exception of the moderate tendency to repeat the same type of offense, this pattern obtains *regardless* of the type of the previous offense.

It is quite possible that like-offense-type repeaters are being "lost" in the noise of minor or nonindex offense commission. A boy may commit several thefts but with several nonindex violations in between. If the choice of offense type is probabilistic, as we are suggesting, such would be the expectation. We may examine the empirical likelihood of *ever* committing the same type of offense again regardless of the types of offenses that may have intervened.

Table 11.10 relates the probability of committing an additional offense of the same type committed before, regardless of the number of different kinds of offenses which may have occurred between the first occurrence and the repeat.[7] If a boy has committed a nonindex offense, his chance of *ever* committing another one is .4590. If he has committed a second nonindex violation, then his chance of a repeat is .5701. If he has committed a third nonindex, his chance of a repeat increases to .6164, and so on. The other offense type entries are read in the same way. This table, in disregarding offense sequences, eliminates the dynamic aspect of offense switching but it does permit us to assess the chance of like-offense repetition.

The probability that another nonindex offense will be committed sometime in a delinquent career is high compared to the other offense probabilities, being between .4590 and .7738. The probability

7. The number of boys who repeated index offenses of each type dropped off rapidly for the offenses of injury, damage, and combination. Therefore, several cells in table 11.10 are empty.

TABLE 11.10

Probability of Ever Committing the Same Type of Offense Disregarding Types of Intervening Offenses

*k*th Repeat	Nonindex	Injury	Theft	Damage	Combi-nation
1st	.4590	.2138	.3349	.0961	.2773
2d	.5701	.3309	.4615	.0000	.4081
3d	.6164	.2978	.4615	.0000	.0000
4th	.6390	.0000	.4722	.0000	.0000
5th	.6578	.0000	.4705	.0000	.0000
6th	.6717	.0000	.4375	.0000	.0000
7th	.6315	.0000	.0000	.0000	.0000
8th	.7738	.0000	.0000	.0000	.0000
9th	.6153	.0000	.0000	.0000	.0000

that an additional injury offense will be committed lies between .2138 and .3309. For theft the range is .3349 to .4722; for damage only one repeat existed, with a probability of .0961, and for combination the probabilities of an additional contact range from .2773 to .4081 for the two repeats.

Under the assumption of a fixed probability matrix we would expect these relatively high probabilities of like offense repeats to exist as the result of the accumulation of offenses. Multiple recidivists will be charged with more index offenses than those who commit fewer violations *just because of the number of times they come in contact with police.*

Seriousness Scores

We would also like to know whether these repeat offenses of the same type are of greater severity. In table 11.11 the mean differences in seriousness scores between each repeat of like-offense types are presented.

Indeed the seriousness score at almost each repetition is greater. Only one nonindex repeat (seventh) was less serious than the one before, two thefts (third and sixth) and the one damage repeat. This increase in seriousness score is significant at least in direction (sign test, $p < .05$). Essentially, each repeat is more serious, but the magnitude of that increase should be put in perspective. It is actually quite small. The increase in seriousness score for all the offenses except the third injury repeat is less than the score assigned to a theft

TABLE 11.11

Mean Difference in Seriousness Score between Repetitions of the Same Offense Type: All Offenders

	Repetition	Mean Seriousness Score Difference[a]
Nonindex	1st	6.453
	2d	0.933
	3d	10.348
	4th	0.591
	5th	6.793
	6th	8.045
	7th	-8.750
	8th	21.123
	9th	10.400
Injury	1st	71.754
	2d	19.851
	3d	144.357
Theft	1st	12.053
	2d	3.314
	3d	-5.778
	4th	48.794
	5th	7.625
	6th	-14.286
Damage	1st	-3.071
Combination	1st	26.918
	2d	64.750

Using sign test $p < .05$, significant.

[a]$\bar{X}$ diff. = (average seriousness score of kth repeat) – (average seriousness score k–1st offense).

of ten dollars.[8] The one injury increment is less than the value of seriousness assigned to a theft of from $10 to $250. So it is clear that although the seriousness of the repeats of like-offenses increases, the amount of that increment is really quite small.

Thus, in one mode of analysis, the transition matrix, the probability that the next offense will be of the same type as the last is

8. See Sellin and Wolfgang, *The Measurement of Delinquency*, p. 298, for a display of seriousness scores for index offenses. We have multiplied all values by 100 to eliminate decimals for scores below 1.0 in the original system.

comparatively small since considerable offense switching occurs at each offense number. On the other hand, when the offense switches are disregarded, the probability that the same type of offense will be repeated an additional time in the future is considerably greater. The severity of that repeat will be only slightly greater as measured by the seriousness score.

So far in this chapter we have suggested that one process operates to generate the transition matrices observed at each offense number, and, with the exception of the moderate diagonal loading or the increased probability of committing the same type of offense again, the probability of committing the next offense by type is nearly independent of the type just committed. We have also seen that boys who commit at least one nonindex, injury, theft, or combination offense are very likely to be officially recorded for an additional one of the same type, regardless of what may have transpired between the original offense and the like-offense repetition. The high probability of ever committing the same offense again obtains after the second, third, and additional repetitions.

We may now examine the transition matrices for the two major subgroups of offenders, whites and nonwhites, in order to determine whether the same kinds of general statements about the transition matrices can still be made.

Transition Probabilities by Race

Matrices 11.11 to 11.18 show the transition probabilities from the first to the eighth transition for whites. Matrices 11.19 to 11.26 show those for nonwhites.

MATRIX 11.11

Transition Probabilities: White *Offenders, First Transition*

$k-1/k$	N	Non-index	Injury	Theft	Damage	Combi-nation	Desist
Nonindex	571	.2960	.0212	.0524	.0120	.0227	.5956
Injury	59	.3417	.0667	.0417	.0250	.0167	.5083
Theft	141	.3563	.0364	.1255	.0162	.0364	.4291
Damage	92	.4063	.0250	.0812	.0375	.0250	.4250
Combination	46	.3875	.0500	.0500	.0375	.0500	.4250
Total	909						

MATRIX 11.12

Transition Probabilities: White *Offenders, Second Transition*

k-1/*k*	*N*	Non-index	Injury	Theft	Damage	Combi-nation	Desist
Nonindex	336	.3764	.0187	.0840	.0233	.0202	.4774
Injury	29	.3636	.0727	.0727	.0000	.0182	.4727
Theft	79	.3543	.0236	.1890	.0236	.0315	.3779
Damage	23	.5455	.0303	.0606	.0000	.0606	.3030
Combination	39	.3725	.0196	.2353	.0196	.1176	.2352
Total	506						

MATRIX 11.13

Transition Probabilities: White *Offenders, Third Transition*

k-1/*k*	*N*	Non-index	Injury	Theft	Damage	Combi-nation	Desist
Nonindex	211	.4331	.0436	.0901	.0233	.0233	.3866
Injury	14	.3333	.1429	.1905	.0000	.0000	.3333
Theft	74	.4271	.1042	.1771	.0208	.0417	.2291
Damage	14	.5263	.0526	.0526	.0526	.0526	.2631
Combination	20	.4231	.0385	.2692	.0000	.0385	.2307
Total	333						

MATRIX 11.14

Transition Probabilities: White *Offenders, Fourth Transition*

k-1/*k*	*N*	Non-index	Injury	Theft	Damage	Combi-nation	Desist
Nonindex	126	.4083	.0321	.0872	.0229	.0275	.4220
Injury	19	.5667	.0000	.0667	.0000	.0000	.3667
Theft	46	.3167	.0333	.3000	.0167	.1000	.2333
Damage	8	.5455	.0000	.0000	.0909	.0909	.2727
Combination	11	.4286	.0714	.1429	.0000	.1429	.2142
Total	210						

MATRIX 11.15

Transition Probabilities: White *Offenders, Fifth Transition*

k–1/*k*	*N*	Non-index	Injury	Theft	Damage	Combi-nation	Desist
Nonindex	87	.4599	.0219	.1168	.0146	.0219	.3649
Injury	4	.2000	.1000	.0000	.0000	.1000	.6000
Theft	28	.3659	.0488	.2195	.0000	.0488	.3170
Damage	6	.7143	.0000	.1429	.0000	.0000	.1428
Combination	13	.5333	.0000	.0667	.0000	.2667	.1333
Total	138						

MATRIX 11.16

Transition Probabilities: White *Offenders, Sixth Transition*

k–1/*k*	*N*	Non-index	Injury	Theft	Damage	Combi-nation	Desist
Nonindex	66	.4516	.0645	.1075	.0215	.0645	.2903
Injury	3	.1667	.1667	.1667	.0000	.0000	.5000
Theft	23	.3704	.0370	.2593	.0370	.1481	.1481
Damage	1	.0000	.0000	.0000	.5000	.0000	.5000
Combination	9	.4000	.0000	.3000	.0000	.2000	.1000
Total	102						

MATRIX 11.17

Transition Probabilities: White *Offenders, Seventh Transition*

k–1/*k*	*N*	Non-index	Injury	Theft	Damage	Combi-nation	Desist
Nonindex	38	.4737	.0351	.1053	.0000	.0526	.3333
Injury	4	.3750	.0000	.1250	.0000	.0000	.5000
Theft	14	.3333	.0000	.2381	.0476	.0476	.3000
Damage	3	.2500	.2500	.2500	.0000	.0000	.2500
Combination	6	.4167	.0000	.0000	.0000	.0833	.5000
Total	65						

MATRIX 11.18

Transition Probabilitics: White *Offenders, Eighth Transition*

$k-1/k$	N	Non-index	Injury	Theft	Damage	Combi-nation	Desist
Nonindex	32	.5116	.0930	.0465	.0000	.0930	.2558
Injury	2	.6667	.0000	.0000	.0000	.0000	.3333
Theft	11	.6154	.0000	.2308	.0000	.0000	.1538
Damage	1	1.0000	.0000	.0000	.0000	.0000	.0000
Combination	2	.2000	.0000	.0000	.0000	.2000	.6000
Total	48						

MATRIX 11.19

Transition Probabilities: Nonwhite *Offenders, First Transition*

$k-1/k$	N	Non-index	Injury	Theft	Damage	Combi-nation	Desist
Nonindex	542	.3986	.0649	.0846	.0232	.0568	.3719
Injury	92	.4028	.0903	.0694	.0278	.0486	.3611
Theft	164	.2954	.0717	.1772	.0464	.1013	.3080
Damage	65	.3804	.0652	.1413	.0326	.0870	.2934
Combination	90	.3500	.0917	.0917	.0500	.1667	.2500
Total	953						

MATRIX 11.20

Transition Probabilities: Nonwhite *Offenders, Second Transition*

$k-1/k$	N	Non-index	Injury	Theft	Damage	Combi-nation	Desist
Nonindex	388	.4444	.0747	.1093	.0237	.0546	.2932
Injury	72	.3981	.0583	.1650	.0388	.0388	.3009
Theft	119	.3960	.0671	.2081	.0201	.1074	.2013
Damage	38	.5000	.0909	.2045	.0455	.0227	.1363
Combination	89	.3981	.0741	.1759	.0278	.1481	.1759
Total	706						

MATRIX 11.21

Transition Probabilities: Nonwhite *Offenders, Third Transition*

k–1/*k*	N	Non-index	Injury	Theft	Damage	Combi-nation	Desist
Nonindex	301	.4645	.0807	.1149	.0220	.0538	.2640
Injury	52	.4358	.1449	.0870	.0435	.0430	.2463
Theft	109	.4632	.0588	.1544	.0294	.0956	.1985
Damage	16	.2800	.2000	.1600	.0000	.0000	.3600
Combination	57	.4478	.0448	.1791	.0448	.1343	.1492
Total	535						

MATRIX 11.22

Transition Probabilities: Nonwhite *Offenders, Fourth Transition*

k–1/*k*	N	Non-index	Injury	Theft	Damage	Combi-nation	Desist
Nonindex	244	.4562	.0781	.1344	.0250	.0687	.2375
Injury	44	.4237	.1017	.0339	.0678	.1186	.2542
Theft	73	.4333	.1000	.1667	.0222	.0889	.1888
Damage	18	.4737	.1579	.2632	.0000	.0526	.0526
Combination	38	.4043	.0851	.1702	.0426	.1064	.1914
Total	417						

MATRIX 11.23

Transition Probabilities: Nonwhite *Offenders, Fifth Transition*

k–1/*k*	N	Non-index	Injury	Theft	Damage	Combi-nation	Desist
Nonindex	183	.4832	.0756	.1387	.0126	.0588	.2310
Injury	34	.4255	.0851	.1702	.0213	.0213	.2765
Theft	60	.5068	.0137	.1644	.0274	.1096	.1780
Damage	15	.6250	.1250	.1250	.0000	.0625	.0625
Combination	35	.4651	.0465	.1860	.0000	.1163	.1860
Total	327						

MATRIX 11.24

Transition Probabilities: Nonwhite *Offenders, Sixth Transition*

k–1/*k*	N	Non-index	Injury	Theft	Damage	Combi-nation	Desist
Nonindex	162	.4653	.1238	.1139	.0545	.0446	.1980
Injury	19	.3704	.1111	.0370	.0370	.1481	.2962
Theft	58	.4603	.0952	.2540	.0159	.0952	.0793
Damage	6	.6667	.0000	.1667	.1667	.0000	.0000
Combination	21	.3793	.0345	.1034	.0000	.2069	.2758
Total	266						

MATRIX 11.25

Transition Probabilities: Nonwhite *Offenders, Seventh Transition*

k–1/*k*	N	Non-index	Injury	Theft	Damage	Combi-nation	Desist
Nonindex	120	.5203	.0878	.1081	.0203	.0743	.1891
Injury	26	.4571	.1714	.0571	.0000	.0571	.2571
Theft	40	.3182	.0455	.3636	.0227	.1591	.0909
Damage	12	.4286	.0714	.2143	.0714	.0714	.1428
Combination	19	.4000	.2000	.1200	.0000	.0400	.2400
Total	217						

MATRIX 11.26

Transition Probabilities: Nonwhite *Offenders, Eighth Transition*

k–1/*k*	N	Non-index	Injury	Theft	Damage	Combi-nation	Desist
Nonindex	104	.5041	.1138	.1382	.0325	.0569	.1544
Injury	18	.4444	.0370	.0741	.0000	.1111	.3333
Theft	35	.4500	.0500	.2000	.0250	.1500	.1250
Damage	5	.6000	.2000	.2000	.0000	.0000	.0000
Combination	15	.2727	.1364	.0909	.0000	.1818	.3181
Total	177						

As in the previous section, which dealt with the total offender group, we have again utilized the chi-square matrix tests to determine whether the adjacent matrices could have been generated by one process. Our interest here is not as general as in the preceding since we wish only to ascertain whether a summary matrix could be used to generalize the transitions for both racial groups, and whether the two groups are different. The problems of small sample size become acute when the offender population is divided in this way. We shall be limited, then, to the simple pair-wise comparison of adjacent matrices, and thus we enter this section with even more caution than before.

TABLE 11.12

Matrix Tests and Chi-square Values for White Offenders: First versus Second out to Seventh versus Eighth Transitions

Transition Comparison	Chi-square	Decision (.05 level)
1st vs. 2d	22.3002	Accept
2d vs. 3d	14.9641	Accept
3d vs. 4th	19.4177	Accept
4th vs. 5th	23.7380	Accept
5th vs. 6th	19.1664	Accept
6th vs. 7th	12.2817	Accept
7th vs. 8th	7.2872	Accept

TABLE 11.13

Matrix Tests and Chi-square Values for Nonwhite Offenders: First versus Second out to Seventh versus Eighth Transitions

Transition Comparison	Chi-square	Decision (.05 level)
1st vs. 2d	19.3473	Accept
2d vs. 3d	15.6508	Accept
3d vs. 4th	8.8075	Accept
4th vs. 5th	20.6554	Accept
5th vs. 6th	27.8526	Accept
6th vs. 7th	20.6677	Accept
7th vs. 8th	11.9108	Accept

Our null hypothesis again will be that one process generates each of the transition matrix pairs at every offense, irrespective of rank. Therefore, the observed differences between the cell entries in each set of comparisons follow from random fluctuation rather than from a number-dependent generating process.

Because for both white and nonwhite groups we have accepted the null hypothesis that the adjacent matrices could have resulted from chance, we again suggest that one process operates to generate the white transition matrices and another process operates to generate the nonwhite matrices.

The summary matrices 11.27 and 11.28 are estimates of these processes for the white and nonwhite transitions respectively.

MATRIX 11.27

Summary Matrix of Offense Transitions: White *Offenders*

k–1/*k*	Nonindex	Injury	Theft	Damage	Combination	Desist
Nonindex	.4263	.0413	.0862	.0147	.0407	.3908
Injury	.3767	.0686	.0829	.0031	.0169	.4578
Theft	.3924	.0354	.2174	.0202	.0568	.2778
Damage	.3735	.0447	.0734	.0851	.0286	.3947
Combination	.3952	.0224	.1330	.0071	.1374	.3049
Desist	.0000	.0000	.0000	.0000	.0000	1.0000

MATRIX 11.28

Summary Matrix of Offense Transitions: Nonwhite *Offenders*

k–1/*k*	Nonindex	Injury	Theft	Damage	Combination	Desist
Nonindex	.4671	.0874	.1178	.0267	.0586	.2424
Injury	.4196	.1000	.0867	.0295	.0734	.2908
Theft	.4154	.0627	.2110	.0261	.1134	.1714
Damage	.4943	.1138	.1844	.0395	.0370	.1310
Combination	.3897	.0891	.1396	.0206	.1376	.2234
Desist	.0000	.0000	.0000	.0000	.0000	1.0000

TABLE 11.14

Matrix Tests and Chi-square Values for White Offenders: Summary Matrix versus First to Eighth Data Matrices

Summary Matrix vs.	Chi-square	Decision
1st data matrix	18.8227	Accept Null
2d data matrix	16.8995	Accept Null
3d data matrix	12.2900	Accept Null
4th data matrix	11.6315	Accept Null
5th data matrix	11.7049	Accept Null
6th data matrix	7.0566	Accept Null
7th data matrix	6.5801	Accept Null
8th data matrix	6.7144	Accept Null

TABLE 11.15

Matrix Tests and Chi-square Values for Nonwhite Offenders: Summary Matrix versus First to Eighth Data Matrices

Summary Matrix vs.	Chi-square	Decision
1st data matrix	16.0188	Accept Null
2d data matrix	7.6060	Accept Null
3d data matrix	10.0433	Accept Null
4th data matrix	9.4924	Accept Null
5th data matrix	13.7456	Accept Null
6th data matrix	10.0481	Accept Null
7th data matrix	11.0600	Accept Null
8th data matrix	5.5330	Accept Null

These matrices may be tested against the data matrices in the same manner as outlined for the all-offender matrix. Tables 11.14 and 11.15 indicate the results of such tests.

In each case we may accept the null hypothesis and conclude that the summary matrix is an adequate fit for the white and nonwhite data matrices. Of course the small sample sizes, particularly for the white group after the third transition, must be remembered with regard to the reliability of the test in this case.

The overall higher level of offensivity which we observed among nonwhites in the static probabilities appears again in this dynamic analysis. The probability of entering the state of desistance is smaller for nonwhites following every offense type, ranging from a low of .1310 after a damage offense to a high of .2908 following an injury, while the range for white offenders extends from .2778 to .4578.

This elevated probability of offense commission among nonwhites is not concentrated in the nonindex category, where the white and the nonwhite values are quite similar, but in the index offenses of injury, theft, damage, and combination. The probability for both whites and nonwhites of following an offense with a nonindex violation lies approximately between .40 and .50, depending on prior offense type, while the probabilities for nonwhites of following any kind of offense with an injury or with a combination of injury, theft, or damage offense are about twice those for whites.

The type of prior offense does not have very great a bearing on the likelihood that the next offense will be a nonindex one, although a nonindex offense is more likely to follow a combination or theft event for whites (~ .39) and a damage offense for nonwhites (.4943). At the other extreme, the whites least likely to commit a nonindex offense next are injury and damage offenders (~ .37), while the nonwhites least likely to go on to a nonindex offense are combination offenders (.3897) – differences that are rather small.

The likelihood that a white offender will commit an injury offense next is greatest if he committed an injury just prior to the new injury (.0686), though the differences between the probability of going from injury to injury and the probabilities of going from damage and nonindex to injury are quite small (.0239 and .0273 respectively). The likelihood that a white offender will commit an injury offense next is smallest if he has just committed a combination offense (.0224). Finally, the likelihood that a white offender will switch to the desistance state is greatest if he has just committed an injury offense (.4518).

Nonwhites are much more likely to follow all types of offenses with an injury event, ranging from .0627 from theft, to .1138 from damage. The diagonal clustering is not evidenced for nonwhites as it was for whites committing injury offenses, for nonwhite transitions to injury offenses are uniformly higher from all offense types. Nonetheless, nonwhites, like whites, are more likely to stop after an injury offense than after any other prior offense type (.2908).

The transitions to theft offenses are characterized by strong diagonal loading (theft to theft probability of .2174 for whites and .2110 for nonwhites). White offenders whose prior offense was a damage are least likely to commit a theft in their next offense (.0734), while nonwhites whose prior offense type was injury are least likely to commit a theft (.0867). The remaining transition probabilities to theft offenses are higher for nonwhites than for whites in every instance.

The probability of desisting is almost as small after a theft offense as after a damage offense: .2778 for whites and .1714 for nonwhites. Thus, these two kinds of property offenses are much more likely to be repeated than are other types of offenses.

The damage-to-damage transitions also exhibit some diagonal emphasis for the nonwhite offenders (.0395) and somewhat greater specialization for the white group (.0851).

Both whites and nonwhites are more likely to commit an offense having components of a combination of injury, theft, or damage if they have just committed such an offense (.1374 for whites, .1376 for nonwhites). Theft offenses are the next most likely type to be followed by a combination event for both whites (.0568) and nonwhites (.1134). In both cases the nonwhites' probabilities are greater than the whites', although for like offenses this difference is insignificant. The probability of desisting is about the same after a combination offense as after a nonindex offense for nonwhites (.2424 and .2234 respectively).

We may also examine the probability of repeating the same type of offense for both racial groups.

As would be expected, the probability of a repeat sometime in a delinquent's career is greater for both whites and nonwhites than the transition matrix values (see above for discussion of similar data for all offenders). Nonwhites not only exhibit a much greater likelihood of a repeat for all offense types than do whites, but they also do more repeating, particularly of injury offenses.

Although nonwhites generally are more likely than are whites to commit an additional nonindex offense at each repetition, the differences are not as great as those found in the remaining index offense types. Thus, the white probability of additional nonindex offense commission lies roughly between .5000 and .6000, while the nonwhite values fall between .6000 and .7000. On the other hand, the probability of one additional injury offense is .1222 for whites and .2620 for nonwhites. The probability that a white will repeat after the second injury offense is 0, while for nonwhites it increases to .3771 for a second repeat and .3255 for a third.

TABLE 11.16

Probability of Ever Committing the Same Type of Offense, Disregarding Types of Intervening Offenses, White Offenders

*k*th Repeat	Nonindex	Injury	Theft	Damage	Combi-nation
1st	.3796	.1222	.2663	.0675	.1777
2d	.4868	.0000	.3442	.0000	.2812
3d	.5286	.0000	.3809	.0000	.0000
4th	.5542	.0000	.0000	.0000	.0000
5th	.6068	.0000	.0000	.0000	.0000
6th	.6071	.0000	.0000	.0000	.0000
7th	.4117	.0000	.0000	.0000	.0000
8th	.8571	.0000	.0000	.0000	.0000
9th	.6666	.0000	.0000	.0000	.0000

TABLE 11.17

Probability of Ever Committing the Same Type of Offense, Disregarding Types of Intervening Offenses, Nonwhite Offenders

*k*th Repeat	Nonindex	Injury	Theft	Damage	Combi-nation
1st	.5653	.2620	.3920	.1255	.3285
2d	.6488	.3771	.5277	.0000	.4434
3d	.6792	.3255	.4912	.0000	.0000
4th	.6852	.0000	.4107	.0000	.0000
5th	.6794	.0000	.5217	.0000	.0000
6th	.6971	.0000	.0000	.0000	.0000
7th	.7070	.0000	.0000	.0000	.0000
8th	.7571	.0000	.0000	.0000	.0000
9th	.6037	.0000	.0000	.0000	.0000
10th	.7812	.0000	.0000	.0000	.0000
11th	.5200	.0000	.0000	.0000	.0000

Whites become increasingly likely to commit an additional theft offense with each repetition, from .2663 for the first repetition to .3809 for the third; nonwhites range between .4000 and .5200 from the first repeat to the fifth. The nonwhite probabilities are noticeably higher.

Damage offenders do not repeat more than once, regardless of race, but nonwhites are almost twice as likely as whites to commit an additional damage event (.0675 for whites and .1255 for nonwhites).

The same pattern exists for combination offenses, where the white probability of a repeat is .1777 for the first repeat to .2812 for the second, with no further combination repetitions. The nonwhite probability of committing the first additional combination offense is .3285, increasing to .4434 at the second repeat.

The likelihood of all offense type repeats is considerably higher for nonwhites than for whites. This difference is particularly dramatic for the serious categories of index crime. Not only is the probability of a repeat greater for nonwhites but the number of repeats is greater.

TABLE 11.18

Mean Difference in Seriousness Score between Offense Repetitions of the Same Type: White Offenders

	Repetition	Mean Seriousness Score Difference
Nonindex	1st	6.817
	2d	-2.225
	3d	10.735
	4th	0.576
	5th	10.750
	6th	-5.853
	7th	3.214
	8th	0.250
	9th	6.375
Injury	1st	127.357
Theft	1st	-3.500
	2d	28.476
	3d	-28.188
Damage	1st	-27.733
Combination	1st	23.500
	2d	37.889

Using sign test $p > .05$, not significant.

TABLE 11.19

Mean Difference in Seriousness Score between Offense Repetitions of the Same Type: Nonwhite Offenders

	Repetition	Mean Seriousness Score Difference
Nonindex	1st	6.115
	2d	3.149
	3d	10.138
	4th	-1.105
	5th	5.232
	6th	12.818
	7th	-11.143
	8th	25.849
	9th	11.406
	10th	-12.680
	11th	19.692
Injury	1st	58.096
	2d	37.977
	3d	144.357
Theft	1st	20.838
	2d	-5.956
	3d	0.625
	4th	43.783
	5th	1.833
Damage	1st	10.630
Combination	1st	27.870
	2d	69.490

Using sign test $p > .05$, significant.

Seriousness Scores by Race

The mean differences in seriousness scores among these race-offense specific repetitions are presented in tables 11.18 and 11.19.

Use of the sign test on the seriousness score differences indicates no real trend for white offenders in the direction of offense severity for the repeats of like-offenses. For nonwhites the opposite is true: there are more increases than would be expected by chance, and so we must conclude that there is escalation in seriousness scores for nonwhite repeats of the same offense. Nonetheless, as we found earlier in this chapter, the magnitude of these increases is not dramatic. Where white repeats of greater severity occur, they are of a smaller magnitude of severity than that of the nonwhite boys in almost every instance.

Summary

We may begin by recalling the two questions which were posed at the beginning of this chapter: (a) Does the type of the offense that a cohort member has committed at the k-1st offense number have any bearing on the probability that he will commit a certain type of offense at the kth number? and (b) Does the same process operate at each offense level (first, second, third, etc.) so that similar transition matrices will be generated when the offenses are classified by type? In short, are the transition configurations such that a homogeneous or number-independent Markov chain can be said to exist?

We have shown that knowledge of the immediately prior offense type (k-1st) does aid in the prediction of the kth type in that there is some tendency to repeat the same type of offense. This inclination, except for theft offenses, is not very strong. Nonetheless, it exists and justifies the inclusion of prior offense type in the model even though the transitions among the offense "switches" are almost independent of prior offense type. We conclude, then, that the probabilities associated with the commission of an offense, when that offense is classified by its components, depend for the most part on the type of the offense just committed. We are also suggesting that the offense history up to the immediately previous offense, or prior to the k-1st offense, has no bearing on the observed probabilities of committing the kth offense. That is, knowledge of the number and type of offenses prior to the k-1st gives us no aid in predicting the type of the next offense.

Because the same process operates at each offense number, we may infer that an offender "starts over," so to speak, each time he commits an offense. Thus we have suggested that the transition probabilities associated with the commission of juvenile offenses may be modeled by a homogeneous Markov chain.

Throughout this section we have stressed caution in interpreting the data. Although such a pose is called for whenever "real" data are examined, it is especially important in our case, when small sample sizes have limited our investigation, particularly in the higher offense numbers.

Our choice of the five categories of offensive behavior was based upon the work of Sellin and Wolfgang in *The Measurement of Delinquency*. We did not expect to find this kind of homogeneity in the offensive behavior exhibited by the transition data matrices. We can only suggest at present that delinquent behavior appears to be probabilistic when viewed through the filter of official records.

It may be that all kinds of delinquencies are being committed most of the time, and what we are observing is really a sample of police behavior whose clearance rates take the form of parameters being functionally dependent upon the type of crime, circumstances surrounding its reporting, age of offender, and numerous other variables which may be related to the process of uncovering crime and apprehending offenders.

The antithesis of this argument, of course, is that the observed counts of offense types that we have exposited here are really accurate indicators of delinquent activity, and, in fact, that this behavior is stochastic. The true state of affairs probably lies somewhere between these two explanations. Part of what we are modeling is police activity and part is delinquent behavior. Surely we are undercounting delinquent events, particularly those of minor severity; but the addition of such "corrected" measures would not materially modify the serious index probabilities to any great extent.

At least for now, lacking anything better, we must work with the official records in our model. Appropriate caution must be exercised, however, until better estimates of delinquent activity by offense type become available.

12 Contingent Probabilities: Age Base

Instead of denoting the transition periods by offense number, as we did in the last chapter, we shall now consider the transitions among three offense-related states by six-month time intervals beginning at age 10. The delinquent cohort members will be classified according to their state at the end of each six-month period until age 18. These states are: (a) "nonindex," (b) "index," and (c) "no-offense."

It will be recalled that one-time offenders, by definition, dropped out after the commission of the first offense and thus were not a part of the discussion after the first transition matrix in the last chapter. We have also eliminated the one-time offenders in this chapter because they reside in a dormant (nonoffender) state after the commission of their first and only offense and can make no further transition. Thus, in this chapter we shall deal only with the 1,862 recidivists.

We have reduced the number of partitions of the offense types from six (nonindex, injury, theft, damage, combination, and desist) to three (nonindex, index, and no-offense) in order to maintain adequate cell size for analysis. Because we are classifying the state of the cohort members over sixteen discrete time periods, the problem of maintaining a sufficient number of observations for each offense state becomes particularly acute. In the offense-specific analysis of chapter 11 this difficulty did not arise, and therefore the six-state model was desirable. A six-state design for the time-base model would have generated matrices in which the cell *N*'s would have been too small for analysis – particularly for injury, damage, and combination offense types.

In chapter 11 we were able to follow the development of offense transition patterns as the cohort offensivity progressed by number of offenses. As a result, we were able to outline the offense transitions for the recidivists as defined by offense number. In this chapter we shall, by the same method, present the offense transition matrices by age group and thus determine whether any significant points in the aging process can be isolated which are related to shifts in the transition probabilities.

The transition matrices by age group and offense type are presented in matrices 12.1 to 12.16 (the static analog of this presentation may be found in chapter 7, in which the relationship between years of age and offensivity is discussed). Table 12.1 displays the chi-square tests for the adjacent matrix comparisons.

MATRIX 12.1

Offense Transition: Age Group 10.0 to 10.5

	Nonindex	Index	No Offense
Nonindex	.114	.071	.815
Index	.072	.060	.868
No offense	.025	.020	.955

MATRIX 12.2

Offense Transition: Age Group 10.5 to 11.0

	Nonindex	Index	No Offense
Nonindex	.113	.151	.736
Index	.024	.167	.810
No offense	.031	.023	.946

MATRIX 12.3

Offense Transition: Age Group 11.0 to 11.5

	Nonindex	Index	No Offense
Nonindex	.103	.086	.810
Index	.076	.132	.793
No offense	.032	.035	.933

MATRIX 12.4

Offense Transition: Age Group 11.5 to 12.0

	Nonindex	Index	No Offense
Nonindex	.065	.161	.774
Index	.101	.145	.754
No offense	.047	.046	.907

MATRIX 12.5

Offense Transition: Age Group 12.0 to 12.5

	Nonindex	Index	No Offense
Nonindex	.058	.115	.828
Index	.106	.192	.702
No offense	.054	.049	.897

MATRIX 12.6

Offense Transition: Age Group 12.5 to 13.0

	Nonindex	Index	No Offense
Nonindex	.101	.101	.798
Index	.143	.143	.714
No offense	.057	.059	.885

MATRIX 12.7

Offense Transition: Age Group 13.0 to 13.5

	Nonindex	Index	No Offense
Nonindex	.170	.143	.688
Index	.113	.122	.765
No offense	.080	.058	.862

MATRIX 12.8

Offense Transition: Age Group 13.5 to 14.0

	Nonindex	Index	No Offense
Nonindex	.154	.114	.732
Index	.153	.127	.720
No offense	.108	.075	.817

MATRIX 12.9

Offense Transition: Age Group 14.0 to 14.5

	Nonindex	Index	No Offense
Nonindex	.205	.110	.685
Index	.161	.161	.678
No offense	.127	.071	.802

MATRIX 12.10

Offense Transition: Age Group 14.5 to 15.0

	Nonindex	Index	No Offense
Nonindex	.231	.132	.636
Index	.229	.167	.604
No offense	.145	.089	.766

MATRIX 12.11

Offense Transition: Age Group 15.0 to 15.5

	Nonindex	Index	No Offense
Nonindex	.266	.147	.587
Index	.227	.102	.671
No offense	.186	.107	.707

MATRIX 12.12

Offense Transition: Age Group 15.5 to 16.0

	Nonindex	Index	No Offense
Nonindex	.294	.144	.562
Index	.223	.158	619
No offense	.213	.116	.671

MATRIX 12.13

Offense Transition: Age Group 16.0 to 16.5

	Nonindex	Index	No Offense
Nonindex	.272	.117	.611
Index	.186	.164	.650
No offense	.239	.113	.648

MATRIX 12.14

Offense Transition: Age Group 16.5 to 17.0

	Nonindex	Index	No Offense
Nonindex	.331	.118	.552
Index	.271	.172	.557
No offense	.273	.102	.625

MATRIX 12.15

Offense Transition: Age Group 17.0 to 17.5

	Nonindex	Index	No Offense
Nonindex	.231	.098	.671
Index	.191	.166	.643
No offense	.183	.097	.720

MATRIX 12.16

Offense Transition: Age Group 17.5 to 18.0

	Nonindex	Index	No Offense
Nonindex	.230	.125	.645
Index	.219	.131	.650
No offense	.133	.072	.795

TABLE 12.1

Matrix Tests and Chi-square Values: Recidivists, 10.0/10.5 versus 10.5/11.0 out to 17.0/17.5 versus 17.5/18.0

Time Interval Comparison (years)	Chi-square	Decision (.05 level)
10.0 to 10.5 vs. 10.5 to 11.0	8.2068	Accept Null
10.5 to 11.0 vs. 11.0 to 11.5	6.7522	Accept Null
11.0 to 11.5 vs. 11.5 to 12.0	10.0941	Accept Null
11.5 to 12.0 vs. 12.0 to 12.5	2.3657	Accept Null
12.0 to 12.5 vs. 12.5 to 13.0	3.9084	Accept Null
12.5 to 13.0 vs. 13.0 to 13.5	10.7175	Accept Null
13.0 to 13.5 vs. 13.5 to 14.0	12.8855	Reject Null
13.5 to 14.0 vs. 14.0 to 14.5	4.8754	Accept Null
14.0 to 14.5 vs. 14.5 to 15.0	9.0260	Accept Null
14.5 to 15.0 vs. 15.0 to 15.5	16.4296	Reject Null
15.0 to 15.5 vs. 15.5 to 16.0	6.8894	Accept Null
15.5 to 16.0 vs. 16.0 to 16.5	5.1629	Accept Null
16.0 to 16.5 vs. 16.5 to 17.0	12.3055	Accept Null
16.5 to 17.0 vs. 17.0 to 17.5	44.8730	Reject Null
17.0 to 17.5 vs. 17.5 to 18.0	19.9620	Reject Null

We would expect, at the outset, that the uniformity in transition probabilities which was apparent when the various offense states were categorized by offense number would not appear when offense number is supplanted by age group, for we know from chapter 8 that the probability of offense commission rises according to a second degree curve up to age 16 and then drops uniformly to age 18. Thus, even though the transition probabilities associated with committing various offenses may not change markedly over time, the probability of remaining in the no-offense state drops dramatically – as the inverse of the plot of the probability of offense commission over age.

The drop is evidenced in matrices 12.1 to 12.16. The probability of remaining in the no-offense state ranges from .955 in the first interval, age 10.0 to 10.5, down uniformly to .625 in the interval from 16.5 to 17.0, and back up to .720 and .795 in the two time periods ending at age 18.

In spite of this increasing trend for law violation with advancing age, there are no significant matrix comparisons for the age intervals 10.0 to 10.5 out to 13.0 to 13.5. The adjacent shifts in the probability of committing no offense are too small to achieve significance, nor are there any special offense pathway probabilities of noticeable magnitude (table 12.1 chi-squares have associated *P* values greater than .05 for these comparisons). We may then conclude that the null hypothesis holds (see chapter 11) and that one generating process operates during this age period from 10.0 to 13.5. Figure 12.1 is the diagrammatic representation of this process.[1]

The time period 10.0 to 13.5 is essentially a stationary one, characterized by large proportions in the no-offense to no-offense transition (.941), high probability of moving from nonindex to no-offense (.778), equally high probability of moving from index to no-offense (.772), equally low probabilities of leaving the no-offense state (.046 to nonindex and .041 to index), and almost equal probabilities of switching or staying within offense types (.091 to .137 for all other combinations). The pattern is one of dormancy; slight rates of offense repetition and lower probabilities of offense type switching.

The first significant shift in the adjacent comparisons appears between the matrices 13.0/13.5 and 13.5/14.0. The main component

1. In chapter 11 we presented the same summary statements in matrix form because the six-way classification was too complex to enable this kind of representation.

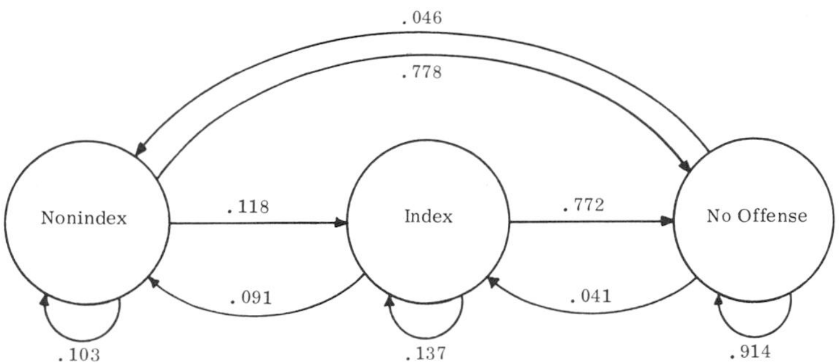

FIGURE 12.1
Digraph for Three-State Model, Ages 10.0/10.5 to 13.0/13.5

in this shift, as we expected earlier, lies in the reduction of the probability of remaining a nonoffender and the concomitant movement to nonindex and index offenses. The same pattern obtains for the transitions from index offenses, while exactly the opposite happens in the transitions from nonindex violations. These various adjustments result in a significant chi-square and are generally in keeping with our earlier noted expectations.

From age group 13.5/14.0 to age group 14.5/15.0 the offense transition matrices fail to achieve significance in the adjacent comparisons.

Another break in the transition probabilities occurs in the 14.5/15.0 to 15.0/15.5 comparison, where again the major component in the shift is the movement out of the no-offense states in the 15.0/15.5 matrix into the two offense categories. Thus, the probability of remaining in the no-offense state drops from .766 to .707. A similar shift appears in the probability of switching from nonindex to no-offense (.636 to .587), while the opposite is true in the probability of going from index to no-offense (.604 to .671). These three components generate the significant chi-square observed in table 12.1.

No additional significant shifts appear in the matrix comparisons out to the 16.5/17.0 matrix. However, the last two comparisons, 16.5/17.0 versus 17.0/17.5 and 17.0/17.5 versus 17.5/18.0, both achieve strong significance, for it is at these ages that the likelihood of returning to the no-offense state increases, and markedly so.[2] The probability of remaining in the no-offense state increases from .625 in the 16.5/17.0 period to .720 in the 17.0/17.5 period to .795 in the 17.5/18.0 period. In fact, all the transitions to the no-offense state, with the exception of the transition from nonindex to no-offense in the 17.5/18.0 matrix, increase over time in these age periods, as, conversely, the transition probabilities of shifting to the offense types decrease. In the 16.5/17.0 period, the probabilities of returning to the no-offense state are .552 from nonindex and .557 from index, while in the 17.0/17.5 period the corresponding values are .671 and .643 and remain essentially unchanged for the 17.5/18.0 period.

We may take the years 14 to 17 as being those in which adolescent delinquency blooms. The process is fairly accurately summarized in figure 12.2. Here we see, in contrast to the process which operates during the earlier period, a decline in the probability of remaining a nonoffender (.914 to .703), a decline in switching to the no-offense state from nonindex (.778 to .606) and index (.772 to .630) offenses. At the same time we see an increase both in like-offense repetition (index to index probabilities increase from .137 to .154, nonindex to nonindex values increase from .103 to .266) and in offense switching (nonindex to index probabilities increase slightly from .118 to .128, while index to nonindex values increase from .091 to .216).

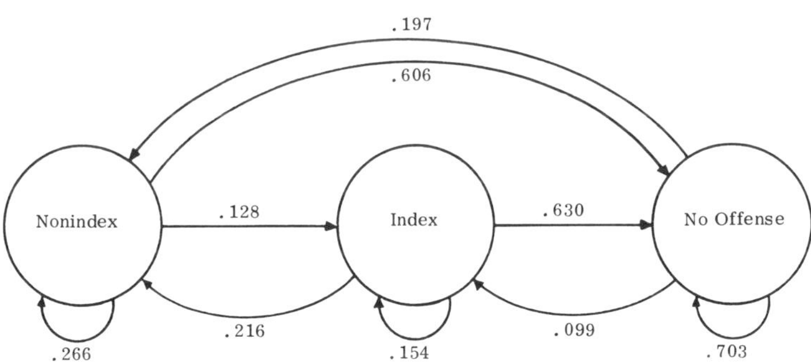

FIGURE 12.2
Digraph for Three-State Model, Ages 14.0/14.5 to 16.5/17.0

2. See figure 8.1 and the accompanying discussion of this decline in late adolescent delinquency.

In summary, the later age group, 14 to 17, is characterized by (a) a general decrease of transition probabilities, leading to the no-offense state, (b) a dramatic increase in the probabilities of switching to a nonindex offense, and (c) an almost negligible increase in the likelihood of committing an index offense, regardless of the initial state.

13 Disposition

Disposition decisions made at various procedural levels affect the composition of samples of juvenile *offenders* and *offenses,* whether the records used are taken from the police, from the courts, or from institutions. For example, although official statistics show that the majority of juveniles who are sent to correctional institutions are from the lower class, self-reporting studies reveal that middle-class juveniles are much involved in delinquency.

Reasonably reliable data on juvenile delinquents and their delinquent acts are available from police files in departments where officers are required to record every contact with juvenile "offenders." Examination of such data may uncover factors involved in the selection of certain juveniles but not others for court action. Thus, the first and most important level at which this screening process begins is the police.

When a juvenile in Philadelphia is apprehended for a delinquent act, the disposition of the offense is handled by the Juvenile Aid Division officer. The choices of the disposition open to him, as to police officers in many sections of the country, are "remedial" (no official arrest, no further processing in the juvenile justice system) or arrest. The decision is governed by five official criteria, as set forth in training posters and other police communications, and three other, informal, criteria. These eight are: (1) previous police contacts as determined by record check; (2) type of offense and the role which the juvenile has played in it; (3) attitude of the victim or complainant; (4) family situation of the offender; (5) community resources which might be utilized; (6) general appearance and attitude of the offender toward the police; (7) possible overcrowding at the Youth Study Center (the detention quarters); and (8) the police officer's anticipation of juvenile court action should an arrest be made.

Before the initial disposition decision is made, the line officer calls headquarters to check on the previous record of the offender as recorded in a master file. The disposition decision is removed from the officer's hands where offenders have what is called a "remedial stop" attached to their records. Such a designation, made by the Juvenile Aid Division staff in the case of some of the more persistent or serious offenders, requires that the next officer handling the juvenile make an arrest. This is the most significant manner in which a prior record can influence the disposition decision. When there is no remedial stop, it is general policy that the officer consider such things as number and seriousness of prior offenses in making his decision.

The frequency distribution of dispositions which were observed for offenses in the cohort study is listed below:

Remedial	6,515
Arrest only	258
Youth Study Center	97
Adjusted	748
Discharged	590
Institution	654
Fine and/or restitution	20
Probation	1,074
Project offense	230
Unknown	28
Total	10,214

An offense was coded as a "project offense" under the disposition category if the offense was recorded and scored separately for analytical purposes. Information was incomplete, unclear, or unknown in 258 cases. Thus, for most purposes in this chapter, our *N* is 9,956.

To simplify analysis we have grouped the categories listed above into the following four: (a) remedial – the unofficial action of the police; (b) arrest – official action by the police, which, for our present analysis, means that no further juvenile justice processing occurred; (c) adjustment – meaning that the case was terminated at the Youth Study Center or was otherwise adjusted or discharged either before reaching the court or at the court hearing; (d) court penalty – those cases in which a relatively severe penalty was imposed, such as probation, fine or restitution, or incarceration in a correctional institution.

Because the initial decision of the police officer is between remedial and arrest, it is useful to consider the remedial decision in comparison with all other dispositions. Much of our analysis is limited to this simple split.

As we pursued analysis of the available data, we became increasingly aware of the differential dispositions based on race.[1] Not all factors that enter into the decisions of police officers or of the personnel at the Youth Study Center are known or available to us. Hence, we recognize the limitations of our data. Inferences drawn from our findings will contain these same limitations. But however we split and spliced the material at hand, nonwhites regularly received more severe dispositions. Perhaps it would be more appropriate to say they received dispositions that caused them to be processed at a later stage in the juvenile justice system, or that required their being under the aegis of official activity longer, or that resulted in a juvenile court penalty. However expressed, nonwhites were less frequently given a remedial disposition.

That nonwhites may have a home environment less conducive to quick return by the police and the court, that further processing at the Youth Study Center might afford fuller opportunities for psychological diagnosis, that probation might provide a means for the community to give a young lad's life a little more supervision than he has had, that incarceration might give a treatment staff a chance to work with the emotional life of a teenager – all these reasons

1. One of the most extensive studies on the topic of differential disposition of juveniles is that of Nathan Goldman, *The Differential Selection of Juvenile Offenders for Court Appearance* (New York: National Council on Crime and Delinquency, 1963).

A recent study that reports no racial differences in disposition by the police or the juvenile court is found in Robert M. Terry, "Discrimination in the Handling of Juvenile Offenders by Social-Control Agencies," *Journal of Research in Crime and Delinquency* 4, no. 2 (July 1967): 218–30.

could be used as generous interpretations of racial differences in disposition from the point of police intervention to court disposal. We do not have information to support or to reject these suggestions. But the rapidity with which the heavy volume of juvenile cases is handled, the virtual absence of defense counsel for juveniles, and the weight of history and previous research on race and official response to race strongly suggest that differential disposition based on race may be the result of discrimination, prejudice, bias.

There is more than race associated with police disposition. One-time offenders as against recidivists, those who commit nonindex offenses as against index offenses, those who commit offenses with seriousness scores under 100, and those from a higher SES are all more likely to receive a remedial disposition. Table 13.1 summarizes these variables.

Because the race variable loomed largest in our analysis of these data, we have chosen this variable as the basis for displaying the data on other variables. Our presentation asks, in effect, whether other factors – generally viewed as aggravating or neutral – rather than race may not be operating to cause more nonwhites than whites to be arrested and further processed throughout the system.

For example, we know more nonwhites are in the lower SES in the cohort. We also know that some of these lower SES boys, com-

TABLE 13.1

Disposition by Four Variables

	Remedial		Other (arrest, etc.)	
	N	%	*N*	%
White	3,339	76.6	1,019	23.4
Nonwhite	3,176	56.7	2,422	43.3
Higher SES	2,310	76.3	715	23.7
Lower SES	4,215	60.7	2,726	39.3
Nonindex Offense	5,133	82.8	1,070	17.2
Index Offense	1,382	36.8	2,371	63.2
Seriousness score:				
Under 100	5,091	86.3	809	13.7
100 and over	1,424	35.1	2,632	64.9

pared to higher SES boys, receive a disposition other than remedial. May not SES level, rather than race, make for the disposition differential? Table 13.2 is revealing. It shows that, regardless of SES, nonwhites are treated essentially the same: about 57 percent have a remedial disposition. SES does make some difference among white boys, for 72 percent of the lower SES are in the remedial category compared to 80 percent from the higher SES. But even lower SES white boys have a significantly higher chance of a remedial disposition than higher SES nonwhite boys. A simple inspection of the table reveals that the race differential is greater than the SES differential.

Nor can it be said that recidivism makes the major difference in disposition. As table 13.3 indicates, nonwhite one-time offenders are much more likely to be processed beyond the police remedial disposition than are white one-time offenders. The same holds true for recidivists.

We have seen that index offenses are more likely to result in arrest, adjustment, or court penalty than are nonindex offenses, and that, indeed, only 39 percent of index offenses receive a remedial disposition. We know from earlier analysis that more nonwhites and more lower SES boys commit index offenses. But our concern now is whether there is any difference in disposition between whites and nonwhites among all index offenders. It is clear again from table 13.4 that nonwhite boys are more frequently arrested, or further disposed beyond a remedial disposition, than are white boys, even when the general category of offense type is held constant. Only 48.1 percent of white boys who had committed index offenses were arrested, compared to 68.4 percent of nonwhite boys. Among those who had committed nonindex offenses, the respective arrest frequencies were 9.3 percent for whites and 20.8 percent for nonwhites.

We have noted the strong relationship between seriousness score and disposition. A division into offenses with scores of 100 and those with scores of 100 and over is the most convenient and telling way to display this association. For offenses under 100, a remedial disposition was given in 88 percent of the cases, and a court penalty was imposed in only 4 percent. For offenses scoring 100 and over, a remedial disposition was given in 37 percent of the cases, and a court penalty was imposed in 37 percent.

But racial differences are still present. Within each seriousness category, nonwhites still receive more severe dispositions. For offenses with a seriousness score of less than 100, 92 percent of whites

TABLE 13.2

Disposition of Offenses by SES and Race

	Lower SES				Higher SES					
	Nonwhites		Whites		Nonwhites		Whites			
Disposition	*N*	%	*N*	%	*N*	%	*N*	%	Total	
Remedial	2,854	56.5	1,351	71.8	322	58.7	1,988	80.3	6,515	65.4
Other	2,195	43.5	531	28.2	227	41.3	488	19.7	3,441	34.6
Total	5,049	100.0	1,882	100.0	549	100.0	2,476	100.0	9,956	100.0

TABLE 13.3

Disposition of One-time and Recidivist Offenses by Race

	One-time					Recidivist				
	Remedial		Arrest			Remedial		Arrest		
	N	%	*N*	%	Total	*N*	%	*N*	%	Total
White	963	86.9	145	13.1	1,108	2.376	73.1	874	26.9	3,250
Nonwhite	352	70.1	150	29.9	502	2,824	55.4	2,272	44.6	5,096

TABLE 13.4

Disposition of Nonindex and Index Offenses by Race

	Nonindex					Index				
	Remedial		Arrest			Remedial		Arrest		
	N	%	*N*	%	Total	*N*	%	*N*	%	Total
Whites	2,665	90.7	274	9.3	2,937	674	51.8	626	48.1	1,300
Nonwhites	2,468	79.2	650	20.8	3,118	708	31.6	1.536	68.4	2,244

and 84 percent of nonwhites are remedialed. For offenses with scores of 100 or more, 50 percent of whites and 30 percent of nonwhites are remedialed (computed from table 13.5).

Socioeconomic status does not greatly affect these conclusions. There are two major ways to view, or control for, these variables when race, SES, seriousness score, and disposition are examined altogether. One approach is to ask whether white boys are treated differently when they fall in the same seriousness score categories but in different SES levels; the same question is asked about nonwhite boys. The answer generally is no (table 13.5). For white boys whose offenses were minor (score less than 100), 91 percent of those in the lower SES and 93 percent in the higher SES were remedialed; for nonwhite boys, 84 percent were remedialed regardless of SES level. For white boys whose offenses were serious (score of 100 or more), 45 percent of those in the lower SES were remedialed and 56 percent of those in the higher SES; for nonwhite boys, 30 percent of those in the lower SES were remedialed and 33 percent of the higher SES.

The other question about race, SES, seriousness score, and disposition is whether white boys are treated differently from nonwhite boys when SES and seriousness scores are the same. Race differences remain but are most noticeable among more serious offenses. There is only an 8 percent difference between lower and higher SES white

TABLE 13.5

Disposition by Seriousness, SES, and Race

Seriousness Score and Disposition	Lower SES				Higher SES			
	Whites		Nonwhites		Whites		Nonwhites	
	N	%	*N*	%	*N*	%	*N*	%
Score less than 100:								
Remedial	1057	90.7	2195	83.9	1594	93.4	245	83.6
Other	109	9.3	421	16.1	113	6.6	48	16.4
Total	1166	100.0	2616	100.0	1707	100.0	293	100.0
Score 100 or more:								
Remedial	294	44.7	659	29.7	394	55.6	77	32.6
Other	364	55.3	1558	70.3	314	44.4	159	67.4
Total	658	100.0	2217	100.0	708	100.0	236	100.0

boys in being remedialed, virtually no difference between lower and higher SES nonwhite boys, but a 26 percent difference between lower SES nonwhite boys and higher SES white boys.

Disposition Contingencies

We now wish to turn to a more dynamic analysis of the relationship between offenses and disposition. We have classified all first through fourth offenses as either index or nonindex and their possible disposition as remedial or court disposition.[2] We have then traced for each offense number the probability of each subsequent offense type and disposition. We now intend a dynamic assessment of the impact of disposition on offense type probabilities.

For this purpose we have altered the clustering of dispositions but still retain a simple dichotomy for most analyses. With remedial we here include every other kind of disposition except a juvenile court penalty. In the earlier section of this chapter we were most concerned with whether the police directly and alone decide disposition, and hence we divided cases into remedial and all other forms. Here we are concerned principally with whether a court penalty (probation, fine, institutionalization), which is tantamount to conviction in criminal court, is related to future delinquency. Therefore, for some sections of this dynamic analysis we shall compare (a) remedials with (b) arrest but adjustment and (c) court penalties; in other sections we shall exclude (b) and examine pure remedials with court penalties; in still others, (a) and (b) will be combined to compare with court penalties.

Tables 13.6 and 13.7 present the probability of disposition and the probability of committing a subsequent offense, given the previous disposition for index and nonindex offenses respectively. These tables indicate that in general the probability of committing a subsequent offense increases consistently from the second through the fifth offense (these probabilities are similar to the probability of a like-offense repeat as described in chapter 11). The tables also show that the more severe the disposition, the higher is the probability of committing a subsequent offense. For example, if an offender receives a remedial for his first index offense, the probability that he will commit a second offense, regardless of type, is .6116, whereas

2. Too few cases remain after the fourth offense to enable any meaningful discussion.

if he receives a severe disposition for an index offense, the likelihood of a second offense increases to .6751. These probabilities continue to rise with subsequent offenses. Similarly, the probability of committing another index offense also increases. In this case, too, the increase in the probability is greater for those who receive court dispositions than for those who are remedialed. Similar trends are noticeable with regard to nonindex offenses, although the number of cases is rather small because court dispositions are not often received for minor offensive behavior.

The decision of a court penalty for a repeat of the same type of offense is most often influenced by previous decisions, the decision immediately preceding the offense having the maximum impact. For instance, if a delinquent receives a court disposition for his first index offense, the probability that he will receive similar treatment for his second index offense is greater than the probability of receiving any other disposition. Similarly, if he had been remedialed for his first index offense, there is a greater probability of receiving a remedial disposition for the second index offense. These facts are demonstrated very clearly by tables 13.6 and 13.7. If an offender receives a remedial disposition for his first index offense and a court disposition for his second, the probability that he will receive a more severe disposition for the third and subsequent offenses is high. But such a definite pattern does not emerge if the court disposition for the first index offense is followed by remedial for the second index offense. Thus, our hypothesis that the disposition immediately preceding the offense influences the subsequent disposition holds partially true, and such a tendency seems to be more stable for those who receive a court disposition.

Since our information about court dispositions is limited, we can list only tentative interpretations. First, the period of institutionalization in most cases is brief. As a result, some offenders have experience in an institution four or five times during their relatively short delinquency careers. Second, those who are placed on probation for a certain period often violate the conditions of probation, and when the offender appears before the court as a result of such violation he usually receives additional probation. Finally, those who are institutionalized or placed on probation appear to be more serious types of delinquents than those who are remedialed. As a result, when an offender with such experience commits another offense, the court is reluctant to be lenient.

TABLE 13.6

Probability of Disposition by Offense Number and Offense Type (Index Offenses)

First Offense				Second Offense			
		Disposition				Disposition	
N	Probability	*N*	Probability	*N*	Probability	*N*	Probability
3475	.3494 (T)	963 R	.8025	589	.6116 (T)	170 R	.6967
1200	.3453 (I)			244	.2534 (I)		
						74 C	.3033
		237 C	.1975	160	.6751 (T)	35 R	.4667
				75	.3164 (I)		
						40 C	.5333

T = Total Offenses; I = Index Offenses; R = Remedial; C = Court Disposition.

We shall now consider conjointly the probability of committing an offense, the mean time interval between subsequent offenses, the type of offense, and the disposition. Table 13.8 presents these data up through the fourth offense.

Let us consider the first offense as an index offense. The probability of committing a nonindex second offense is greater (.3558) than that of committing an index offense (.2377) if the offender has been remedialed for his first index offense. More or less the same occurs when the disposition is "adjusted" by the police ("other").

Third Offense				Fourth Offense			
		Disposition				Disposition	
N	Probability	N	Probability	N	Probability	N	Probability
---- 134	.7882 (T)	34 R	.5862	27	.7941 (T)	9 R	.4737
58	.3412 (I)			19	.5588 (I)		
						10 C	.5263
		24 C	.4138	18	.7500 (T)	5 R	.6250
				8	.3333 (I)	3 C	.3750
---- 60	.8108 (T)	13 R	.3939	12	.9231 (T)	4 R	.8000
33	.4459 (I)			5	.3846 (I)	1 C	.2000
		20 C	.6061	14	.7000 (T)	2 R	.2500
				8	.4000 (I)	6 C	.7500
---- 26	.7429 (T)	9 R	.6000	9	1.0000 (T)	1 R	.2500
15	.4286 (I)			4	.4444 (I)	3 C	.7500
		6 C	.4000	6	1.0000 (T)	1 R	.3333
				3	.5000 (I)	2 C	.6667
---- 31	.7750 (T)	3 R	.1875	2	.6667 (T)	1 R	.5000
16	.4000 (I)			2	.6667 (I)	1 C	.5000
		13 C	.8125	13	1.0000 (T)	1 R	.1000
				10	.7692 (I)	9 C	.9000

Remedial includes other dispositions, viz., discharged, acquitted, adjusted, etc.

But if the offender is institutionalized or placed on probation for his first index offense, the probability of his committing a second index offense increases to .3164. If the first offense is nonindex, no matter what the disposition is, the second offense, if committed, is more likely to be nonindex than index. Moreover, the probability of second offense commission is almost independent of the type of the punishment administered for that first nonindex offense.

The sequence of second to third offense provides information for all three offenses, for the second disposition, and for the probability

TABLE 13.7

Probability of Disposition by Offense Number and Offense Type (Nonindex)

First Offense		Disposition		Second Offense		Disposition	
N	Probability	*N*	Probability	*N*	Probability	*N*	Probability
3475	.3494 (T)	2213 R	.9727	1083	.4894 (T)	720 R	.9717
2275	.6547 (NI)			741	.3348 (NI)		
						21 C	.0283
		62 C	.0273	30	.4839 (T)	18 R	.8571
				21	.3387 (NI)		
						3 C	.1429

T = Total Offenses; NI = Nonindex Offenses; R = Remedial; C = Court Disposi-

of the third offense. In all instances, except when the offender's first two offenses were nonindex, recidivism rates are fairly high. Furthermore, the first three offense combination types – that is, I-I-I and I-I-N; N-I-I and N-I-N; and I-N-I and I-N-N, in the second-to-third offense sequence – also indicate that in general, when the second offenses are disposed of by court penalty, the probability of a third offense following such disposition is about as high as or higher than in cases given other dispositions.

The data also show that offenders who receive a severe disposition for their second offense are more likely to commit a third index

Third Offense				Fourth Offense			
		Disposition				Disposition	
N	Probability	N	Probability	N	Probability	N	Probability
427	.5762 (T)	294 R	.9671	190	.6463 (T)	114 R	.9268
304	.4103 (NI)			123	.4184 (NI)		
						9 C	.0732
		10 C	.0329	6	.6000 (T)	6 R	1.0000
				6	.6000 (NI)	0	.0000
9	.4286 (T)	6 R	1.0000	2	.3333 (T)	2 R	1.0000
6	.2857 (NI)			2	.3333 (NI)	0 C	.0000
		O	.0000				
14	.7778 (T)	6 R	.7500	6	1.0000 (T)	4 R	.8000
8	.4444 (NI)			5	.8333 (NI)	1 C	.2000
		2 C	.2500	0	.0000	0	.0000
2	.6667 (T)	0	.0000	0	.0000	0	.0000
2	.6667 (NI)						
		2 C	1.0000	1	.5000 (T)	1 R	1.0000
				1	.5000 (NI)		
						0	.0000

tion. Remedials include other dispositions, viz., discharged, acquitted, adjusted, etc.

offense than those who receive other dispositions for their second offense in the three situations demonstrated by offense sequence combinations I-I-I, N-I-I, and I-N-I. Here the probabilities of committing an index offense by those who have received a court disposition for their second offense are .4298, .3140, and .4333 respectively.

Data patterns in third-to-fourth offense sequence are not as well defined as the above, although it is clear that court dispositions have little deterrent effect. The impact of offense switching, which we discussed in chapter 11, tends to color the disposition data, especially as the number of cases declines in the higher offense numbers. None-

TABLE 13.8

Contingent Probability of Offense, Mean Time Interval (in Months) between Two Subsequent Offenses by Type of Offense and Disposition Immediately Preceding the Offense

Offense Sequence	Offense Disposition	Number	Probability	Mean Time Interval	Offense Disposition	Number	Probability	Mean Time Interval	Desistance Probability
1st to 2d Offense	I(R)→ I	155	.2377	19.06	I(R)→ N	232	.3558	22.58	.4065
	I(C)→ I	75	.3164	10.16	I(C)→ N	85	.3586	15.27	.3250
	I(O)→ I	89	.2861	20.60	I(O)→ N	113	.3633	19.68	.3506
	N(R)→ I	314	.1527	16.98	N(R)→ N	692	.3365	17.67	.5108
	N(C)→ I	9	.1451	10.98	N(C)→ N	21	.3387	16.52	.5162
	N(O)→ I	28	.1783	16.29	N(O)→ N	49	.5096	16.25	.5096
2d to 3d Offense	I–I(R)→ I	49	.4083	9.97	I–I(R)→ N	47	.3917	13.89	.2000
	I–I(C)→ I	49	.4298	8.18	I–I(C)→ N	42	.3684	10.71	.2018
	I–I(O)→ I	24	.2824	12.08	I–I(O)→ N	40	.4706	11.98	.2470
	N–I(R)→ I	34	.2411	13.27	N–I(R)→ N	63	.4468	13.17	.3121
	N–I(C)→ I	27	.3140	9.57	N–I(C)→ N	38	.4419	10.66	.2441
	N–I(O)→ I	38	.3065	12.90	N–I(O)→ N	37	.2984	11.39	.3951
	I–N(R)→ I	76	.2289	10.52	I–N(R)→ N	136	.4096	10.51	.3615
	I–N(C)→ I	13	.4333	12.03	I–N(C)→ N	10	.3333	7.98	.2334
	I–N(O)→ I	17	.2500	13.64	I–N(O)→ N	20	.2941	9.34	.4559
	N–N(R)→ I	116	.1779	8.03	N–N(R)→ N	269	.4126	9.11	.4095
	N–N(C)→ I	3	.1250	14.06	N–N(C)→ N	8	.3333	13.73	.5417
	N–N(O)→ I	13	.1512	5.42	N–N(O)→ N	43	.5000	11.75	.3488

3d to 4th Offense[a]	I–I–I(R)→ I	16	.5000	10.48	I–I–I(R)→ N	12	.3750	7.01	.1250
	I–I–I(C)→ I	29	.4328	6.18	I–I–I(C)→ N	22	.3284	6.14	.2388
	I–I–I(O)→ I	14	.5185	4.95	I–I–I(O)→ N	8	.2963	5.87	.1852
	N–I–I(R)→ I	6	.1579	13.34	N–I–I(R)→ N	22	.5789	9.07	.2632
	N–I–I(C)→ I	11	.3056	5.63	N–I–I(C)→ N	18	.5000	13.55	.1944
	N–I–I(O)→ I	11	.4400	13.38	N–I–I(O)→ N	9	.3600	5.91	.2000

I = Index Offense; R = Remedial Disposition; C = Court Disposition; O = Other Disposition; N = Nonindex Offense

[a]In this offense sequence all the possible combinations of offenses and dispositions have not been presented Only those combinations which seemed numerically large enough have been shown.

theless, we can conclude from the probabilities in table 13.8 that serious dispositions have little or no influence on the choice of the type of the next offense or even on the decision to continue or desist from further delinquent behavior. In fact, serious delinquent behavior more often follows a court appearance than not.

We now seek to determine whether the number of previous offenses influences the disposition. Table 13.9 shows the sequence of offenses, court disposition, and the probability of a severe disposition of each offense. The probability of receiving a court disposition for the first time varies between a low of .0829 at the fifth offense and a high of .1129 at the fourth offense. It is interesting to note that the probability of a first court disposition at the first offense is almost the same (.0860) as the probability at the fifth offense. The slight variation between the probabilities of a first court disposition at each offense seem to suggest that the number of previous police contacts has little to do with the type of disposition. The data also show a consistent increase in the probabilities of second, third, and fourth court dispositions at each offense. For example, the probability of a first court disposition at the third offense is .1048, whereas the probabilities of a second or a third court disposition at the third offense are .1587 and .3214 respectively.

Table 13.9 also shows that, once an offender has received a court disposition, he is most likely to receive another court disposition in connection with his immediately following offense. For example, the probability of a second court disposition at the second offense is .1873 and declines to .1587, .1104, and .0850 at the third, fourth, and fifth offense respectively. An identical situation emerges in the case of probabilities of third and fourth court dispositions. The probability increases steadily and sharply from the first through the fifth offenses, and at the fifth offense the probability of a fifth court disposition is .6000.

Table 13.10 displays the probability of a remedial disposition at each offense, from the first through the fourth. The probabilities of a second, third, or fourth remedial disposition increase at each offense. But, unlike the probabilities of a court disposition, the probability of a first remedial disposition is greatest at the first offense and smallest at the fourth offense. In fact, the probability of a second remedial disposition for the second offense is less than half of the probability for the first offense. These probabilities increase at the third and fourth offenses but not significantly.

TABLE 13.9

Offense Number and Probability of Court Disposition

Offense Number	First Disposition (Prob. and *N*)	Second Disposition (Prob. and *N*)	Third Disposition (Prob. and *N*)	Fourth Disposition (Prob. and *N*)	Fifth Disposition (Prob. and *N*)
First	.0860 299				
Second	.1063 198	.1873 56			
Third	.1048 127	.1587 70	.3214 18		
Fourth	.1129 98	.1104 55	.2222 24	.5556 10	
Fifth	.0829 52	.0850 46	.1655 23	.2500 8	.6000 6

TABLE 13.10

Offense Number and Probability of Remedial Disposition

Offense Number	First Disposition (Prob. and N)	Second Disposition (Prob. and N)	Third Disposition (Prob. and N)	Fourth Disposition (Prob. and N)	Total Number of Offenses
First	.7793 2708				3,475
Second	.1359 253	.3663 992			1,862
Third	.0627 76	.1392 274	.4315 428		1,212
Fourth	.0276 24	.0491 87	.2458 206	.4346 186	868

In most instances a court disposition does not reduce recidivism. Data presented in table 13.11 further support this conclusion. Of the 1,200 first index offenses, 237 or about 20 percent were given a court disposition. Following these 237 cases through the fifth offense reveals certain important results. One hundred and sixty or about 68 percent of the offenders who received a court disposition for their first offense committed a second offense, and nearly 47 percent of these were index offenses. Over 53 percent of these second offenders received a court disposition for the second time. Approximately 77 percent of those who received a court disposition for the second time violated the law for the third time, and the majority of them committed a third index offense. Over 81 percent of these received a court disposition for the third time, and all were subsequently arrested for the fourth time. Thus, it seems that two factors – seriousness of the offense and severe disposition – are associated with a substantial proportion of recidivism.

Compared to index offenses, a very low proportion of nonindex offenses receive a court disposition. Only 62, or less than 3 percent, of the first nonindex offenses committed by our cohorts, compared to 20 percent of the first index offenses, received a court disposition. Moreover, after nonindex offenses have been given a court disposition, recidivism declines.

We cannot, on the basis of these data alone, say that recidivism declines because of the type of offense. Recidivism declines even more when the offense is serious but receives a lenient disposition, such as a remedial; yet the decline in recidivism is relatively greater when a minor offense is given a lenient disposition. Data presented in tables 13.12 and 13.13 support this argument. For instance, over 90 percent of the first nonindex offenses were given a remedial disposition. About 49 percent of these were followed by another offense, over two-thirds of which were nonindex. From the first offense to the fifth, the proportion of recidivists increases and the percentage of those receiving a remedial disposition decreases, but these changes do not seem to be highly significant. A greater proportion of subsequent offenses are nonindex, and this proportion remains almost constant from the second offense through the fifth. Thus, though a lenient disposition does not necessarily prevent an offender from committing another offense, it does not seem to encourage a repeat either, for the majority of leniently treated offenders do not become worse. Furthermore, as can be seen in table 13.8,

TABLE 13.11

Number of Index Offenses from First through Fifth: Disposition and Desist Rate: Court Disposition

Offense Number	Total Offenses		Index Offenses	Percentage of Index Offenses to Total Offenses	Court Disposition to Index Offenses		Desist Rate
	N	%	*N*		*N*	%	
First	3475	34.94	1200	34.53	237	19.75	
Second	160	67.51	75	46.88	40	53.33	.3249
Third	31	77.50	16	51.61	13	81.25	.2250
Fourth	13	100.00	10	76.92	9	90.00	.0000
Fifth	9	100.00	6	66.67	6	100.00	.0000

TABLE 13.12

Number of Nonindex Offenses from First through Fifth: Disposition and Desist Rate: Remedial Disposition

Offense Number	Total Offenses		Nonindex Offenses	Percentage of Nonindex Offenses to Total Offenses	Remedial Disposition to Nonindex Offenses		Desist Rate
	N	%	*N*		*N*	%	
First	3475	34.94	2275	65.47	2056	90.37	
Second	1006	48.93	692	68.79	605	87.43	.5107
Third	350	57.85	244	69.71	208	85.25	.4215
Fourth	131	62.98	90	68.70	73	81.11	.3702
Fifth	39	53.42	28	71.79	22	78.57	.4658

TABLE 13.13

Number of Index Offenses from First through Fifth: Disposition and Desist Rate: Remedial Disposition

Offense Number	Total Offenses		Index Offenses	Percentage of Index Offenses to Total Offenses	Remedial to Index Offenses		Desist Rate
	N	%	*N*		*N*	%	
First	3475	34.94	1200	34.53	652	54.33	
Second	387	59.36	155	40.05	75	48.39	.4064
Third	60	80.00	27	45.00	10	37.04	.2000
Fourth	9	90.00	6	66.67	3	50.00	.1000
Fifth	3	100.00	1	33.33			

the desistance rate of those leniently treated is relatively higher than in any other situation discussed above.

So far we have attempted to measure the effectiveness of various dispositions in terms of the probability of committing subsequent offenses. Another measure consists of the time interval between two consecutive offenses, from the first through the fourth. We would expect that, if the more severe dispositions constitute an effective containing force, the time interval between two consecutive offenses receiving severe dispositions would be greater than the time interval between offenses receiving milder dispositions. On the contrary, as table 13.8 shows, the average time interval between consecutive offenses is less when the earlier case has been given a court penalty than when it has received any other disposition. This trend follows through from first-to-second offense to third-to-fourth offense. Thus, we observe that the mean time interval between the first and second index offenses is 10.16 months when the first offense has been disposed of by a court penalty, but 19.06 months when the first has been given a remedial disposition, and 20.60 months when any other kind of disposition has been used. A similar trend is noticeable between first offense (when nonindex) and second offense (when index), and between first offense (index) and second offense (nonindex). With a few exceptions, this same pattern is found in the rest of the table. For example, the mean time interval between third and fourth index offenses (when the first two offenses were also index offenses) is 6.18 months if the disposition was a court penalty, compared to 10.48 months if the case received a remedial disposition. The time interval was 5.63 months when a court penalty was given for the third offense, the first having been nonindex and the second and third index, compared to 13.34 months when the third was given a remedial disposition and 13.38 months when any other disposition was given.

The mean time interval between two consecutive offenses when the first offense was disposed of by a court penalty actually amounts to less than the figures suggest, because those who received a court penalty were either committed to institutions or placed on probation. These constraining forces do not exist in most cases receiving other dispositions. The findings further strengthen our earlier interpretation that the period of institutionalization in most cases is brief and that those who receive a court penalty are serious and persistent delinquents.

The patterns observed in this analysis lead to two hypotheses which stand apart in their points of reference. The first hypothesis assumes the preexistence of a "hard core" offensive population prior to its contact with the judicial process; the second hypothesis refers to the judicial process as a factor which activates and eventually patterns persistent criminal behavior.

The first hypothesis assumes that uniformity in the transition of offense types that receive incarceration or probation as a consistent mode of disposition from the first offense to the fourth is an indication of commitment to future offensivity. If we assume the existence of potentially persistent offenders prior to their first contact with the judicial process, the court's first disposition (incarceration or probation) becomes an adequate screening process. The court, in effect, selects the potential "hard core" offenders from among the first-time offenders when the severity of its first disposition corresponds to the expected seriousness of future offensive behavior and when this expected seriousness is demonstrated by the probability of the offenders' committing subsequent offenses.

The second hypothesis holds the judicial experience as its point of reference. It is here assumed that the court disposes of first offenders mainly in terms of the immediate seriousness of the offense that has been committed, and disposition is not related to expected offensivity as in the first hypothesis. The population of first offenders who receive a disposition of incarceration or probation is assumed to be, at this stage, the same as the population of first offenders which is remedialed. The consequent patterning of the probability of committing a second serious offense and subsequent ones is not a prior property of the population disposed by incarceration but is a result of a process that takes place *after* the court's disposition. That is, incarceration or probation fail to curb offensivity and, in fact, trigger the patterning of higher probabilities of committing subsequent serious offenses (table 13.8).

To conclude, the first hypothesis assumes the presence of different populations of first offenders who are adequately screened by the court. The post-release behavior, represented by higher probabilities of committing subsequent serious crimes, confirms the prior judgment of the court.

The second hypothesis, in contrast, regards first offenders as all possessing similar properties, with the first disposition subsequently becoming the differential variable. That is, the type of first disposition dynamically affects the pattern of future expectancies of deviant behavior. Specifically, the "hard" type of disposition (incarceration or probation in contrast to remedial or other disposition) opens up a process whereby first offenders become persistent serious offenders.

Thus, we cannot conclude from an analysis of subsequent offensivity that the dispositions afforded juvenile offenders are serving the purposes for which they were designed. It would appear that on the one hand the judicial process has been able to screen the hard core offenders fairly well; on the other hand the judicial process and the correctional system do not seem to function effectively to restrain, discourage, or cure delinquency. Not only do a greater proportion of those who receive a severe disposition violate the law, but these violations are serious and rapid. The inferences which can be drawn from this analysis are not conclusive, for other factors which may affect the disposition decision are likely to affect not only the probability of committing a second, third, or any subsequent offense but also the length of time between offenses. With this analysis, however, we are on the threshold of a more accurate and valid evaluation of the juvenile justice system.

14 Summary

Our analytical pose in this study has followed two paths: descriptive and inferential. We have outlined some of those characteristics of delinquents and nondelinquents which could be gleaned from official school and police records and have related them to the extent and character of delinquency in a birth cohort. We have developed "true" probabilities of committing delinquent acts – true in the sense that the base is a continuous, longitudinal data stream.

In order to provide enough cases for assessing our probability model we decided to obtain information on *all* boys born in 1945 who lived in Philadelphia at least between their tenth and their eighteenth birthdays. This complete enumeration (within the limits of our knowledge and accuracy of the school and police records) yielded 9,945 boys, of whom 3,475 had at least one recorded police contact.[1]

From the school records we obtained most of the background data such as: name, birth date, race, name of parents or guardians,

1. See chapters 1–3 for discussion of the cohort concept and of the data gathering procedures.

addresses, country of origin for parents and subject, I.Q. scores, achievement level, number of unexcused absences, behavior (if incorrigible), highest grade completed, and termination date. From the records of the Juvenile Aid Division of the Philadelphia Police Department we obtained information on the number, type, and dates of offenses committed by members of the cohort, as well as the full descriptions of the events, including aspects of physical injury, property theft or damage, use of weapons, disposition of the case, and any other relevant information about the event, victim, or offender which was deemed important for this and future analysis. Finally, as an additional check on the whereabouts of the cohort members during the time period ending with the eighteenth birthday, we checked the selective service registration for Philadelphia residency at the terminal year.

Through a collation of these three data banks we were able to account for the physical location of the cohort members at least from the tenth birthday – and generally from birth – through the eighteenth birthday.

Of the 9,945 cohort subjects, 3,475 or some 35 percent of the boys were involved with the police at least once to the extent that an official recording of the act resulted, while 6,470 or 65 percent never had any such experience. Seven thousand and forty-three (71%) boys were white, and 2,902 (29%) were nonwhite. Of the whites, 2,071 or 28.6 percent were classified as offenders while 1,458 or 50.2 percent of the nonwhite boys were likewise designated. Slightly more than half (54%) of the cohort members were from the higher socioeconomic status (SES) group, of whom 26.5 percent were delinquent: 46 percent of the cohort were in the lower SES classification, of whom 44.8 percent were delinquent.

After examining the relationship between the various background variables of race, SES, types of schools attended, residential and school moves, highest grade completed, I.Q., achievement level, and the state of being delinquent or not, we concluded that the variables of race and SES (of somewhat lesser importance) were most strongly related to the offender-nonoffender classification. The remaining variables in the school records had little or no relationship to delinquency status. For example, the variable of achievement level[2] is inversely related to delinquency, that is, high achievers are much less

2. Defined in chapter 3.

likely to be classified as offenders than are low achievers. However, the relationship between race and achievement is such that most of the variation between achievement and delinquency status is explained by race, for being a poor achiever is highly related to being nonwhite. This relationship also exists between race and the remaining background variables, with the exception of SES.

Thus we found a nexus of factors related to race and delinquency which we referred to as a "disadvantaged" position. The nonwhite delinquent boy is likely to belong to the lower socioeconomic group, experience a greater number of school and residential moves (that is, be subject to the disrupting forces of intracity mobility more than the nondelinquent) and have the lowest average grade completed, the lowest achievement level, and the lowest I.Q. score.

We were then led to divide the cohort further into groups of nonoffenders, one-time offenders, and recidivists. Of the delinquents in the cohort, 54 percent were recidivists and 46 percent one-timers.

In comparing the three groups on the various background variables, we found that the recidivists, one-time offenders, and nonoffenders lie on a continuum. Recidivists experience the greatest school and residential mobility, attain the lowest I.Q. scores and achievement levels, and complete the least number of school years. Nonoffenders lie on the other end of the continuum, and one-timers fall between the two.

Recidivists are more likely to be low SES nonwhites than are one-time offenders or nonoffenders. Low SES boys have a higher rate of multiple than of single offense commission, but the reverse is true among high SES boys. Nonwhites exhibit a higher multiple offender rate, 328.4 as against 173.3 for one-timers, while the white multiple rate is 129.1 as against 157.6 for one-timers. When race and SES are considered jointly, low SES white boys have a higher rate of recidivism than of one-time offense commission, and high SES white boys are more likely to be one-time offenders. Such was not the case with nonwhites. Both high and low SES nonwhite youths generated higher rates of recidivism than of one-time violative behavior. In terms of the offense rate, rather than the offender rates discussed above, the nonwhite rate is about three times as high as that of the whites (1,983.4 compared to 632.9), while the offense rate for the whole cohort is 1,027 offenses per 1,000 cohort members.

In addition to describing certain characteristics of offenders we may also outline some facets of the offenses, particularly those of the severe or "index" variety. Nonwhite rates for offenses against both body and property are higher than those of whites, especially for attacks of robbery. Although low SES boys exhibited higher rates for these kinds of offenses than did high SES boys, the differentials were not so great as those according to race.

Because recidivists are more than twice as likely to commit index offenses than are one-time offenders, the index crime rate of recidivists is higher than that of one-timers; such is the case regardless of race or SES. Nonetheless, the spread between the white one-time and recidivist index crime rates is about three times the nonwhite spread, indicating that a proportionately greater number of index crimes are being committed by one-time, nonwhite boys. On the basis of SES rather than race, the spread between one-time and recidivist rates is only about twice as great among high SES boys as among low SES boys.

In this study an additional dimension has been added for the assessment of offense severity, the S–W seriousness score.[3] Thus, when we examined the relative seriousness of injury offenses, we observed that the more serious forms of bodily harm are committed by nonwhites. The highest injury mean seriousness score follows from attacks by low SES, recidivist, nonwhite offenders (241.9), while the lowest injury mean seriousness score results from attacks by high SES, one-time, nonwhite offenders (100.00). Within each SES level across racial groups, the differences in weighted rates of injury and mean seriousness scores are insignificant for one-time offenders, although the weighted rate based on seriousness score indicates that the 14 homicides committed by nonwhite recidivists represent more community harm than the total seriousness for all of the 465 acts of physical injury perpetrated by all white offenders during their juvenile years.

Most damage offenses are trivial (under $10 in value). The median amount of damage done by whites is $14.63 and is higher than that inflicted by nonwhites ($11.43). About two-fifths of the theft offenses involve amounts of less than $10. White boys commit fewer thefts but steal more per offense.

We undertook an additional subgrouping of the offenders by defining as chronic offenders those boys who committed more than

3. See appendix D.2 for a discussion of the Sellin-Wolfgang seriousness scoring system.

four violations. This group of 627 chronic offenders (18% of the total number of offenders) was responsible for over one-half of all offenses. The nonchronic recidivists (more than one offense but less than five) accounted for 36 percent of the offenders but for only 33 percent of the offenses.

Because there were proportionately three times as many nonwhite recidivists as white recidivists, nonwhites were much more likely than whites to appear in both the chronic and nonchronic offender groups. In fact, nonwhites were most overrepresented in the chronic category, being found five times as frequently as were whites, and in the nonchronic group, twice as frequently.

When SES is controlled, the same pattern emerges. Within both SES levels, nonwhites are more likely than whites to be recidivists, and of the recidivists, nonwhites are more likely than whites to be chronic offenders. Within both races, low SES boys are more likely to be chronic offenders than are high SES boys, although the differences between SES groups, holding race constant, are not so great as the differences between whites and nonwhites.

Chronic offenders in the cohort had a greater number of residential moves, lower I.Q. scores, a greater percentage classified as retarded, and fewer grades completed than did either the nonchronic or the one-time offenders, even when race and SES are considered.

The relationship between the total number of offenses a boy commits and the mean seriousness score of those offenses is direct and positive. The mean seriousness score of one-time offenders is lower than that of the nonchronics, which in turn is lower than that of the chronic offenders. However, it does not follow that, as a delinquent commits more offenses, his seriousness score necessarily escalates. On the contrary, we found that the seriousness score for all offenses, excepting attacks against the person by nonwhites, remained practically constant and in a few instances (certain damage, combination, and injury offenses committed by whites) actually diminished as the number of offenses increased.[4]

If, as we have suggested, the probabilities of offense commission when classified by type (nonindex (N), injury (I), theft (T), damage (D), and combination of I, T, or D) are relatively constant over offense number,[5] then the average seriousness score per person must be greater for those boys who commit many offenses because they

4. See chapter 10.
5. See chapter 11.

are likely to commit a greater number of more serious offenses. Thus we are not saying, in general, that offense careers escalate in seriousness as the number of offenses increases, but that the simple addition of serious offenses will force up the average score per person for recidivists – particularly for chronics.

The relationship between offense number and offense severity, however, is not so easily explained, for we know from the dynamic analysis of offense histories (chapter 11) that, once a boy has committed an index offense, the likelihood of a repeat sometime in his career is much greater than the initial probability of commission, be it injury, theft, or a combination of these offense types. This inference is based on the assumption that a constant probability matrix of offense transitions obtains for each offense number (the first, second, third offense, and so on).[6] Thus the probability of a serious offense repeat sometime in a delinquent's career must be positively related to increasing offense number.

Nevertheless, with the exception of injury offenses committed by nonwhites, which are typified by a strong positive relationship between offense number and severity, it is not readily apparent from the plots of offense severity by type of offense (chapter 10) that repeats of index offenses are likely to be more serious with each additional commission, for these plots refer to the severity of offenses regardless of the type or types of previous offenses. Under such conditions, escalation does appear in some offense types but it is of a very small magnitude.

If, on the other hand, the type of previous offense is considered, then the repeat of the same type of offense (if it occurs) is very likely to be more serious.[7] The magnitude of that increase depends upon offense type and race (comparatively large for nonwhite injury and white theft repeats, rather small for nonindex repeats, and nonexistent for damage repeats).

Thus we see that the accumulation of seriousness scores by cohort members is a complex phenomenon, being a function of (a) the number of offenses under the assumption of a fixed transition matrix, (b) some increase in seriousness score of repeats of like offense types, and (c) a weak propensity toward offense type specialization.

6. See chapter 11. In the study to follow this one, we shall develop and outline the mathematical derivation of those probabilities by building upon our findings with regard to the stationarity of the offense transition matrices.

7. See chapter 11.

We may discuss briefly here some of the findings introduced above concerning the offense transition matrices. First, it will be recalled, we discovered that the probability of offense commission when classified by type (nonindex, injury, theft, damage, and combination of I, T, D) varies very little from the initial probability vectors (probabilities associated with the commission of the first offense) over the first fifteen offenses when the type of previous offense is disregarded.[8] This is a very significant finding, for it implies that the delinquents in this cohort are not shifting in any uniform way to the index offenses as offense number increases. If such shifts were to exist, the probabilities of offense commission for those types of offenses having such increased likelihoods of occurrence would become higher with each additional offense. Thus we would have evidence for a hypothesis of "channeling" along these index pathways. Although the slopes of the regression lines of offense probability on offense number are positive for most offense types and for all race and SES groups, the increment per offense number is quite small, offering us little support for the above hypothesis.[9]

If we carry this mode of analysis further by including the type of prior offense through the medium of the offense transition matrix, we uncover an even more surprising result. The offense transition matrices appear to be independent of offense number and, in fact, the same process seems to operate at each step in the offense histories. There is no "break" after which the offenders specialize along some discernible pathways. Indeed, with the exception of a small tendency of like offense repetition (particularly for theft offenses), the choice of the next offense follows the first offense probability vectors as mentioned above. The same conclusion holds for all offenders taken together and for whites and nonwhites separately.

Thus we concluded that the probability of offense commission, when classified by type, is independent of offense number. Conversely, the probability of desisting from further delinquency is also unrelated to the number of offenses committed, especially after the first two offenses.

Substantively, white boys are less likely than nonwhites to follow an offense with an act of physical violence, and whites are about twice as likely as nonwhites to desist from further delinquency after each offense.

8. See chapter 10 for the exposition of this area.
9. See chapter 10.

We may now turn to the relationship of age to offense commission. The proportion of offenses committed of the total, and the proportion of boys violating the law, increase steadily from age 10 to just under age 16. From that point to age 18 the proportions decrease. These findings obtain for all race-SES combinations.

Another way of looking at this likelihood of offense commission over age is to use the probability of remaining in a state of desistance,[10] which declines from .955 between 10 and 10½ years of age uniformly to .675 at age 17 and back up to .720 and .795 from 17½ to 18 years of age. The likelihood of violent criminality increases with age, while the likelihood of property offense commission irregularly increases and decreases over age. Overall, the offense switch matrices based on age groups indicate that the likelihood of all types (nonindex and index) of delinquent events increases during the years 14 to 17, and that the trend toward index offensivity is not at all marked (as we would expect from our findings on the probability of offense commission over offense number).[11]

In comparing across race and SES we find that both whites and nonwhites commit a greater number of violent crimes as they age, although the rate of increase is greater for nonwhites. On the other hand, the number of property offenses declines with age for nonwhites and remains unchanged for whites. For low SES boys, violence increases while property theft and damage decrease as age advances. For high SES boys only violence increases, though only to a small extent, while property, theft, and damage remain unchanged.

Although the likelihood of offense commission is directly related to age, it must be stressed that those boys who commit many offenses are doing so within rather short time spans. We found (chapter 10) that the mean age at commission of the first offense on out to the fifteenth, for those boys who went that far, ranged from about age 15 at the first offense to a little over age 16 at the fifteenth for all offense types taken together. Although some boys who started their delinquent careers at an early age and continued to accumulate many offenses may be lost in the mean ages at commission of the early offenses due to the influx of large numbers of one-time offenders at age 15–16, such would not be the case for the higher offense numbers, where the age dispersion would seem to be much less.

10. See chapter 12.

11. See chapter 12 for the discussion of these age-based offense transition probabilities.

In terms of a crude offender rate based on age at onset of delinquency, 72 percent of the delinquents experienced their first police contact between the ages of 12 and 16. The probability of *first* offense commission increases from age 7 to age 14, sharply peaks at age 16, and decreases to age 18. These probabilities obtain for all race-SES combinations.

We have briefly analyzed the disposition of offenders taken into custody by the police. Some were given a remedial disposition, which means that the police recorded the delinquent behavior but did not further process the case for consideration by the juvenile court. Others were arrested formally and had their cases "adjusted" at an intake interview; still others were formally dealt with by means of a court penalty, such as probation or incarceration. Variables associated with a greater likelihood of a court penalty included being nonwhite, being of low SES level, committing an index offense, being a recidivist, and committing an offense with a relatively high seriousness score. However, in an effort to determine the relative effect of each of these variables, we had to conclude that the most significant factor related to a boy's not being remedialed by the police, but being processed to the full extent of the juvenile justice system, is his being nonwhite. That differential treatment based on race occurs is once again documented from this cohort study.

Finally, we may briefly note that the effect of disposition on the offense histories of the cohort members is unclear. It appears that the juvenile justice system has been able to isolate the hard core offender fairly well. Unfortunately, the product of this encounter with sanctioning authorities is far from desirable. Not only do a greater number of those who receive punitive treatment (institutionalization, fine, or probation) continue to violate the law, but they also commit more serious crimes with greater rapidity than those who experience a less constraining contact with the judicial and correctional systems. Thus, we must conclude that the juvenile justice system, at its best, has no effect on the subsequent behavior of adolescent boys and, at its worst, has a deleterious effect on future behavior. For it is clear that, if a selection process is operating which routes hard core delinquents into the courts and correctional institutions, no benefit is derived from this encounter, for the subsequent offense rates and seriousness scores show no reduction in volume and intensity. If the other process is in operation – that of random entrance into the juvenile justice system from the delinquent population –

then we would expect either (1) no difference in subsequent offense rate and seriousness scores between those who were treated and those who were not, under the hypothesis that the justice system has no effect, or (2) higher subsequent offense rates and more serious offenses committed by those who were treated when compared to those who were not, under the hypothesis that the juvenile justice system is in fact doing more harm than good.

The task of tying this array of data together is difficult indeed, for this study of interrelationships offers a myriad of investigative avenues, of which we have explored only a few. We have, however, isolated several detrimental conditions which indirectly accompany the delinquent state, such as withdrawal from school without graduating, poor school achievement, weak performance on I.Q. tests, repeated intracity migration, and membership in the lower socioeconomic groups. We say that these factors are indirectly related to delinquency because they are strongly correlated with race, specifically with being nonwhite, which in turn relates to the likelihood of (a) being an offender, (b) being a recidivist or chronic offender, and (c) being an offender who commits serious violent crimes.

Although we have no data which may accurately be called etiological, we may at least suggest that the strength of these interrelationships among the various background and delinquency variables is sufficient to permit our discussing some appropriate implications. We know that boys who commit many offenses, some of them very serious, are very likely to be nonwhite members of the low socioeconomic group. We also know that only 35 percent of these particular boys desist from further delinquency after their first contact with the law. With this knowledge in mind, as unsurprising as it may be, it seems appropriate to suggest that community action programs which have as their goals the alleviation or modification of the abovementioned conditions may also influence the course of juvenile delinquency within the subject areas. It has not been within the scope of the present investigation to comment on the character or form of such a program. Our data are such that we may refer only to those aspects of officially recorded existence which seem to be related to delinquent behavior.

If, on the other hand, an intervention program were to be suggested, the target of which would be the individual child rather than the community, some insight into the timing of such a program might be gained from the offense transition matrices in chapter 11. For it was in this chapter that we discussed the probabilities associated with various crime types in our investigation of the Markovian properties of the cohort offense histories.

We found that the offense transition matrices did not vary significantly over offense number. We also discovered that the choice of the type of the next offense is only very slightly related to the type of the prior offense or offenses. This finding leads us to the conclusion that the type of the next offense – be it injury, theft, damage, combination, or nonindex – cannot well be predicted by examination of the prior offense history, at least when that history is represented by our typology. There is practically no evidence to support a hypothesis of the existence of offense specialization among juvenile delinquents.

We are able to assert, however, that once an offense has been committed, the probability of a repeat of the same type of violation is somewhat greater than the likelihood of the initial offense. But as we earlier pointed out, these increased probabilities of repeats of the same type of offense can be explained, under the assumption of a stationary transition process, as the product of the accumulation of a large number of offenses rather than as the product of any special proclivity toward offense specialization. Thus, in order to prevent the occurrence of serious crimes in a delinquent boy's future, efforts should be made to prevent all forms of recidivism.

The most relevant question, then, is at what point in a delinquent boy's career an intervention program should act. One answer would be that the best time is that point beyond which the natural loss rate, or probability of desistance, begins to level off. Because 46 percent of the delinquents stop after the first offense, a major and expensive treatment program at this point would appear to be wasteful. We could even suggest that intervention be held in abeyance until the commission of the third offense, for an additional 35 percent of the second-time offenders desist from then on. Thus we could reduce the number of boys requiring attention in this cohort from 3,475 after the first offense, to 1,862 after the second offense, to 1,212 after the third offense, rather than concentrating on all 9,945 or some other large subgroup (such as nonwhites or lower SES boys) under a blanket community action program. Beyond the third offense, the desistance probabilities level off.

We intend in another research project, now underway, to extend this line of thinking, through the techniques of linear programming, by developing a set of decision functions which will permit the location of optimal intervention points in view of many factors such as age, seriousness score, transition probabilities, and other background variables. The proposed model should be much more complete, for we shall be expanding the scope of the study to include more extensive background information to be gathered from field interviews with a large sample of the original birth cohort.

This study of delinquency in a birth cohort was not originally designed to be etiological; it did not seek to predict, nor was it meant to evaluate the way in which society's agencies respond to or dispose of juvenile law violators. Yet in our descriptive statistics and through the use of a Markov model we have found broad sociological variables related to higher frequencies of certain kinds of delinquency, we have generated a model for prediction of future delinquency at specific points in time, and we have produced findings from which efficient timing of intervention schemes might logically be inferred. The posture of these inferences may still be in the form of new sets of hypotheses. But, most importantly, they are derived from probabilities based on a dynamic longitudinal analysis of a birth cohort traced through time.

Appendixes

APPENDIX A.1

Registration Card (side 1)

LAST NAME | FIRST NAME | MIDDLE NAME | DATE OF BIRTH (MONTH, DAY, YEAR) | EVIDENCE OF AGE (INDICATE BY X)*: BIRTH CERTIFICATE, BAPTISMAL CERTIFICATE, PASSPORT, OTHER DOCUMENTARY PROOF†, OPINION OF MEDICAL INSP.‡, SIG.‡ | RACE (IND. BY X)*: WHITE, NEGRO, OTHER

*FIRST NAME OF FATHER | CHK. IF DEC. | *FIRST NAME OF MOTHER | CHK. IF DEC. | *FULL NAME OF STEP-PARENT OR GUARDIAN | COUNTRY OF BIRTH*: CHILD; IF U. S. GIVE CITY AND STATE, FATHER, MOTHER

RESIDENCE **

	NUMBER	STREET	ZONE	TELEPHONE		NUMBER	STREET	ZONE	TELEPHONE
1	*	*	*	*	7				
2					8				
3					9				
4					10				
5					11				
6					12				

ADMITTED BY "O"		DISMISSED BY "O"		ADMITTED BY "R" OR "O"		DISMISSED BY "O"		ADMITTED BY "R" OR "O"		DISMISSED BY "O"	
DATE*	SOURCE*	DATE	CODE NO.	DATE	SOURCE	DATE	CODE NO.	DATE	SOURCE	DATE	CODE NO.
1		2		3		4		7		8	
				5		6		9		10	

*ORIGINAL ENTRIES, TYPE. **IN CASE OF TRANSFER, DISMISSING SCHOOL ENTER NEW ADDRESS. (DISMISS D 2, USE RED INK.)

DATE MO. DAY YEAR	GRADE-SECTION	TEACHER FIRST NAME	TEACHER LAST NAME	ROOM NUMBER	SCHOOL	DATE MO. DAY YEAR	GRADE-SECTION	TEACHER FIRST NAME	TEACHER LAST NAME	ROOM NUMBER	SCHOOL
*	*	*		*	*						

FILL OUT FOR ORIGINAL ADMISSION AND FOR EACH READMISSION OR TRANSFER. FOR TRANSFER, GIVE GRADE-SECTION TO WHICH PUPIL IS TRANSFERRED. IN KINDERGARDEN, GRADES 1 TO 6, AND SPECIAL CLASSES MAKE ENTRIES FOR EACH CHANGE OF GRADE-SECTION OR TEACHER. FOR DISMISS UNDER D 1 ENTER NEW SCHOOL IN RED INK.

BIRTH CERTIFICATE No. .... SOURCE ....

FORM EHV 1—REGISTRATION CARD, BOYS—SCHOOL DISTRICT OF PHILADELPHIA (APR. 1955)

†SPECIFY .... ‡SIG. MED. INSP. (OVER)

APPENDIX A.1

Registration Card (side 2)

DATE MO. DAY YEAR	GRADE-SECTION	TEACHER FIRST NAME	TEACHER LAST NAME	ROOM NUMBER	SCHOOL	DATE MO. DAY YEAR	GRADE-SECTION	TEACHER FIRST NAME	TEACHER LAST NAME	ROOM NUMBER	SCHOOL

REMARKS (DATED):

APPENDIX A.2

Cumulative Record (side 1)

LAST NAME	FIRST NAME	MIDDLE NAME	DATE OF BIRTH MONTH DAY YEAR	EVIDENCE OF AGE: BIRTH CERTIFICATE (CHECK) / OTHER (SPECIFY)	DATE ENTERED GRADE 1 IN ANY SCHOOL SYSTEM	BOY / GIRL / IND. BY X

FIRST NAME OF FATHER	CHK. IF DEC.	FIRST NAME OF MOTHER	CHK. IF DEC.	FULL NAME OF STEPPARENT OR GUARDIAN	COUNTRY OF BIRTH: CHILD, IF U. S. GIVE CITY AND STATE	FATHER	MOTHER

GRADE								
ARITHMETIC								
READING								
WRITTEN EXPRESSION								
SPELLING								
HANDWRITING								
SOCIAL STUDIES								
SCIENCE								

DATE		DATE	REMARKS
	FIRST COUNSELING CONTACT		
	PSYCHOLOGICAL EXAMINATION		
	PSYCHOLOGICAL EXAMINATION		
	NON-APPARENT PHYS. DEFECTS		

ENROLLMENT AND RESIDENCE RECORD

DATE MO. DAY YEAR	SCHOOL-KINDERGARTEN TO GRADUATION. INCLUDE ALL SCHOOLS IN PA., PUBLIC, PRIVATE, AND PAROCHIAL.*	CODE ADM. DIS. ETC.	GRADE	RESIDENCE - ENTER ORIGINAL ADDRESS AND ALL CHANGES, INCLUDING OUT-OF-CITY ADDRESSES, OR AT LEAST NAME OF CITY.

*INDICATE SOURCE BY "BEGINNER" OR NAME OF LAST CITY OR STATE IN RESIDENCE COLUMN. INDICATE ALL SCHOOL, GRADE, AND RESIDENCE. INDICATE "GRADUATIO

SCHOOL ATTENDED WITH TRANSFERS, GIVING NEW

FORM EH 6—CUMULATIV .CORD SCHOOL DISTRICT OF PHILADELPHIA (JUNE 1962)

APPENDIX A.2

Cumulative Record (side 2)

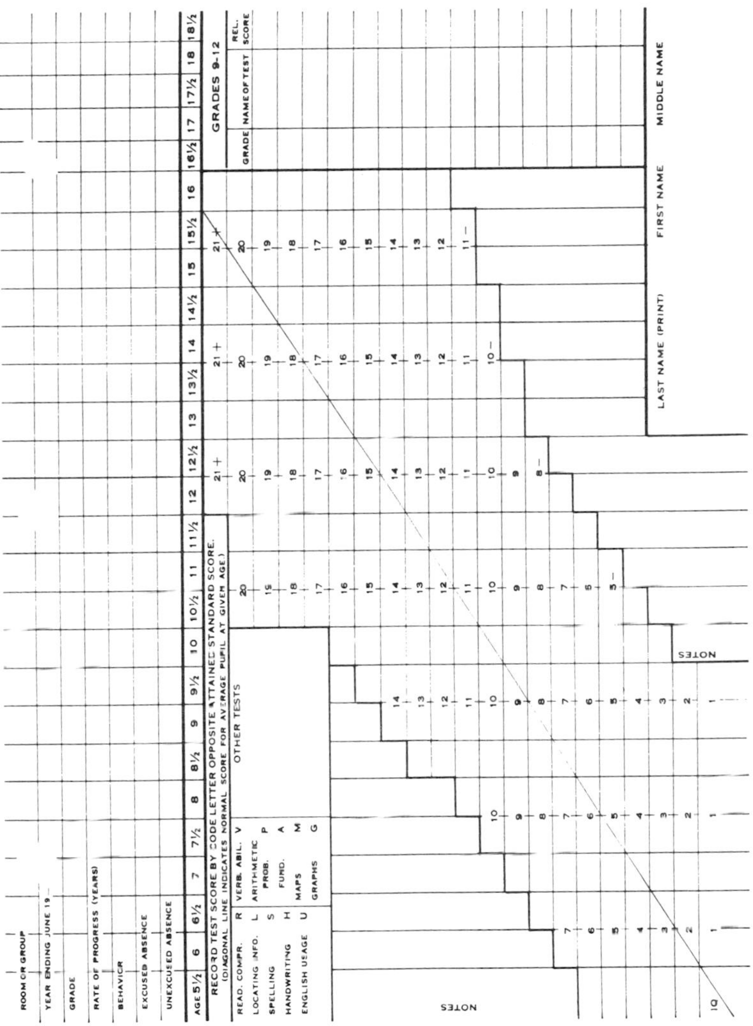

APPENDIX A.3

Application for Records

LAST NAME	FIRST NAME AND INITIALS	DATE OF BIRTH		
		MONTH	DAY	YEAR

PHILADELPHIA PUBLIC SCHOOL FORMERLY ATTENDED:	DATE OF DISMISSAL		
	MONTH	DAY	YEAR
............SCHOOL, DISTRICT............			

FIRST NAME OF FATHER *	CHK. IF DEC.	FIRST NAME OF MOTHER *	CHK. IF DEC.	FULL NAME OF STEP PARENT OR GUARDIAN

* FULL NAME IF DIFFERENT FROM THAT OF CHILD.

TO THE DIRECTOR OF THE DIVISION OF PUPIL PERSONNEL AND COUNSELING:

PLEASE FORWARD THE CUMULATIVE AND OTHER RECORDS OF THE ABOVE-NAMED

CHILD TO THE ....SCHOOL, DISTRICT............,

LOCATED AT ...., ZIP CODE............

............, 19............

....
PRINCIPAL

FORM EH 62—APPLICATION FOR RECORDS, FORMER PUPILS—SCHOOL DISTRICT OF PHILADELPHIA (NOV. 1969)

APPENDIX A.4

Permanent Record (side 1)

WEST PHILADELPHIA CATHOLIC HIGH SCHOOL FOR BOYS, PHILADELPHIA, PA.

RECORD OF　　　　　　PARISH　　　　　　COURSE

ADDRESS　　　ZONE　　　PHONE {HOME / NEAREST　　　CHANGED TO　　　RANK IN CLASS

Picture

CREDITS

FIRST SEC.				SECOND SEC.				THIRD SEC.				FOURTH SEC.				REPEATING			
19	19			19	19			19	19			19	19			19	19		
HOME ROOM	1ST	2ND	CR.	HOME ROOM	1ST	2ND	CR.	HOME ROOM	1ST	2ND	CR.	HOME ROOM	1ST	2ND	CR.	HOME ROOM	1ST	2ND	CR.
REL.				REL.				REL.				REL.							
ENG.				ENG.				ENG.				ENG.							
TOTAL CREDITS				TOTAL CREDITS				TOTAL CREDITS				TOTAL CREDITS				TOTAL CREDITS			

NO. OF DAYS ABSENT	1ST YR.	2ND YR.	3RD YR.	4TH YR.
TIMES LATE	1ST YR.	2ND YR.	3RD YR.	4TH YR.

STUDY CONDITIONS

NOTABLE ACCOMPLISHMENTS

SERVICE TO SCHOOL　　OFFICES

EXTRA CURRICULAR WORK　　HRS. PER WEEK

ATHLETIC

NON-ATHLETIC

PERSONAL QUALITIES

CHECK √	HIGH +2	HIGH +1	NORM. 0	LOW —1	LOW —2
APPEARANCE					
INITIATIVE					
LEADERSHIP					
SELF-RESTRAINT					
EFFORT					
SENSE OF RESPONSIBILITY					
ABILITY TO GET ALONG WITH OTHERS					
COOPERATION					

Form 1 — Permanent Record

APPENDIX A.4

Permanent Record (side 2)

LAST NAME | FIRST NAME | MIDDLE NAME | PLACE OF BIRTH | DATE OF BIRTH MO. DAY YR.

FATHER'S FIRST NAME | NATIONALITY | RACE | RELIGION | LIVING—YES NO

MOTHER'S FIRST NAME | NATIONALITY | RACE | RELIGION | LIVING—YES NO

OCCUPATION OF FATHER 1 | FIRM ADDRESS | FIRM PHONE NO.

2

OCCUPATION OF MOTHER

LANGUAGE SPOKEN IN THE HOME →	BEFORE 10	AFTER 10

CHECK HOME CONDITIONS

EX.	GOOD	MEDIUM	FAIR	POOR

SCHOOL FROM WHICH ADMITTED

LEFT SCHOOL | DATE | REASON

GRADUATION DATE | TRANSFERRED TO

CERTIFICATION TO

NO. BROTHERS OLDER | YOUNGER

NO. SISTERS OLDER | YOUNGER

NO. WHO HAVE ATTENDED COLLEGE

IF PARENTS SEPARATED | DATE

VACCINATION CERTIFICATE | DATE

MENTAL ABILITY AND OTHER STANDARDIZED TESTS

DATE	EXACT TITLE	FORM	SCORE	RATING

OBSERVATIONS:—

APPENDIX B

Offense Number,[1] Crime Code, and Derived Scores for Nonindex Offenses

(a) Offense No.	(b) Crime Code	(c) Manual Score
87	1,005	207
88	1,101	87
89	1,201	353
90	1,202	31
91	1,203	114
92	1,301	131
93	1,302	77
94	1,305	148
95	1,401	220
100	1,403	192
101	1,405	95
103	1,405	356
104	1,406	36
105	1,407	0.4
106	1,408	357
107	1,409	431
108	1,410	0.2
109	1,601	1,010
110	1,601	1,643
111	1,602	141
112	1,602	1,061
113	1,603	113
114	1,603	477
115	1,703	40
116	1,710	149
117	1,802	0.4
118	1,804	63
119	1,901	48
120	1,903	22
121	1,904	19
122	1,909	22

1. This heading refers to the number assigned that offense in the list of offense descriptions found in *The Measurement of Delinquency*, pp. 381–86.

(a) Offense No.	(b) Crime Code	(c) Manual Score
123	2,001	58
124	2,002	0.5
125	2,103	74
126	2,104	253
127	2,105	36
128	2,109	36
129	2,601	510
130	2,616	518
131	2,619	0.3
132	2,621	60
133	2,622	0.8
134	2,623	122
135	2,624	30
140	2,646	842
141	2,653	33

APPENDIX C

Intercorrelation Matrix of Cohort Background Variables

	(1) Race	(2) No. of Moves	(3) Status of Handi-capped	(4) Highest Grade Completed	(5) No. of Different Schools	(6) First I.Q. Score	(7) Income Census Tract
(1)	1.000	.377	.010	-.397	.386	-.402	-.587
(2)		1.000	.002	-.367	.670	-.279	-.275
(3)			1.000	-.021	.056	-.009	-.010
(4)				1.000	-.329	.468	.352
(5)					1.000	-.244	-.232
(6)						1.000	.377
(7)							1.000

APPENDIX D.1

Notes Concerning the Computation of Weighted Rates

In *The Measurement of Delinquency* study we suggested formulae for the computation of weighted rates of delinquency. (See T. Sellin and M.W. Wolfgang, *The Measurement of Delinquency* (New York, John Wiley and Sons, Inc., 1964, Table 70, p. 307). Here we have at our disposal data from a cohort population. Hence we have used the cohort population or parts thereof as the denominator in the computation of weighted rates.

The formulae used are as follows:

	Formula	*Explanation*
A	$\frac{\Sigma fs}{pc} \times k$	$\frac{\text{Seriousness Summed Over Events}}{\text{Cohort Population}} \times 1{,}000$
B	$\frac{\Sigma fs}{pw} \times k$	$\frac{\text{Seriousness Summed Over Events}}{\text{White Cohort Population}} \times 1{,}000$
C	$\frac{\Sigma fs}{pnw} \times k$	$\frac{\text{Seriousness Summed Over Events}}{\text{Nonwhite Cohort Population}} \times 1{,}000$
D	$\frac{\Sigma fs}{pwl} \times k$	$\frac{\text{Seriousness Summed Over Events}}{\text{Lower SES White Cohort Population}} \times 1{,}000$
E	$\frac{\Sigma fs}{pnwl} \times k$	$\frac{\text{Seriousness Summed Over Events}}{\text{Lower SES Nonwhite Cohort Population}} \times 1{,}000$
F	$\frac{\Sigma fs}{pwh} \times k$	$\frac{\text{Seriousness Summed Over Events}}{\text{Higher SES White Cohort Population}} \times 1{,}000$
G	$\frac{\Sigma fs}{pnwh} \times k$	$\frac{\text{Seriousness Summed Over Events}}{\text{Higher SES Nonwhite Population}} \times 1{,}000$

Formula	Explanation	
H $\frac{\Sigma fs}{pl} \times k$	$\frac{\text{Seriousness Summed Over Events}}{\text{Lower SES Population}}$	$\times$ 1,000
I $\frac{\Sigma fs}{ph} \times k$	$\frac{\text{Seriousness Summed Over Events}}{\text{Higher SES Population}}$	$\times$ 1,000

Thus *A* is the weighted rate for the general cohort; *B* and *C* are race-specific weighted rates; *D, E, F,* and *G* are race-SES-specific weighted rates; and *H* and *I* are SES-specific weighted rates.

When we computed rates using any of the above formulae, we found the results to have very large numbers to the left of the decimal. In order to simplify the terms we have divided all of the serious scores by 100 and used the resulting number as the weighting factor.

An example will help to illustrate the point. The mean seriousness score for all events committed by the cohort is 114.15. There were 10,214 events and 9,945 boys at risk. Using formula *A* we calculate a weighted rate as follows:

$$\frac{114.15 \times 10{,}214}{9{,}945} \times 1{,}000$$

which yields a weighted rate of 117, 237.6 per 1,000 subjects. Using the variation of formula *A* (as described above) we calculate a weighted rate as follows:

$$\frac{10{,}214 \times 1.1415}{9{,}945} \times 1{,}000$$

which yields a weighted rate of 1,172.4 per 1,000 subjects.

Certain weighted rates computed yield smaller numbers than do the simple rates. It should be clear to the reader that this effect occurs because of our altered weighting factor. That is, when seriousness scores fall below 100, the weighting factor will be less than 1. For example a seirousness score of 67 yields a weighting factor of 0.67.

Finally, it should be clear that this alteration (division by 100) does not affect internal comparisons among weighted rates.

APPENDIX D.2

A Note on the Findings Based on the Use of the Seriousness Score

The seriousness of a delinquent act was found to be related to race, SES level, delinquency status, type of offense, rank of offense, victimization, and age of onset as summarized below: (1) Juvenile delinquents engage mostly in nonindex events and petty thefts. Eighty-seven percent of the delinquent events, regardless of race or income, fall into seriousness score categories below 300. (2) In general, whites commit less serious crimes than nonwhites. The proportion of whites in the categories of offenses that score less than 100 is larger than nonwhites, while it is smaller in the categories of offenses that score over 100. This racial difference is consistent when SES level and delinquency status are held constant. (3) A distinct difference between mean seriousness scores as well as weighted rates, compared to raw offenses and crude weights, occurs when we split the delinquent population into one-time offenders and recidivists. This difference obtains when we account for both races and SES levels. (4) More serious forms of bodily harm are committed by nonwhites. The highest mean injury score is found among nonwhite recidivists in the lower income category (241.93). (5) Within each respective SES level across racial groups, the difference in weighted rates of mean injury seriousness score diminishes for one-time offenders and increases for recidivists. The greatest difference is not between races or SES levels but between one-time offenders and recidivists within the nonwhite group. (6) The weighted rate based on the injury scoring system of the gravity of crime indicates that the 14 homicides committed by nonwhites represent more community harm than all the combined 456 acts of physical injury committed by whites during the juvenile years. With respect to type of offense and seriousness score, we found that: (7) The mean seriousness score per offense increases as the number of offenses committed per person increases, and with each group of offenders (one-time, recidivists, and chronic), the nonwhites always committed more serious offenses than did the whites. One-time offenders exhibit lower seriousness scores than do recidivists, and recidivists exhibit lower seriousness scores than chronic offenders. The one exception to the pattern occurs in the nonwhite high SES level, where the recidivist seriousness score is slightly above that of the chronic offenders (the seriousness score of the recidivists was affected by the inclusion of two high scores in a small number of offenses). (8) The seriousness scores for higher SES youths are lower than those for lower SES youths for one-time offenders, chronic offenders and white recidivists. (9) Injury, combination, theft, damage, and nonindex offenses lie in that order from the most to the least serious, while within offense types the score is found to vary by race. Nonwhites exceed whites in the severity of injury, combination and, nonindex offenses (greater proportion of harm against the person), while the whites exceed the nonwhites in the mean seriousness score for theft and damage (property loss).

Whites in the higher SES level committed a higher percentage of primary and face-to-face victimization than whites in the lower SES category but of less severity. Nonwhites in the lower income group committed the most serious injury offenses (face-to-face victimization).

The introduction of age and SES indicates that generally the nonwhite lower SES boys commit the most serious offenses. However, when the weighted offender rate is considered, we find that it is the nonwhite higher SES boys who increase from age 7 to age 17, having the highest weighted offender rates of all race-income categories at ages 16 and 17.

In sum, the analysis of the relationship between the number of offenses and mean seriousness score by type of offense within age of onset categories, controlling for the effect of race, leads to several conclusions: White offenders within age of onset categories consistently exhibit higher mean seriousness scores in the damage, theft, and combination categories, while nonwhites are higher for nonindex and injury offenses. Furthermore, the mean injury seriousness scores explain in part the positive relationship which we found earlier between the nonwhite all-offender seriousness score and age of onset. Thus, it is the injury score which contributes to this positive increase. The mean seriousness scores for nonindex and injury offenses tend to be greater for the lower SES boys across age of onset categories, while it is smaller for theft, damage, and combination. Or, for the high SES boys, the magnitude of seriousness score for theft, damage, and combination is greater than that of the lower SES boys.

In analyzing the mean seriousness by offense number and type of offense, a pattern emerged showing a tendency for increasing mean seriousness score, as the number of the offense increases from the first to the fifteenth. This upward trend is most pronounced for the injury offenses. The combination offenses increase less than the injury type but more than the nonindex, which, like theft and damage offenses, does not increase as the rank of the offense increases. When these three types of offenses are combined, a negative slope results, which indicates that the mean seriousness score decreases as the rank number increases.

When all offense types are combined, the nonwhite seriousness score is higher than the white score for all offense numbers. A sharp increase occurs for injury offenses in the nonwhite group over the fifteen offenses, compared to a decrease in the white group. A similar but not as pronounced trend emerges for the combination offenses. The mean seriousness score for damage offenses decreases for both groups.

Across SES levels we find that, regardless of income level, the nonwhites commit more serious offenses in general and especially against the person, while the white boys commit more serious property offenses. Disregarding race, high SES boys often commit more serious offenses than low SES boys.

The technique of assigning seriousness scores to offenses was also utilized in examining disposition. Holding all other variables constant, one would expect that offenses with higher seriousness scores would incur a more serious disposition than offenses with lower seriousness scores. It was found that offenses with a seriousness score of less than 100 constituted over 78 percent of all remedials, and over 86 percent of all offenses with such a score were so disposed. Court sentencing, considered in the present study to be the most severe disposition, was imposed in only 4 percent of the offenses with a seriousness score of less than 100. On the other hand, 55 percent of the offenses with a seriousness score of 100 or more were followed by a remedial disposition, compared to 37 percent by a court sentence.

APPENDIX D.3

A Note on the Classification of Delinquents by Average Seriousness Score Classifications

In order to distinguish further between degrees of offender seriousness, we have classified the 3,475 delinquents into six categories on the basis of their average offense seriousness score. The categories consist of delinquents with (a) an average score of 1; (b) an average score greater than 1 but less than 30; (c) an average score from 30 to less than 80; (d) an average score from 80 to less than 150; (e) an average score from 150 to less than 400; (f) an average score of 400 or more.

These categories were determined after a careful analysis of the distribution and components of the average seriousness scores. Category *a* was selected because it contained, almost exclusively, one-time curfew delinquents (84% of the delinquents in that category).

Category *b* was selected because of the clustering of disorderly conduct scores (score = 19) and the existence of a break in the distribution at a score of 24. Category *c* contains those offenders whose average score was comprised primarily of other nonindex offenses (86% of all their offenses). Categories *d* and *e* were selected on the basis of major clusterings in the average score distributions at scores of 100 and 152, while category *f* (and therefore the upper limit of category *e*) was determined residually, so as to maintain a high mean score, while at the same time maximizing the number of delinquents in the category. The subject background variables (chapter 4) were then analyzed within each of these delinquent seriousness score categories (table D.3.1).[1]

Previous analysis of the relationship between subject variables and indexes of extensive delinquency have stressed the linearity of the relationship (see the discussion of chronic delinquents in chapter 6 and the analysis of delinquents-nondelinquents in chapter 4 and of one-time recidivist delinquents in chapter 5). The present analysis does not support a linear description of the relationship but rather suggests that the relationship between the average delinquent seriousness scores and background characteristics is curvilinear, most frequently described by a third-degree curve. For example, we note that the mean number of offenses per average score category is: $a = 1.19$; $b = 2.01$; $c = 3.39$; $d = 4.87$; $e = 3.5$; and $f = 2.01$. Thus, the same mean number of offenses obtains in the most serious and the next to least serious categories. Although the upper tail of the curve does not attain the same magnitude as the lower tail, the direction of the relationship is supportive of the curvilinear contention (this type of magnitude difference is also consistent with regard to most of the background variables presented in table D.3.1). Of course, the decline in number of offenses committed by the more serious categories could be related to the time spent in an institution, thereby limiting the opportunity for the accumulation of offenses.

This form of relationship holds if we consider the within-classification distributions by race, SES, exit code, disciplinary status, and between-classification comparisons of the mean first I.Q., mean number of moves, and mean school grade completed. Thus, category *d* has the highest proportion of nonwhite delinquents (55.5%), the lowest proportion in the higher class (30.1%), the lowest mean I.Q. (99.0), the highest mean number of moves (3.2), the lowest mean

1. These categories were not further divided into racial and/or SES groups as our interest is in between-category classifications as opposed to within/between comparisons.

TABLE D.3.1

Average Score Subject Classifications by Background Variables

Characteristic	a 1 (N = 760)	b 1–30 (N = 579)	c 30–80 (N = 637)	d 80–150 (N = 667)	e 150–400 (N = 714)	f 400+ (N = 118)
$\bar{X}$ Number Offenses	1.19	2.01	3.39	4.87	3.50	2.01
Race:						
White (%)	69.6	71.2	61.7	44.5	46.1	50.0
Nonwhite (%)	30.4	28.8	38.3	55.5	53.9	50.0
SES						
I–III (%)	45.5	53.3	57.6	69.9	68.5	66.9
IV–V (%)	54.5	46.7	42.4	30.1	31.5	33.1
Mean first I.Q.	105.1	103.5	100.8	99.0	99.2	101.1
Mean number of moves	2.3	2.3	2.8	3.2	3.1	2.6
Mean grade completed	10.9	10.4	9.8	9.2	9.4	9.8
School exit type:						
Graduate (%)	59.7	51.1	35.2	26.1	27.6	36.4
Dropout (%)	40.3	48.9	64.8	73.9	72.4	63.6
Disciplinary status						
No (%)	96.2	95.5	84.8	71.2	74.8	81.4
Yes (%)	3.8	4.5	15.2	28.8	25.2	18.6

grade completed (9.2), the lowest proportion of graduates (26.1%), the lowest proportion of nondisciplinary assignments (71.2%). These values of category *d* represent the peaks of the relationships, with the lower categories (*a*, *b*, and *c*) gradually increasing to this point and the higher categories (*e* and *f*) decreasing from the values observed in category *d*.

This relationship has particular relevance to our consideration of the most serious delinquents (N = 118), those with an average score of 400 or above. We observe that category *f* is most like (i.e., closest in value to) category *e* with regard to racial and SES distributions, most like category *c* with regard to mean I.Q., mean number of moves, mean grade completed, exit code distribution, and disciplinary status, and most like category *b* with regard to the mean number of offenses ($\bar{X}$ = 2.01 for each). Perhaps, the most striking finding is equal representation of whites and nonwhites in category *f*. Given the disproportionate representation of nonwhites in the delinquent population, the equality of representation of whites and nonwhites in category *f* is further evidence of the observations in chapters 5 and 6 concerning the differences between whites and nonwhites relative to participation in serious delinquency.

In sum, the classification of delinquents into categories based on the average seriousness of their delinquencies presents a different conceptualization of the relationship between significant background variables and delinquency than does the relationship generated when delinquency is measured only in terms of the quantity of delinquent behavior. The current analysis suggests that seriousness and background variables are curvilinearly related, while the number of offenses and background variables (e.g., as in the discussion of one-time offenders and recidivists) and the number of offenses and seriousness scores are linearly related (e.g., as in the discussion of chronic offenders). The unit of measurement must, therefore, be clearly specified before one can adequately predict the form of the relationship between background variables and delinquency.

When a qualitative measure of seriousness is utilized, we observe that the most serious delinquents occupy a more positive position on the continuum of background variables than do other, less serious delinquents. Furthermore their offensivity is considerably less extensive than that of less serious delinquents.

APPENDIX E

Multiple Regression Analysis of Subject Background Variables and Delinquency

A stepwise regression procedure was used which computes a series of multiple regression equations by reexamining all of the variables at each step according to predetermined criteria.[1]

In the first set of equations we attempted to predict the observed values of the dependent variable with a multiple determination by ten independent variables. The latter with this notation were:

X_1 = race
X_2 = number of address moves
X_3 = school exit
X_4 = handicapped
X_5 = highest grade completed
X_6 = number of school moves
X_7 = absenteeism
X_8 = achievement
X_9 = first I.Q.
X_{10} = income

Among the various dimensions of delinquency taken as the dependent variable were number of offenses, delinquency status, and total or average seriousness scores.

Because not all the information for those characteristics was available for all the subjects,[2] another set of regressions was run with only seven independent variables. In this way we were able to maximize, within the limits of the data, the number of cases entered into each equation. The variables dropped were exit code, absenteeism, and achievement level (X_3, X_7, and X_8). Since these variables are more or less highly interrelated with the other school variables, mainly with highest grade completed, we did not expect to lose much explanatory power by eliminating them. The second set of independent variables was:

1. For a detailed description of the program used, its computational and machine procedure, see: *BMD: Biomedical Computer Programs,* ed. W.J. Dixon (Berkeley and Los Angeles: University of California Press, 1967). A discussion of the method may be found in M.A. Efroymsen, "Multiple Regression Analysis," in *Mathematical Methods for Digital Computers,* ed. A. Ralston and H.S. Wilf (New York: John Wiley, 1960), part 5.

2. We will indicate for each equation the number of subjects that were entered into the regression.

TABLE E.1

Intercepts, Coefficients and R^2 *of Regressions, Set Number One*

Y	*N*	*I*	X^1	X^2	X^3
1. Number of offenses	(3,350)	3.767	0.557	−0.035	0.001
2. Offender, nonoffender	(3,350)	0.518	0.075	0.000	0.007
3. 0, 1, >1 offense	(3,350)	1.023	0.163	−0.002	0.011
4. Total seriousness score	(3,350)	493.589	97.869	6.313	−0.496
5. Average seriousness score	(3,350)	74.562	19.111	1.197	0.601
6. Average seriousness score offenders only	(1,128)	103.462	27.226	1.882	0.426

X_1 = race
X_2 = number of moves
X_3 = handicapped
X_4 = highest grade completed
X_5 = number of school moves
X_6 = first I.Q.
X_7 = income

In table E.1 the regression coefficients and the total R^2 for the equations with the independent variables are presented. The strongest relationships as evaluated by their R^2's are for the predictions of the total number of offenses and the closely related prediction of the delinquency status broken down into three subgroups: nonoffenders, one-time offenders, and recidivists, followed by the dichotomy of offender-nonoffender. The explanatory power of the equations decreases when we attempt to predict seriousness scores. For the total seriousness score, an R^2 of .1864 was obtained (nonoffenders included) and for the average seriousness score, .1213. When we eliminated the nonoffenders to determine whether the variables were able to discriminate degrees of offensivity, the smallest R^2 (.0659) resulted.

Looking now at the role played by each variable, we note that race, highest grade completed, number of school moves, income, and exit code produced consistent significant contributions to the R^2 in the six equations of this set. Table E.2 displays the percentages of R^2 accounted for by each of these four variables in each equation.

Highest grade completed and exit code (which are highly interrelated) account for the largest proportion of explained variation in all but one case, the average seriousness score of offenders. Race replaces school when only the delinquent group is considered. As we shall see, this finding is consistent with the analysis of the second set of equa-

X^4	X^5	X^6	X^7	X^8	X^9	X^{10}	R^2
-0.558	-0.326	0.331	0.018	0.021	-0.004	-0.081	.2678
-0.028	-0.021	0.034	-0.000	-0.018	-0.001	-0.014	.1953
-0.096	-0.058	0.075	-0.000	-0.009	-0.002	-0.032	.2585
-36.616	-45.753	36.652	1.636	2.352	-0.085	-16.586	.1864
6.477	-5.233	3.747	-0.181	-1.395	0.062	4.793	.1213
30.136	-4.495	1.279	-0.269	-3.928	0.433	-8.951	.0659

TABLE E.2

Percentage of the Variation Explained by Significant Variables in Set One

Equation	Race %	Highest Grade %	School Moves %	Income %	Exit Code %
1	5	72	19	.....	.....
2	12	3	5	.....	78
3	14	5	7	1	73
4	9	70	18	1	.....
5	18	70	4	2	.....
6	65	18	.....	8	.....

tions. SES plays a poor role, but this should be qualified by the high interrelation between race and income.

In the second set of equations we dropped exit code, absenteeism, and achievement level. By so doing our total N increased from 3,350 to 7,900 subjects about which we had comparable information. Table E.3 displays the coefficients, intercepts and R^2's of this set of equations.

Here again it is clear that a higher proportion of variation was explained when the variables were related to the category scales of delinquency status or with the total number of offenses than when they were asked to account for the variation in seriousness scores. The highest R^2 (.2453) was obtained between the categories of nonoffender and chronic recidivist and the seven independent variables. On the opposite end, the smallest R^2 (.0319) obtains between the average seriousness score of chronic offenders and their background char-

TABLE E.3

Intercepts, Coefficients and R^2 of Regressions, Set Number Two

Y	N	I	X^1	X^2	X^3	X^4	X^5	X^6	X^7	R^2
1. Nonoffender, >4 offenses	(5777)	0.089	0.096	0.008	−0.202	−0.076	0.065	−0.001	−0.026	.2453
2. Number of offenses	(7900)	3.950	0.334	0.040	−0.762	−0.290	0.234	−0.005	−0.102	.2122
3. <Five, ≥five offenses	(2601)	1.424	0.054	0.005	−0.131	−0.039	0.039	−0.000	−0.010	.1902
4. Nonoffender, 1, >1 offenses	(7900)	1.632	0.089	−0.003	−0.243	−0.080	0.077	−0.004	−0.049	.1744
5. Offender, nonoffender	(7900)	0.936	0.049	−0.002	−0.119	−0.037	0.038	−0.002	−0.027	.1219
6. Total seriousness score	(7900)	456.911	72.932	7.274	−77.525	−38.471	29.807	−0.121	−16.306	.1594
7. Total score, chronics	(468)	1424.928	259.229	−3.255	−236.347	−32.297	55.319	−4.362	−46.309	.0954
8. Average seriousness score	(7900)	106.069	15.661	−0.193	−1.883	−5.576	4.441	−0.163	−4.728	.0755
9. Average seriousness score, chronics	(408)	139.000	17.359	−0.264	−35.666	0.890	2.230	−0.229	−6.513	.0319

TABLE E.4

Percentage of the Variation Explained by Significant Variables in Set Two

Equation	Race %	Highest Grade %	School Moves %	Income %
1	4	77	17	1
2	4	76	18	1
3	4	71	24	0
4	1	73	16	6
5	1	70	16	8
6	1	73	18	7
7	62	17	15	3
8	22	68	6	4
9	71	2	7	16

acteristics. This difference may be explained by the fact that the small range of variation of most of the independent variables is better able to indicate association in a less partitioned and elaborated scale (as the ones in equations 1–5) than in a higher and more complex form of scale as the S–W seriousness scores.

Variables 1, 4, 5 and 7 (race, highest grades, school moves, and income) made the most significant contribution to R^2 (table E.4).

They are the same as those in the first set of equations. We can speak also of the same pattern in the percentage distribution of variation explained by these four variables. Excepting the seriousness scores (total and average) of the chronic offenders, the school characteristics have the strongest power of prediction when taken together. In the case of the chronics it is again the race variable that accounts for degrees of offensivity.

APPENDIX F

Age and Offense Probability

The cohort data include information on the number of individuals in each age category, beginning with the 84th month (7 years of age) and ending with the 215th month (17.9 years of age), who have committed at least one offense. This means that the age distributions of those committing at least two, three, four, five or six offenses are also available. In the following analysis we shall consider the relationship between age and offense number for (1) all offenses, (2) only index offenses, (3) only nonindex offenses excluding curfew violations, and (4) only curfew violations.[1] Our emphasis will be on the judgment of the extent of the relationship for each of the offenses specified (eta^2), and on the most efficient depiction of the relationship (curve-fitting).

A substantial proportion of the variance in the frequency of committing an offense is associated with the variance in age.[2] Table F.1 presents the correlation ratios for each of the frequencies from at least one to six offenses with age for each of the four offense classifications described above. With the exception of the relationship between age and first offense in the total offenses category, and age and fifth curfew-only offense, it appears the proportion of explained variation remains fairly stable as we move from one to at least five offenses across offense types. The explanatory power of age declines, however, at the sixth offense for all offense types, especially for curfew-only offenses.

The correlation ratio is a measure of the scatter about the yearly means of monthly frequencies. As we are primarily interested in the contour of the relationship, we shall shift our analysis from variation explained to the estimation of regression equations to depict the shape of the relationship. The regression model will provide us with predictive estimates while the correlational model measures the variability around the regressed values.

Since there is no estimating equation for the correlation ratio, and therefore no satisfactory way of making monthly estimates of the dependent variables, we chose the total number of offenses within

TABLE F.1

Corrected Correlation Ratios for Frequency of at Least One to Six Offenses and Age

At Least	Total Offenses	Index Only	Nonindex, less Curfew	Curfew Only
1 Offense	.901	.657	.789	.366
2 Offenses	.793	.659	.788	.243
3 Offenses	.755	.702	.660	.235
4 Offenses	.793	.618	.628	.297
5 Offenses	.732	.613	.632	.171
6 Offenses	.637	.488	.446	.040

1. It is necessary to consider curfew violations separately because they are restricted by statute in Philadelphia to those under 17 years of age.

2. The contours of the regression of frequency of offense over age and of moving probability of offense over age are identical.

each twelve-month interval, rather than the path of the yearly means of monthly frequencies, as our observed values. We are permitted to do this since our dependent variable consists of frequencies rather than scale values; it thus makes sense simply to sum up the frequencies in a particular interval and employ this total as the interval value. Only a distinct cyclical pattern could make this procedure inadvisable; however, none was found.

By grouping our data into twelve-month intervals we reduce the chance fluctuations to which smaller (monthly) frequencies are subject; the observed distribution may therefore be more accurately fitted by regression equations, which, in turn, permits superior summarization or reconstruction of the data. Most importantly, the one-month interval admits of no interpretative advantages. Notwithstanding the attenuation of cases, this very refined breakdown tells us no more about the regressions in which we are interested than does the cruder, yearly one.

Having chosen a twelve-month interval, we must now transform yearly frequencies into probabilities. The probability of committing at least one offense of the four types specified above in each successive age interval is obtained by dividing the number of offenders in a particular interval by the total number in the cohort *minus* the number committing at least one offense in the previous intervals. Thus, as we move from one age unit to the next, the base becomes smaller. It is against this moving base that we compute the monthly probabilities of committing at least one offense. This same procedure is employed to compute the yearly probabilities of committing at least two to six offenses.

In tables F.2 to F.5 we have displayed the yearly probabilities for one to six offenses for all offenses, index offenses, nonindex offenses less curfews and curfew offenses.

We had anticipated variations in the relative shape of the distributions between different offense types and minimum variance among the distributions within offense types. However, we note only two significant variations in the data: (1) the earlier peaking for index offense probabilities for offenses 1 and 2; and (2) the absence of a decline in the probability of a fourth or fifth nonindex offense at age 17. The similarity in the relationship between index and curfew-only offenses at ages 16 and 17 was most unexpected. We had anticipated that the decline from age 16 in the total offenses was due to the relative impossibility of committing a curfew offense after age 16 was completed, and that other offense types, in particular index offenses, would not reflect this form of relationship. As noted above, we observed that the decline occurred in all cases except the fourth and fifth nonindex offenses.

TABLE F.2

Yearly Probability of Offense Commission, All Offenses

	Observed Probabilities					
Age	1st Offense	2d Offense	3d Offense	4th Offense	5th Offense	6th Offense
7–7.9	.0020	.0002	.0002	.0001	.0001	.0001
8–8.9	.0056	.0007	.0002	.0001	.0001	.0000
9–9.9	.0126	.0030	.0012	.0006	.0004	.0003
10–10.9	.0184	.0046	.0022	.0016	.0003	.0007
11–11.9	.0245	.0088	.0044	.0017	.0011	.0007
12–12.9	.0323	.0130	.0064	.0045	.0025	.0021
13–13.9	.0456	.0194	.0111	.0083	.0059	.0031
14–14.9	.0562	.0288	.0192	.0114	.0099	.0068
15–15.9	.0733	.0434	.0264	.0188	.0134	.0104
16–16.9	.0952	.0509	.0351	.0245	.0177	.0141
17–17.9	.0503	.0301	.0216	.0188	.0127	.0093

TABLE F.3

Yearly Probability of Offense Commission, Index Offenses

	Observed Probabilities					
Age	1st Offense	2d Offense	3d Offense	4th Offense	5th Offense	6th Offense
7–7.9	.0013	.0001	.0000	.0000	.0000	.0000
8–8.9	.0027	.0005	.0001	.0000	.0001	.0000
9–9.9	.0068	.0014	.0005	.0003	.0003	.0003
10–10.9	.0077	.0026	.0012	.0006	.0004	.0002
11–11.9	.0111	.0048	.0023	.0008	.0005	.0005
12–12.9	.0147	.0072	.0031	.0027	.0015	.0011
13–13.9	.0144	.0093	.0056	.0039	.0033	.0018
14–14.9	.0178	.0103	.0087	.0039	.0042	.0027
15–15.9	.0209	.0128	.0100	.0068	.0054	.0029
16–16.9	.0179	.0108	.0091	.0083	.0059	.0042
17–17.9	.0116	.0092	.0060	.0062	.0038	.0031

TABLE F.4

Yearly Probability of Offense Commission, Nonindex Offenses (less Curfew)

	Observed Probabilities					
Age	1st Offense	2d Offense	3d Offense	4th Offense	5th Offense	6th Offense
7–7.9	.0007	.0001	.0002	.0001	.0001	.0001
8–8.9	.0028	.0002	.0001	.0001	.0000	.0000
9–9.9	.0054	.0015	.0007	.0003	.0001	.0000
10–10.9	.0095	.0019	.0009	.0010	.0004	.0005
11–11.9	.0107	.0035	.0014	.0008	.0003	.0002
12–12.9	.0087	.0045	.0020	.0010	.0008	.0006
13–13.9	.0174	.0070	.0041	.0028	.0021	.0009
14–14.9	.0233	.0126	.0072	.0061	.0044	.0029
15–15.9	.0259	.0206	.0115	.0076	.0059	.0065
16–16.9	.0303	.0220	.0171	.0104	.0080	.0066
17–17.9	.0259	.0168	.0138	.0110	.0084	.0055

TABLE F.5

Yearly Probability of Offense Commission, Curfew Offenses

	Observed Probabilities					
Age	1st Offense	2d Offense	3d Offense	4th Offense	5th Offense	6th Offense
7–7.9	.0000	.0000	.0000	.0000	.0000	.0000
8–8.9	.0001	.0000	.0000	.0000	.0000	.0000
9–9.9	.0002	.0001	.0000	.0000	.0000	.0000
10–10.9	.0009	.0001	.0001	.0000	.0000	.0000
11–11.9	.0021	.0004	.0007	.0001	.0003	.0000
12–12.9	.0076	.0012	.0012	.0008	.0002	.0004
13–13.9	.0110	.0027	.0012	.0015	.0004	.0004
14–14.9	.0101	.0051	.0029	.0012	.0012	.0011
15–15.9	.0171	.0083	.0041	.0040	.0019	.0009
16–16.9	.0301	.0139	.0073	.0051	.0034	.0030
17–17.9	.0016	.0009	.0004	.0009	.0001	.0002

TABLE F.6

Number and Percent of Offenses by Offense Type, Offense Number and Age (15, 16, and 17)

	A First Offense						B Second Offense					
	180–191.9		192–203.9		204–215.9		180–191.9		192–203.9		204–215.9	
	N	%	N	%	N	%	N	%	N	%	N	%
Index	193	32.4	162	22.6	103	30.0	123	30.4	103	23.0	87	34.7
Nonindex (without Curfew)	238	39.9	271	37.7	225	65.6	199	49.3	208	46.6	155	61.7
Curfew only	165	27.7	285	39.7	15	4.4	82	20.3	136	30.4	9	3.6
Total	596		718		343		404		447		251	

	C Third Offense						D Fourth Offense					
	180–191.9		192–203.9		204–215.9		180–191.9		192–203.9		204–215.9	
	N	%	N	%	N	%	N	%	N	%	N	%
Index	98	39.0	88	27.1	58	30.1	67	36.8	81	34.9	60	34.3
Nonindex (without Curfew)	112	44.6	165	50.8	131	67.9	75	41.2	101	43.5	106	60.6
Curfew only	41	16.4	72	22.1	4	2.0	40	22.0	40	21.6	9	5.0
Total	251		325		193		182		232		175	

	E						F					
	Fifth Offense						Sixth Offense					
	180–191.9		192–203.9		204–215.9		180–191.9		192–203.9		204–215.9	
	N	%	N	%	N	%	N	%	N	%	N	%
Index	54	41.2	58	34.1	37	30.8	29	28.4	42	30.7	31	35.6
Nonindex (without Curfew)	58	44.3	78	45.9	82	68.4	64	62.8	65	47.4	54	62.1
Curfew only	19	14.5	34	20.0	1	.8	9	8.8	30	21.9	2	2.3
Total	131		170		120		102		137		87	

The relative degree of the decline is not constant across offense types. It is most clear in curfew offenses, less so in index offenses, and most negligible in nonindex offenses. Table F.6 contains the number and percent of offenses by offense types for the 15-, 16-, and 17-year-old age periods for the six offenses. The "curfew effect" is observable in the sharp decline in the proportion of curfew offenses at ages 15 and 16 compared to the proportion at age 17. The corresponding result at all offense numbers is a large increase in the proportion of 17-year-old offenses that are nonindex and a smaller increase in the proportion of index offenses. However, as the above analysis indicated, the across age effect is constant for the period 16–17, namely an overall decline in the frequency of offenses with the previously noted exception of fourth and fifth nonindex offenses (16 = 101, 17 = 106, 16 = 78, 17 = 82 respectively). In sum, the decline at age 15 or 16 is a "real" effect in the sense that it cannot be explained solely by reference to the "curfew effect," though changes in the number of curfew offenses at age 17 do contribute significantly to the overall decrease.

APPENDIX G.1

Static Offense Probabilities: By Race

The First Offense

In keeping with the procedure followed in discussing the background variables of the cohort, we here compare the probabilities for the two significant racial groups of white and nonwhite.

Of all whites in the cohort, .2867 had at least one encounter with the police while .5017 of the nonwhites experienced a similar event. In each category of offensivity, the probability of committing an offense is higher for nonwhites than for whites. Thus, the probability (of the total cohort) of committing a nonindex offense is .2974 for nonwhites and .2005 for whites. For an injury offense the probabili-

TABLE G.1.1

First Offense Probabilities by Type of Offense: White and Nonwhite

	All Types	Non-index	Injury	Theft	Dam-age	Combi-nation
White (total cohort)	.2867	.2005	.0170	.0351	.0227	.0114
Nonwhite (total cohort)	.5017	.2974	.0496	.0817	.0317	.0414
White (offenders only)	1.0000	.6994	.0594	.1223	.0792	.0396
Nonwhite (offenders only)	1.0000	.5927	.0989	.1628	.0632	.0824

ties are .0496 for nonwhites and .0170 for whites; for a theft offense the probabilities are .0817 for nonwhites and .0351 for whites; for a damage offense the probabilities are .0317 for nonwhites and .0227 for whites; and for a combination offense the probabilities are .0414 for the nonwhites and .0114 for the whites.

In considering the first offense probability distributions for offenders only (table G.1.1) we see that nonwhites are more likely to be involved in injury, theft, and combination first offenses than are whites. Whites are more likely to have committed nonindex or damage first offenses, although the damage probabilities are quite similar (.0792 for whites and .0632 for nonwhites). In short, about 40 percent of all nonwhite first offenses involve index components, while 30 percent of white first contacts are index events.

The proportion of offenders who committed only one offense is much smaller in the nonwhite group (.3455) than in the white (.5498) (table G.1.2).

For all offense types the proportion of one-time offenders is much higher in the white group than in the nonwhite. Although white offenders were slightly more prone to commit a damage offense than were the nonwhites, they were also more likely to stop after that offense (.7938 were one-timers) than was either racial group after any other offense type. At the other extreme, only 10 percent of the nonwhite offenders stopped after committing a combination first offense – the lowest proportion for either group and offense type.

The data here present a dismal picture for nonwhites relative to whites. Fifty percent of all nonwhites got into trouble at least once with the law compared to 29 percent of the whites. And only 35 percent of nonwhites stopped after the first offense compared to 55 percent of the whites. Not only did smaller proportions of the nonwhites stop, but these boys were concentrated in those offense groups containing or likely to contain components of bodily harm – injury and combination – with the respective desisting probabilities of .2847 and .1000.

TABLE G.1.2

Proportion of One-time Offenders by Race and Type of Offense

	All Types	Non-index	Injury	Theft	Damage	Combi-nation
White	.5498	.5446	.5417	.4858	.7938	.3625
Nonwhite	.3455	.3638	.2847	.3713	.5217	.1000

TABLE G.1.3

Static Probability of Committing k*th Offense: Whites and Nonwhites*

k (Number of Offense)		All Types[a] (N,I,T,D,C)	Non-index[b]	Injury[c]	Theft[d]	Damage[e]	Combination[f]	Desisted (stopped after kth offense)
2	White	.4502	.3185	.0272	.0629	.0163	.0253	.5498
	Nonwhite	.6545	.3770	.0707	.1023	.0302	.0742	.2592
3	White	.5566	.3784	.0231	.1056	.0209	.0286	.4434
	Nonwhite	.7408	.4292	.0724	.1427	.0262	.0703	2592
4	White	.6581	.4308	.0599	.1186	.0217	.0277	.3413
	Nonwhite	.7577	.4533	.0836	.1275	.0269	.0666	.2421
5	White	.6306	.4114	.0300	.1231	.0210	.0450	.3695
	Nonwhite	.7794	.4449	.0879	.1364	.0299	.0804	.2205
6	White	.6571	.4429	.0286	.1286	.0095	.0476	.3428
	Nonwhite	.7841	.4844	.0647	.1511	.0144	.0695	.2159
7	White	.7391	.4130	.0580	.1522	.0290	.0870	.2608
	Nonwhite	.8134	.4526	.1070	.1346	.0428	.0765	.1865
8	White	.6372	.4216	.0294	.1275	.0098	.0490	.3627
	Nonwhite	.8157	.4624	.1015	.1504	.0188	.0827	.1842
9	White	.7384	.5231	.0615	.0769	.0000	.0769	.2616
	Nonwhite	.8156	.4654	.0968	.1382	.0230	.0922	.1844
10	White	.7291	.4167	.0625	.2292	.0000	.0203	.2713
	Nonwhite	.8531	.4576	.1243	.1864	.0113	.0734	.1470

11	White	.7142	.4571	.0000	.1429	.0000	.1143	.2857
	Nonwhite	.8079	.4636	.0795	.1589	.0066	.0993	.1921
12	White	.7200	.5200	.0000	.0800	.0800	.0400	.2800
	Nonwhite	.8196	.4754	.0984	.0902	.0492	.1066	.1802
13	White	.7222	.3333	.0555	.2222	.0555	.0555	.2780
	Nonwhite	.7300	.4200	.0600	.1300	.0200	.1000	.2700
14	White	.9230	.4615	.0000	.0769	.1538	.2308	.0770
	Nonwhite	.8767	.5342	.1370	.0822	.0137	.1096	.1233
15	White	.5833	.4167	.0000	.0833	.0000	.0833	.4167
	Nonwhite	.7187	.4531	.0312	.1406	.0000	.0937	.2814

Regression estimates:

White: [a]$Y = .0160X + .5396$, [b]$Y = .0049X + .3829$, [c]$Y = -.0020X + .0481$
Nonwhite: $Y = .0057X + .7349$, $Y = .0043X + .4186$, $Y = .0003X + .0842$

White: [d]$Y = .0018X + .1082$, [e]$Y = .0040X - .0041$, [f]$Y = .0073X + .0044$
Nonwhite: $Y = -.0006X + .1387$, $Y = -.0012X + .0325$, $Y = .0028X + .0615$

Second to Fifteenth Offense: Whites and Nonwhites

In the following discussion, which compares whites and nonwhites on the static probabilities, it will be evident that the greater propensity for offense commission among nonwhites which exists for the first offense distributions, when classified by type, persists throughout the remaining fourteen offenses. As indicated in table G.1.3 and figure G.1.1, the probabilities of committing any type of offense are greater at each rank number if the nonwhite group alone is being considered. Conversely, the probability of desisting is higher for whites at each offense rank.

The probability of committing all types of offenses ranges from about .57 to about .78 from the second to the fifteenth offense for whites, while the range for the same interval is between .75 and .82 for the nonwhites. Although the probability of committing any kind of offense rises more sharply over offense number for whites (b = .0160) than for nonwhites (b = .0057), the least squares estimates for the absolute values are consistently below the nonwhite trace.[1]

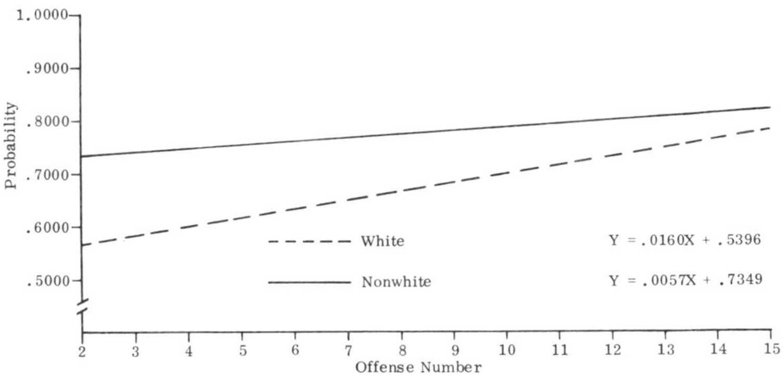

FIGURE G.1.1
Regression Estimate of Probability of Committing Second to Fifteenth Offense by Race (All Offense Types)

1. It must be remembered that we offer these regression estimates guardedly because of their susceptibility to end point bias when the number of cases is small. This problem becomes especially burdensome as we subdivide the cohort in various ways. Thus, it can be seen by inspection that the magnitude of the positive slope of the white regression is to a large extent generated by the comparatively small probabilities of committing a second and third offense and the extremely high probability of committing a fourteenth offense. Because so few boys arrive at the high offense end points, the meaning of divergent values at those points is difficult to assess.

The slopes of the nonindex regression lines are almost equal (.0043 for nonwhites, .0049 for whites) although the intercept points are slightly different. The estimated range is .39 to .45 for whites and .43 to .48 for nonwhites. Thus, nonwhites are about 4 percent more likely to commit nonindex offenses than are whites.

Relative to the likelihood of committing a nonindex offense, the probabilities of index offensivity are small, although for the offenses of injury and combination the differences between whites and nonwhites are substantial.

For injury offenses, the estimated range in offense probability of whites is .0441 down to .0200 over the fifteen offenses, while for nonwhites the range varies from .0848 to .0887, roughly unchanging. Nonwhites are about twice as likely to commit injury offenses as are whites in the early part of their careers and about four times as likely in the later stages.

At the outset of their delinquency, nonwhites are somewhat more likely to commit theft offenses (.1375) than are whites (.1118). But unlike other nonwhite offensivity, the slope of this regression is -.0006, very slightly negative. As a result, the probabilities of white and nonwhite theft commission are very close at the fifteenth offense. The white probability ranges from about .1118 to .1352 over the fifteen offenses, while the nonwhite declines from .1375 to .1297.

For both racial groups the probabilities associated with damage offenses are exceedingly small (.01 to .03) for the first eleven offenses, although the nonwhite offense probabilities are slightly higher than the white at each instance. From the twelfth to the fifteenth offense some increase in likelihood of offense commission is apparent, but these values should be considered with caution because so few boys were involved in damage events at these ranks.

At the outset of combination offenses, the white and nonwhite probabilities are somewhat disparate, having regression estimates of .0190 and .0671 respectively. However, due to the magnitude of the white offense-by-offense increase in probability, the values at the fifteenth offense are nearly the same (.1139 for whites and .1035 for nonwhites). Nevertheless, until the thirteenth offense the nonwhite trace is consistently above the white.

In sum, the elevated likelihood of nonwhite offensivity across all offense types which exists in the first offense distributions persists through all offense types at practically all offense ranks. This difference is particularly noticeable for the categories of nonindex, injury, and, to a somewhat lesser degree, combination. Not only does the nonwhite group exhibit a greater propensity toward all types of offense commission but this characteristic is most apparent in the violent index offenses.

The probability of desisting at each offense rank ranges approximately from .45 to .30 for the white group and from .25 to .18 for nonwhites over the fifteen offenses. At each offense rank, then, nonwhites are only about 0.6 as likely to stop as are the whites.

Mean Seriousness Score

Table G.1.4 and figure G.1.2 (for all offenses) present the mean seriousness score comparisons for whites and nonwhites by type of offense. When the average of all types of offenses is considered, the nonwhite value exceeds that of the white at each offense rank except the seventh where they are essentially the same. Thus the regression estimate of white offense severity ranges from 101.66 to 109.68 over the fifteen offenses, while the nonwhite values average 122.20 to 158.93 on the same range.

Nonindex and theft offense severity increase very slightly over the fifteen offenses for both racial groups, although the nonwhite rates of increase are about twice the white rates (1.59 vs. 0.79 for nonindex and 1.94 vs. 1.02 for theft). The estimated nonindex seriousness scores for whites range from 24.49 to 35.60 from the first to the fifteenth offense while those for the nonwhite range from 27.51 to 49.76. Conversely, the nonwhite estimates of theft severity are lower than those of the white group despite their greater offense-by-offense increase, having mean score estimates of 171.53 to 198.68, compared to 212.47 and 226.81 for whites.

Such is not the case for those offenses involving violence to the person. The category of injury is characterized in the raw data by a rapid rise in white offense severity in the first five offenses from about 300 to 630, followed by an equally rapid decline to zero out to the fifteenth offense level. In contrast, the nonwhite group seriousness scores exhibit a fairly smooth increase from about 340 to 520 at the tenth offense, followed by a moderate decline into the 300s to the thirteenth offense and a rapid rise to 900 at the fifteenth offense. The differential in injury seriousness score between the two groups is rather dramatic when the estimated slopes are compared: 18.68 *increase* per offense number for nonwhites and 33.02 *decrease* per offense number for whites. As a result, the estimated seriousness scores range from 332.75 to 593.75 for nonwhites and from 486.06 down to 23.85 for whites. It is clear from these data that the main component of the increase in the all-offense plot is the magnitude of the nonwhite slope for injury offenses.

Combination offenses, which, it will be remembered, may include components of injury, exhibit tendencies similar to injury-only offenses for the two racial groups, though the differential is not nearly so outstanding. The white seriousness scores decline rather smoothly from an estimated 330.14 to 252.38 at about 5.56 seriousness score points per offense. Over the same interval the nonwhite scores advance from 272.26 to 399.29 at a rate of 9.07 points per offense. The difference between the two groups is not very great when considered over the first eleven offenses, with the whites committing somewhat more serious offenses for the first four offenses and nonwhites doing the same for all of the remaining offenses excepting the seventh and the eleventh. Nonetheless, the nonwhite rate of increase in seriousness score per offense for both injury and combination offenses is approximately twice as great as the white rate of decline for those offenses. For injury offenses, nonwhites on the average inflicted harm which was 18.69 points more serious at each rank number, while whites were likely to have perpetrated bodily harm of 33.02 seriousness score points lower than in the prior offense. Similarly, for offenses involving some combination of injury, theft, or damage, the nonwhite increase per offense was 9.07, while the white offense seriousness score declined 5.56 points per offense.

Finally, for the damage category, both racial groups on the average commit these offenses at reduced seriousness scores with advancing offense number, although as the data indicate, for the first eight offenses little change is apparent. The nonwhite decrease in seriousness score per offense is about one-half the white (–5.52 versus –11.03), yielding an estimated seriousness score range of 184.44 to 107.23 for nonwhites and 227.19 to 72.80 for whites.

In this discussion of mean seriousness score for various types of offenses by offense number we have seen that, overall, nonwhites are more likely to commit more serious offenses at each offense number and that the severity of their offenses advances at a greater rate than that of the whites. This characteristic is particularly evident for offenses involving bodily injury and somewhat less so for events having components of injury, theft, or damage. Although this differential still obtains for the categories of nonindex and damage, it is less marked than that observed for combination offenses. The exceptions in this string of uniformities are those offenses involving theft, where it appears that white boys steal more valuable articles than do nonwhite youths.

In sum, then, we can say that over time white thefts are somewhat more serious than are nonwhite thefts, while injuries inflicted by nonwhite boys are more serious than those inflicted by white offenders. The seriousness of other property offenses and nonindex events decreases or changes little over time.

TABLE G.1.4

Mean Seriousness Score of kth *Offense by Type of Offense and Race*

k (Number of Offense)		All Types[a] (N,I,T,D,C)	Non-index[b]	Injury[c]	Theft[d]	Damage[e]	Combination[f]
1	White	82.10	20.35	320.47	195.15	162.37	304.77
	Nonwhite	111.29	29.20	339.68	170.42	148.73	282.12
2	White	89.46	26.77	278.95	193.13	171.33	364.31
	Nonwhite	126.31	26.06	381.91	178.76	160.18	305.96
3	White	94.21	25.12	391.48	198.60	177.58	321.88
	Nonwhite	124.51	34.83	365.39	188.79	148.16	284.58
4	White	124.66	28.16	536.67	211.80	161.27	342.21
	Nonwhite	127.44	37.25	388.85	173.83	167.11	308.51
5	White	114.32	25.85	630.00	213.95	153.43	287.93
	Nonwhite	139.64	41.21	371.81	173.23	159.87	366.09
6	White	88.39	21.66	166.67	196.48	550.00	277.80
	Nonwhite	123.54	29.87	469.70	190.38	150.00	303.00
7	White	146.89	26.70	450.00	209.95	200.00	387.67
	Nonwhite	146.80	35.09	454.34	159.00	162.43	347.36
8	White	98.19	29.40	300.00	210.77	200.00	255.60
	Nonwhite	162.23	40.82	589.41	164.72	200.00	303 64
9	White	100.88	38.06	350.00	214.00	0.00	215.60
	Nonwhite	152.82	36.93	503.24	218.03	193.00	262.25
10	White	118.60	52.50	300.00	181.91	0.00	200.00
	Nonwhite	157.57	25.58	521.27	174.36	200.00	315.38

11	White	119.96	20.06	0.00	260.00	0.00	344.50
	Nonwhite	120.56	36.49	300.00	181.42	74.00	275.07
12	White	91.61	44.23	0.00	250.00	137.00	300.00
	Nonwhite	172.67	44.48	392.25	191.45	200.00	513.38
13	White	122.61	40.33	100.00	213.00	200.00	200.00
	Nonwhite	143.07	48.07	367.83	224.77	150.00	299.60
14	White	121.83	31.33	0.00	200.00	137.00	266.67
	Nonwhite	191.59	64.10	606.70	205.83	74.00	298.25
15	White	71.37	20.20	0.00	100.00	0.00	300.00
	Nonwhite	180.48	49.59	900.00	181.67	0.00	571.50

Regression estimates:

White:	[a] $Y = .5722X + 101.0937$,	[b] $Y = .7939X + 23.6962$,	[c] $Y = -33.0150X + 519.0750$
Nonwhite:	$Y = 2.6234X + 119.5802$,	$Y = 1.5890X + 25.9207$,	$Y = 18.6900X + 313.3966$
White:	[d] $Y = 1.0240X + 211.4480$,	[e] $Y = -11.0280X + 238.2220$,	[f] $Y = -5.5550X + 335.7000$
Nonwhite:	$Y = 1.9390X + 169.5930$,	$Y = -5.5150X + 189.9590$,	$Y = 9.0730X + 263.1910$

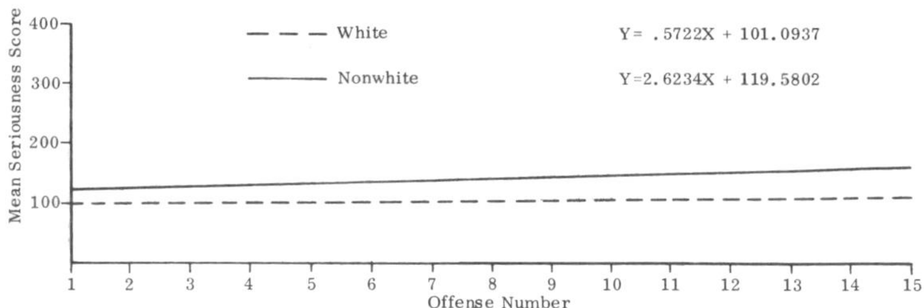

FIGURE G.1.2
Regression Estimate of Mean Seriousness Score of First to Fifteenth Offense by Race (All Offense Types)

Mean Time between Offenses

The mean times between offenses by the various offense types follow fairly closely the function log $Y = b \log X + a$ wnen the data are broken down by racial group (table G.1.5 and figure G.1.3). This configuration is the same as that presented earlier in our discussion of mean times between offenses for the cohort taken as a whole. As with those regression lines, these fits tend to overestimate the time interval between the first and second offense, although the remaining estimated times conform more adequately when sufficient data points exist.

Nonindex offenses, due to their numerousness, generate smooth decay lines for both groups and thus enable us to estimate the curves very closely.[2] The drop-off rates are very similar for both groups, ranging from about one and one-half years between the first and second offense, to eleven months for the second-to-third, to five to three months out to the fourteenth-to-fifteenth offense. The average age at commission ranges for nonwhites from about 168 months or 14 years at the first offense, to 190 months or almost 16 years at the fifteenth offense; and for whites from about 180 months or 15 years, at the first offense, to 203 months or about 17 years at the fifteenth offense.

The data for injury offenses are much more scattered than those for nonindex offenses. However, we can say that in general the mean

2. The two equations are: $\log Y = -.7875 \log X + 1.4102$, and $\log Y = -.9312 \log X + 1.5037$.

time between any type of offense and an injury that follows it is slightly greater for both whites and nonwhites than it is for each corresponding white or nonwhite nonindex offense. Internally, the difference between whites and nonwhites is difficult to assess due to the scatter of the white data, although it does appear that the mean time between offenses tends to be a little shorter for nonwhites than for whites. As a result of the sharp drop after the eighth offense for whites, the regressions on these data after the fifth offense place the mean time line of the whites about 1.2 months below that of the nonwhite offenders. Indeed, this characteristic seems to persist throughout all offense types, as we would expect, for the group which begins its delinquency career at a later age must necessarily have a higher repetition rate to enable the accumulation of the same number of offenses. The age at commission of injury offense ranges from 14 (167 months) to 17.3 (209 months) for nonwhites and 14.7 (176 months) to 17 years (208 months) for whites. At each offense rank white boys tend to be 6 to 18 months older than the nonwhites.

The mean times to theft offenses are smaller after the fourth offense for whites, averaging about 1½ to 2 months as based on the estimated values. As with injury, white offenders also begin theft offenses later than do nonwhites – 14.5 years (174 months) versus 13.7 years (164 months).

Damage offense mean times are also plagued by rather wild swings in the data. The regression estimates indicate that the mean times to damage offenses are about equal for whites and for nonwhites and are practically identical to those enumerated for nonindex offenses. The starting ages for both groups are lower for damage offenses (12.6 years or 152 months for nonwhites, and 12.8 years or 154 months for whites) than for the other categories of offensivity, with white offenders tending to be about 7 to 11 months older than the nonwhites at most of the subsequent ranks.

After the fifth offense, the estimated values yield differences averaging about 1.6 months less time to a combination offense for whites than for nonwhites. As with the other offense types, the age of onset of combination offensivity is later for whites than for nonwhites (14.3 years or 171 months versus 13.2 years or 160 months).

In comparing the various types of offenses against one another by racial groups, we find little variation in the shape and elevation of the various traces. The distributions have several features in common: (a) whites tend to be older than nonwhites both at the age of onset and at subsequent offense ranks; (b) up to the fourth or fifth offense the white mean times between offenses tend to be greater than the nonwhite across all offense types; and (c) after the fourth or fifth offense the white mean transition times tend to be shorter than the nonwhite by about 1 to 2 months.

TABLE G.1.5

Cohort Mean Time between Offenses

Offense Sequence		Non-index[a]	Injury[b]	Theft[c]	Damage[d]	Combination[e]
1 – 2	White	19.14	16.91	16.22	17.29	19.06
	Nonwhite	17.91	18.78	16.93	16.44	15.96
2 – 3	White	11.16	11.70	13.16	7.71	9.06
	Nonwhite	10.17	11.86	8.43	7.00	8.69
3 – 4	White	8.64	6.30	7.34	11.00	9.01
	Nonwhite	7.66	9.30	8.33	6.83	5.72
4 – 5	White	6.42	12.97	6.56	6.20	6.20
	Nonwhite	7.49	6.04	6.11	4.76	6.61
5 – 6	White	5.34	7.72	7.05	8.10	4.95
	Nonwhite	5.39	8.43	5.97	5.70	6.73
6 – 7	White	5.00	9.75	3.20	5.85	6.18
	Nonwhite	5.30	4.91	6.56	6.80	5.84
7 – 8	White	5.19	9.03	3.21	36.10	2.36
	Nonwhite	5.24	5.49	4.76	1.32	6.74
8 – 9	White	3.90	6.12	1.10	0.00	5.22
	Nonwhite	4.82	4.84	2.61	6.36	5 00
9 – 10	White	4.86	1.30	6.81	0.00	1.60
	Nonwhite	3.89	4.80	6.08	6.10	4.74
10 – 11	White	3.49	0.00	1.04	0.00	4.10
	Nonwhite	4.07	4.77	4.88	0.20	2.97

11 – 12	White	4.58	0.00	0.10	1.30	0.10
	Nonwhite	3.08	5.42	6.45	6.03	9.98
12 – 13	White	5.17	0.30	1.17	18.40	14.30
	Nonwhite	4.03	6.43	6.64	3.75	4.16
13 – 14	White	2.20	0.00	0.00	7.30	3.97
	Nonwhite	3.29	4.15	2.25	7.50	1.79
14 – 15	White	1.20	0.00	0.10	0.00	0.10
	Nonwhite	3.28	12.30	4.79	0.00	6.15

Regression estimates:

White: [a]$\text{Log } Y = 1.5037 - .9312 \log X$, [b]$\text{Log } Y = 1.5466 - .9112 \log X$,
Nonwhite: $\text{Log } Y = 1.4002 - .7875 \log X$, $\text{Log } Y = 1.2622 - .4888 \log X$,

White: [c]$\text{Log } Y = 1.7892 - 1.4522 \log X$, [d]$\text{Log } Y = 1.4052 - .9174 \log X$,
Nonwhite: $\text{Log } Y = 1.2693 - .5848 \log X$, $\text{Log } Y = 1.3066 - .7587 \log X$,

White: [e]$\text{Log } Y = 1.4909 - .9689 \log X$
Nonwhite: $\text{Log } Y = 1.2503 - .5647 \log X$

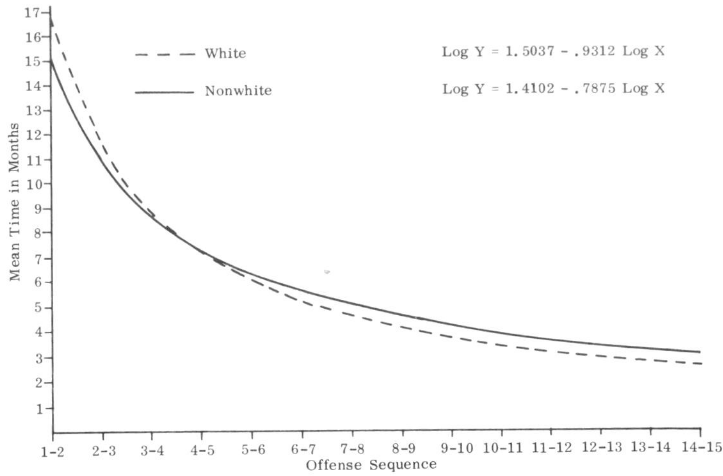

FIGURE G.1.3
Regression Estimate of Mean Time between Offenses by Race and SES

APPENDIX G.2

Static Offense Probabilities: By SES and Race Combined

The First Offense

In this and the following sections, we shall examine the same kinds of data for the first to the ninth offenses as we did in the prior discussions of the fifteen offenses (chapter 10), except that now the additional variable of income group (SES) will be added.[1] Our purpose will be to ascertain the extent of the influence of socioeconomic position on: (a) the likelihood of offense commission, (b) the seriousness of offensivity, and (c) on the timing of offenses. To this end we shall divide the white and the nonwhite offenders into the two SES groups, high and low, as discussed earlier.

The likelihood of committing any type of first offense for the total cohort follows the same pattern of advancing offense probability for the white-high, white-low, nonwhite-high, nonwhite-low groups that we observed earlier in certain other variables when classified by race and income. In table G.2.1 the white-high SES first offense probability is .2554, the white-low SES probability is .3584, the nonwhite-high SES probability is .3646, and the nonwhite-low

1. We shall not examine offense numbers beyond the ninth in this appendix because too few cases existed in many of the categories when the data were divided by the four race-income groupings.

TABLE G.2.1

First Offense Probabilities by Type of Offense, Race, and SES Group

	All Types	Nonindex	Injury	Theft	Damage	Combination
Cohort:						
White-high	.2554	.1856	.0137	.0302	.0179	.0080
White-low	.3584	.2346	.0248	.0463	.0336	.0192
Nonwhite-high	.3646	.2205	.0393	.0349	.0240	.0458
Nonwhite-low	.5274	.3118	.0516	.0904	.0331	.0405
Offenders:						
White-high	1.0000	.7268	.0535	.1182	.0703	.0312
White-low	1.0000	.6545	.0691	.1291	.0939	.0534
Nonwhite-high	1.0000	.6048	.1078	.0958	.0659	.1257
Nonwhite-low	1.0000	.5912	.0978	.1714	.0628	.0768

SES value is .5274. Thus about 26 percent of the white-high income group and 53 percent of the nonwhite low income group had at least one police contact. Income level is not as mitigating an influence on the racial differential in offensivity as would be hoped, since in each income group the likelihood of offense commission is substantially higher for the nonwhites – 11 percent higher than the whites in the high SES group and 17 percent higher in the low SES group, although within both racial groups high SES boys are less likely to be picked up by the police than are low SES boys. In fact, for the total cohort across all offense types, low SES boys are more likely to become classified as offenders within each racial group than are high SES boys. (Nonwhite combination is the exception in that the probabilities for both SES groups are almost the same, .0458 for high and .0405 for low).

The nonwhite probabilities classified by offense type are also higher than the white, even when SES level is held constant (although for theft offenses high SES whites and nonwhites exhibit similar probabilities of .0302 and .0349, and for damage offenses low SES whites and nonwhites have probabilities of .0336 and .0331 respectively). As we found in our discussion of the white and the nonwhite groups in the preceding section, we also now observe noticeable differences between the racial groups when SES is considered on those offenses involving or possibly involving bodily harm – the offenses of injury and combination. Thus the probability of a high SES, white, first offense of injury is .0137, while the corresponding nonwhite value is .0393; for low SES whites: .0248; and for low SES nonwhites: .0516. It is highly unlikely that high SES white boys will commit a combination first offense (.0080), while it is considerably more likely that high SES nonwhites will (.0458). The same is true of low SES whites and nonwhites: .0192 and .0405 respectively.

The probabilities of committing property offenses are similar for the race-SES groups with the exception of low SES theft offensivity, where nonwhites are about twice as likely as whites of gaining a police record (.0904 compared to .0463).

And again, in the minor nonindex offense category, nonwhites are more likely to be involved in such acts in both SES groups than are whites. For high SES nonwhites the probability of committing a nonindex offense is .2205, while it is .1856 for high SES whites; and for low SES nonwhites, the value is .3118, while it is .2346 for low SES whites.

If we now look at the offense probability distributions by type of offense for offenders only (also in table G.2.1), clearly the most likely first offense type is nonindex. Here again white offenders are more likely to choose a nonindex first offense than are nonwhites, regardless of SES group. Thus, 73 percent of the high SES white boys, 65 percent of the low SES white boys, 60 percent of the high SES nonwhite boys, and 59 percent of the low SES nonwhite boys committed a nonindex first offense. Conversely, the opposite ordering for index offense probabilities must follow.

The concentration of both nonwhite SES groups in the injury and combination categories compared to the whites is especially conspicuous in the offenders-only distribution. The high and low SES nonwhite probabilities for injury offenses are .1078 and .0978 respectively, while the corresponding probabilities for the high and low SES whites are .0535 and .0691. Additionally, the high and low SES values for nonwhites involved with combination first offenses are .1257 and .0768, while the respective white values are .0312 and .0534.

The proportion of white boys in both SES groups involved in property damage exceeds that of nonwhites in both groups (for high SES, .0703 and .0659; for low SES, .0939 and .0628). High SES whites and low SES nonwhites are more likely to be involved in thefts than are their corresponding opposite racial SES groups (.1182 compared to .0958, and .1714 compared to .1291).

Thus, we find again a propensity in the nonwhite group when compared to the white on SES level for violent offensivity and for infractions having components of injury, theft, or damage, while white offenders are slightly more likely to be involved in property offensivity. This finding, along with the higher probability in both SES groups of nonwhite commission of almost all offense types, supports our earlier statement of the dismal position of the urban nonwhite boy and his chances of being apprehended by the police.

TABLE G.2.2

Proportion of One-time Offenders by Race, SES, and Type of Offense

	All Types	Nonindex	Injury	Theft	Damage	Combi-nation
White-high	.5902	.5901	.5672	.4865	.8864	.3590
White-low	.4837	.4622	.5094	.4848	.6806	.3658
Nonwhite-high	.4311	.3960	.5000	.1875	.6364	.6190
Nonwhite-low	.3344	.3596	.2540	.3846	.5062	.0100

The proportion of offenders stopping after the first offense is highest for the high SES white group (.5902) followed by the low SES white group (.4837), the high SES nonwhite group (.4311), and the low SES nonwhite group (.3344). Thus, recidivism, disregarding first offense type, is considerably more likely for nonwhites in both SES groups. The same ordering exists for nonindex offenses with essentially the same proportion of one-time offenders for each race-SES group.

About 50 percent of the high SES white, low SES white, and high SES nonwhite offenders who started with an injury event desisted after the commission of that offense. On the other hand, only 25 percent of the low SES nonwhite offenders desisted after an injury first offense. About 36 percent of the white boys in both SES groups desisted after a combination first offense, while 62 percent of the nonwhite, high SES boys desisted. Only one low SES nonwhite boy out of a hundred (.0100) did not go on to further delinquency after a combination first offense. About 75 percent of the low SES nonwhite boys who began their delinquency careers with an offense involving injury, and about 99 percent of the low SES nonwhite boys who started with some combination of injury, theft, or damage, went on to commit an additional delinquent act.

Boys who begin their delinquency careers with property damage are the least likely to commit additional acts, regardless of SES level. Eighty-eight percent of the high SES whites, 68 percent of the low SES whites, 64 percent of the high SES nonwhites, and 51 percent of the low SES nonwhites desisted from further offensivity after a damage first offense. These desistance rates are the highest ones in each race-SES group.

In both white SES groups, 48 percent of the boys stopped after a theft first offense. About 38 percent of the low SES nonwhites stopped, and only 19 percent of the high SES nonwhites stopped after a theft first offense – the second lowest of all the groups.

Thus, white boys of both SES groups are more likely to desist after almost any form of delinquency than are nonwhite boys of the corresponding SES groups, particularly if the white boys are of the high SES damage first offense group, and the nonwhite boys of the low SES injury or combination first offense group. Nonwhite high SES offenders who commit theft first offenses are likely to recidivate (only .1875 desisted), as are nonwhite low SES injury first offenders (.2540 desisted) and nonwhite, low SES, combination first offenders (.0100 desisted).

Second to Ninth Offense

Our concern in this discussion of the second to the ninth offense probability distributions is the same as in the exposition of the first offense probabilities: Do the racial differentials for offenses beyond the first, across all offense types, still obtain when socioeconomic status is considered? We shall, as we did earlier, rely on the linear least squares estimates of the various probabilities, since the number of data points for the various classifications by race, income, offense type, and rank become unmanageably large if only the raw information is considered. The roughness in the plots, which was evident in the race classification by offense type at the higher offense ranks, becomes especially noticeable because of small class numbers when we further divide by income group. The regression estimates, therefore, although they tend to mask the fairly rapid rise in offense probability which appears at the second or third offense in many categories, offer the basis for simple summary statements which typify most of the offense probability distributions. With that in mind, we continue in this section to offer the reader data plots, regression lines, and raw data tables, even though we shall be concerned primarily with the regression estimates.[2]

The first offense probability ordering for all offense types, which we outlined in the immediately preceding section, persists at least through to the ninth occurrence for the four race-income groups (table G.2.3 and figure G.2.1). The white, high SES probability ranges from .5014 at the second offense to .7079 at the ninth, while that for the white, low SES ranges from .5577 to .7740; the nonwhite, high SES probability ranges from .6406 to .8639, and that for the nonwhite, low SES ranges from .7075 to .8370. Essentially, these differences are functions of the starting probabilities represented by the *Y*-intercepts, since the slopes across all race-income groups are similar, ranging between .02 and .03. Thus, regardless of the race-

2. Thus the probabilities discussed in this section are regression estimates, not raw data values.

income classification, the *increase* per offense rank in probability is almost identical among the groups. Nonetheless, the two white SES groups cluster in a lower likelihood of offense commission, while the two nonwhite SES groups lie even closer together in the higher. Socioeconomic status does account for some of the variation across rank within race groups but not between. We can say, however, that although nonwhites exhibit a greater inclination to offense commission at the outset than do whites, regardless of income group, the rate of increase in offense probability is similar across the four groups up to the ninth offense.

What has been found above must also hold in a converse manner for the probability of desisting after the kth offense, since the probability of stopping and the probability of going on to a subsequent offense must sum to one. Thus, at each offense rank the likelihood of stopping is greatest for high SES whites, followed by low SES whites, high SES nonwhites, and low SES nonwhites, in that order and ranging from .50 to .30 for high SES whites over the eight offenses, to .30 to .16 for low SES nonwhites over the same interval.

Similar findings hold for nonindex offenses over the eight offenses and four race-income groups. Thus, the probability of nonindex offense commission ranges from .3563 to .4508 for high SES whites, .3519 to .5118 for low SES whites, .3800 to .5634 for high SES nonwhites, and .4163 to .4719 for low SES nonwhites. High SES nonwhites are more likely than high SES whites to commit nonindex offenses at each rank number, while low SES whites are less likely than low SES nonwhites up to the sixth offense and more likely from the seventh to the ninth.

The injury offense probabilities across the eight offenses again indicate that the likelihood of nonwhite offensivity is greater than the white within each of the SES groups. The range in offense probabilities for high SES whites is .0140 to .0721,[3] while that for high SES nonwhites is .0594 to .1014. Similarly, the range for low SES whites is .0441 and .0310, while that for low SES nonwhites is .0710 to .1014.

The likelihood of nonwhite theft offensivity is also higher than that for whites of each SES group, although for the high SES group the difference is not great. The probability range for high SES white theft offensivity is .0955 to .1062, while that for high SES nonwhites is .1156 to .1050. The difference between the ranges of the low SES racial groups is greater, being .0955 to .1062 for whites and .1228 to .1532 for nonwhites.

3. See appendix G.1, n. 1, on end point bias and its effect on interpretation of the data.

TABLE G.2.3

Static Probability of Committing k*th Offense by Race and SES*

Number of Offense			All Types[a] (ΣN,I,T,D,C)	Non-index[b]	Injury[c]	Theft[d]	Damage[e]	Combination[f]	Desisted (stopped after *k*th offense)
2	White	L	.5163	.3520	.0338	.0664	.0299	.0338	.4837
	White	H	.4097	.2979	.0231	.0607	.0079	.0199	.5903
	Nonwhite	L	.6656	.3785	.0729	.1055	.0310	.0775	.3344
	Nonwhite	H	.5688	.3652	.0538	.0778	.0239	.0479	.4312
3	White	L	.6061	.3939	.0328	.1161	.0277	.0353	.3939
	White	H	.5185	.3664	.0155	.0974	.0155	.0233	.4315
	Nonwhite	L	.7494	.4358	.0722	.1456	.0279	.0675	.2506
	Nonwhite	H	.6631	.3684	.0736	.1157	.0105	.0947	.3369
4	White	L	.6875	.4458	.0625	.1375	.0166	.0250	.3125
	White	H	.6315	.4172	.0563	.1015	.0263	.0300	.3685
	Nonwhite	L	.7604	.4510	.0902	.1275	.0248	.0668	.2396
	Nonwhite	H	.7301	.4761	.0158	.1269	.0476	.0634	.2699
5	White	L	.6424	.3636	.0545	.1393	.0181	.0666	.3576
	White	H	.6190	.4583	.0059	.1071	.0238	.0238	.3810
	Nonwhite	L	.7730	.4355	.0879	.1329	.0327	.0838	.2270
	Nonwhite	H	.8478	.5434	.0869	.1739	.0000	.0434	.1522
6	White	L	.6415	.4622	.0094	.0943	.0000	.0754	.3585
	White	H	.6730	.4230	.0480	.1634	.0192	.0192	.3270
	Nonwhite	L	.7883	.4920	.0608	.1534	.0132	.0687	.2117
	Nonwhite	H	.7435	.4102	.1025	.1282	.0256	.0769	.2565

7	White	L	.7353	.3970	.0588	.1911	.0294	.0583	.2647
	White	H	.7428	.4285	.0571	.1142	.0285	.1142	.2572
	Nonwhite	L	.8154	.4463	.1040	.1442	.0469	.0738	.1846
	Nonwhite	H	.7931	.5172	.1379	.0344	.0000	.1034	.2069
8	White	L	.7000	.4400	.0200	.1600	.0200	.0600	.3000
	White	H	.5769	.4038	.0384	.0961	.0000	.0384	.4231
	Nonwhite	L	.8065	.4567	.0946	.1522	.0205	.0823	.1935
	Nonwhite	H	.9130	.5217	.1739	.1304	.0000	.0869	.0870
9	White	L	.8000	.6000	.0285	.0857	.0000	.0857	.2000
	White	H	.6667	.4333	.1000	.0666	.0000	.0666	.3333
	Nonwhite	L	.8214	.4540	.1071	.1428	.0255	.0918	.1786
	Nonwhite	H	.7619	.5714	.0000	.0952	.0000	.0952	.2331

Regression estimates:

White, High SES: ${}^{a}Y = .0295X + .4424$, ${}^{b}Y = .0134X + .3294$, ${}^{c}Y = .0083X - .0026$
White, Low SES: ${}^{a}Y = .0309X + .4959$, ${}^{b}Y = .0228X + .3062$, ${}^{c}Y = -.0019X + .0478$

Nonwhite, High SES: ${}^{a}Y = .0319X + .5768$, ${}^{b}Y = .0262X + .3276$, ${}^{c}Y = .0060X + .0474$
Nonwhite, Low SES: ${}^{a}Y = .0185X + .6705$, ${}^{b}Y = .0080X + .3995$, ${}^{c}Y = .0044X + .0623$

White, High SES: ${}^{d}Y = .0015X + .0925$, ${}^{e}Y = -.0015X + .0237$, ${}^{f}Y = .0077X - .0006$
White, Low SES: ${}^{d}Y = .0056X + .0930$, ${}^{e}Y = -.0027X + .0326$, ${}^{f}Y = .0071X + .0160$

Nonwhite, High SES: ${}^{d}Y = -.0015X + .1187$, ${}^{e}Y = -.0040X + .0355$, ${}^{f}Y = .0053X + .0473$
Nonwhite, Low SES: ${}^{d}Y = .0043X + .1141$, ${}^{e}Y = -.0003X + .0297$, ${}^{f}Y = .0023X + .0636$

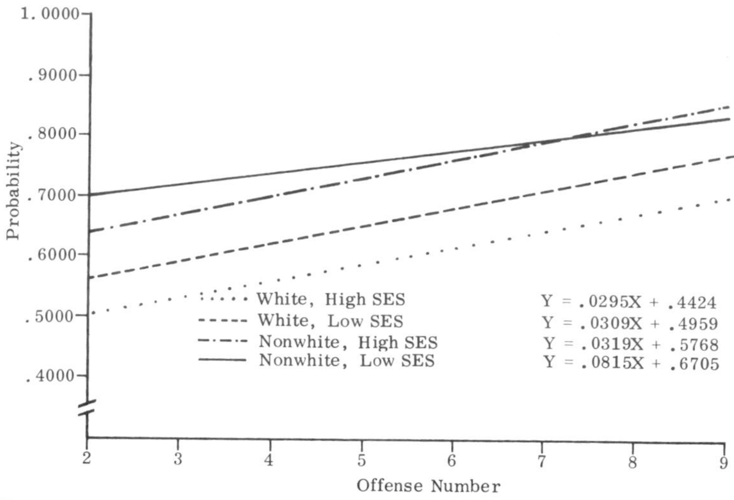

FIGURE G.2.1

Regression Estimate of Probability of Committing Second to Ninth Offense by Race and SES (All Offense Types)

Offenses which contain only a component of damage are very low incidence events in this cohort. All four race-income groups commit damage offenses at declining rates at each offense rank. Thus, the slopes of the regression lines are –.0040 per offense number for high SES nonwhites (the greatest rate of decrease for this type of offense), –.0027 for the low SES whites, –.0015 for high SES whites, and –.0003 for low SES nonwhites (the smallest rate of decline in this offense category). The likelihood of damage offensivity for high SES whites ranges from .0206 to .0097, and for low SES whites, from .0272 to .0083. For high SES nonwhites it ranges from .0275 to .0006, and for low SES nonwhite, from .0290 to .0266 (practically no change from the second to the ninth offense).

The probability of committing offenses involving combinations of injury, theft, or damage is again greater within SES groups for nonwhite boys for the second to the ninth offense. The probability for high SES white boys ranges from .0148 to .0690, while for high SES nonwhites the range is .0578 to .0950. For the low SES whites the probabilities are .0302 to .0799, and for the low SES whites, .0682 to .0843.

In summary, we can say that in addition to the greater initial likelihood of being involved in an offense, nonwhite boys are more likely to go on to a subsequent offense at almost any offense number and to practically any offense type than are white boys, regardless of socioeconomic level. This differential is particularly evident for those offenses involving injury or combinations of injury, theft, or damage.

Mean Seriousness Score

In addition to the greater likelihood of nonwhite offensivity observed above, we also find that nonwhites are committing more serious offenses than are whites, irrespective of income level. In table G.2.4 and figure G.2.2 it is clear that such is the case for the mean seriousness scores of all offense types from the first to the ninth. High SES white offenders advanced in seriousness scores from 80.25 to 122.07 over the nine offenses, while high SES nonwhites advanced from 124.79 to 164.75. Additionally, low SES white seriousness scores increased from 107.49 to 109.10, while low SES nonwhite scores increased from 112.10 to 155.14. Seriousness scores for high SES whites, high SES nonwhites, and low SES nonwhites increased about 5 points per offense number, while those for low SES whites increased only .20 points per offense number.

Nonindex offensivity, which manifests low seriousness scores of rather limited range, exhibits the same increases in scores between race groups within SES categories, although the differences are small. High SES whites committed nonindex offenses of severity ranging from 20.38 to 31.17, while those of high SES nonwhites ranged from 37.08 to 54.39. Low SES white scores ranged from 24.58 to 31.58, and low SES nonwhite scores, from 29.49 to 32.27.

The data for injury offenses is marked by large swings for all the race-SES groups except low SES nonwhite, where the almost even advance in seriousness score from 331.51 to 529.27 is self-evident in the raw data. High SES nonwhite injury offensivity swings from a high of 826.75 at the eighth offense to a low of 0.0 at the ninth (no high SES nonwhites committed a ninth offense having only a component of injury). Both high and low SES whites have data peaks and valleys which, while not of the same magnitude as those associated with high SES nonwhite injury, are nonetheless substantial. However, the least squares lines through these points do enable us to make the necessary comparisons, though with caution.

High SES white offenders committed injury offenses which ranged from 308.95 to 323.64 for the first to the ninth offense. For high SES nonwhites the values declined from 440.159 to 359.831 over the same interval – still much in excess of the high SES white values. The low SES white scores ranged from 410.04 to 417.60, while the low SES nonwhite scores rose from 331.51 to 529.27. Thus it appears that within SES levels the race differentials in offense seriousness scores still persist for injury offenses.

The high SES white seriousness scores for theft offenses advanced from 192.52 to 227.54, while the high SES nonwhite scores declined from 198.79 to 177.10 from the first to the ninth offense. A similar finding appears in damage offensivity, where the high SES white seri-

TABLE G.2.4

Mean Seriousness Score by Race and SES

Number of Offense			All Types (ΣN,I,T,D,C)	Non-index[b]	Injury[c]	Theft[d]	Damage[e]	Combination[f]
1	White	L	93.79	23.83	341.17	195.09	151.44	284.76
	White	H	74.94	18.44	304.10	195.20	171.32	325.82
	Nonwhite	L	109.82	29.13	343.23	171.77	147.35	264.76
	Nonwhite	H	122.69	29.74	314.83	151.75	158.91	363.95
2	White	L	94.06	28.04	294.46	214.96	155.65	287.62
	White	H	85.91	25.86	265.03	178.49	207.40	444.08
	Nonwhite	L	126.66	26.67	383.37	177.65	166.20	305.31
	Nonwhite	H	105.05	21.18	366.67	190.38	100.00	314.13
3	White	L	101.59	24.57	409.31	201.65	179.45	284.14
	White	H	87.56	25.58	362.50	195.80	175.00	365.92
	Nonwhite	L	119.94	31.42	374.27	186.38	150.17	263.22
	Nonwhite	H	170.75	71.26	286.71	216.18	100.00	422.22
4	White	L	136.40	34.96	626.67	208.73	125.00	329.67
	White	H	113.12	21.59	446.67	215.56	182.00	351.63
	Nonwhite	L	127.70	35.86	381.76	172.28	167.19	304.65
	Nonwhite	H	124.76	50.70	800.00	189.75	166.67	350.00
5	White	L	150.41	29.95	677.78	206.70	124.67	265.36
	White	H	77.52	22.65	200.00	223.22	175.00	350.00
	Nonwhite	L	138.18	39.95	361.74	168.40	159.87	366.88
	Nonwhite	H	144.05	51.92	480.00	212.50	0.0	350.00

6	White	L	77.11	18.63	200.00	185.30	0.0	284.75
	White	H	99.33	25.02	160.00	203.06	550.00	250.00
	Nonwhite	L	119.63	30.02	481.83	180.71	140.00	300.08
	Nonwhite	H	163.73	28.13	400.00	302.60	200.00	328.33
7	White	L	125.24	22.81	375.00	177.46	250.00	334.75
	White	H	167.71	25.02	525.00	262.75	150.00	414.13
	Nonwhite	L	149.64	33.14	496.84	160.37	162.43	335.64
	Nonwhite	H	116.78	52.40	125.00	100.00	0.0	433.33
8	White	L	102.80	28.00	400.00	213.00	200.00	226.00
	White	H	92.80	30.20	250.00	207.20	0.0	300.00
	Nonwhite	L	153.26	39.62	548.13	163.62	200.00	299.00
	Nonwhite	H	245.95	51.92	826.75	178.33	0.0	350.00
9	White	L	93.25	41.95	400.00	217.33	0.0	226.00
	White	H	111.55	31.77	333.33	209.00	0.0	200.00
	Nonwhite	L	157.75	34.60	503.60	222.89	193.00	252.50
	Nonwhite	H	103.19	54.25	0.0	150.00	0.0	350.00

Regression estimates:

White, High SES: ${}^{a}Y = 5.2270X + 75.0250$, ${}^{b}Y = 1.3498X + 19.0254$, ${}^{c}Y = 1.8360X + 307.1120$
White, Low SES: ${}^{a}Y = .2011X + 107.2886$, ${}^{b}Y = .8725X + 23.7064$, ${}^{c}Y = .9440X + 409.1010$

Nonwhite, High SES: ${}^{a}Y = 4.9956X + 119.7947$, ${}^{b}Y = 2.1661X + 34.8997$, ${}^{c}Y = -10.0401X + 450.2000$
Nonwhite, Low SES: ${}^{a}Y = 5.3808X + 106.7158$, ${}^{b}Y = .9722X + 28.5181$, ${}^{c}Y = 24.7200X + 306.7860$

White, High SES: ${}^{d}Y = 4.3780X + 188.1410$, ${}^{e}Y = 16.4910X + 261.4230$, ${}^{f}Y = -15.6780X + 411.8980$
White, Low SES: ${}^{d}Y = .2100X + 201.1610$, ${}^{e}Y = -7.6100X + 169.8510$, ${}^{f}Y = -6.0600X + 310.6380$

Nonwhite, High SES: ${}^{d}Y = -2.7110X + 201.4980$, ${}^{e}Y = -18.3710X + 172.4750$, ${}^{f}Y = .8710X + 358.0810$
Nonwhite, Low SES: ${}^{d}Y = 1.9800X + 168.3300$, ${}^{e}Y = 4.6880X + 141.6940$, ${}^{f}Y = 1.2050X + 293.0900$

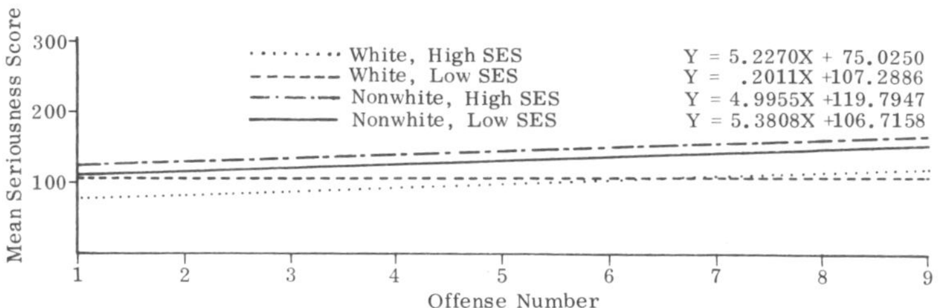

FIGURE G.2.2
Regression Estimate of Mean Seriousness Score of First to Ninth Offense by Race and SES (All Offense Types)

ousness scores decline from 244.93 to 113.00, while the high SES nonwhite scores decline from 154.10 to 7.14. A similar finding follows in low SES theft offensivity between the two race groups. Low SES white theft offense severity remained practically unchanged over the nine offenses, 201.37 to 203.05, while low SES nonwhite severity advanced somewhat, from 170.31 to 186.15. The exception to this pattern of higher seriousness scores for property offenses committed by whites appears in damage offenses involving low SES racial groups. Here, low SES white damage offense seriousness scores dropped from 162.24 to 101.35 from the first to the ninth offense, while low SES nonwhite scores increased from 146.38 to 183.89.

For offenses involving combinations of injury, theft, or damage, high SES white scores dropped from 396.22 to 270.80 from the first to the ninth offense, while high SES nonwhite scores increased from 358.95 to 365.92. Over the same interval, low SES white combination scores declined from 304.58 to 256.10, while low SES nonwhite combination scores rose slightly, from 294.39 to 303.94. Thus, within SES groups, nonwhites exhibit somewhat higher seriousness scores than do whites, while between SES groups, high SES offenders have higher scores than do low SES boys.

We have found in this discussion of offense seriousness scores for the first nine offenses that, for all offense types taken together (Σ N, I, T, D, C), nonwhite offenders in our cohort have committed more serious offenses than have white offenders. This difference also obtains to a greater or lesser degree for those events containing elements of nonindex offensivity, for injury offenses, and for combinations of injury, theft, or damage. On the other hand, with the exception of low SES damage offenses, whites were involved with property offenses having greater seriousness scores than those associated with nonwhites, regardless of SES level.

Disregarding race, it is of interest to note that in many instances high SES boys committed more serious offenses than did low SES boys. Thus, for all offense types considered together, high SES nonwhites committed offenses which ranged from 124.79 to 164.75, while the low SES nonwhites' offenses ranged from 112.10 to 155.14. High SES nonwhites' nonindex offenses were more serious than were low SES nonwhites' nonindex offenses (37.08 to 54.39 compared to 29.49 to 32.27), and high SES whites' nonindex scores were about the same as those of the low SES white boys. High SES white theft scores were higher (192.52 to 227.54) than were those of low SES whites (201.37 to 203.05). Similar scores follow for high SES nonwhite theft scores (198.79 to 177.10) compared to low SES nonwhite theft scores (170.31 to 196.15). High SES white damage offenders committed more serious offenses (244.93 to 113.00) than did low SES white damage offenders (162.24 to 101.36). Both high SES racial groups committed more serious combination offenses than did their corresponding low SES counterparts (high SES nonwhites, 358.95 to 365.92; low SES nonwhites, 294.30 to 303.94; high SES whites, 392.22 to 240.80; low SES whites, 304.58 to 256.10).

The interaction among race, income, offense type, offense rank, and seriousness score is not a simple one. Nonwhite offenders commit more serious offenses in general, and more offenses against the person in particular, regardless of income level. White boys commit more serious offenses against property than do nonwhites, regardless of income level. But, as we outlined above, within racial groups high SES boys often commit more serious offenses than do low SES boys.

Mean Time between Offenses

The data for the mean time between offenses with this additional classification of income group, still follow the form of the function $\log Y = a + b \log X$, as have the other mean time classifications outlined earlier. Of course the manifold categorization of race, income group, offense rank, and offense type does cause problems in that many more offense types and ranks are sparsely populated. This difficulty has been present throughout this race-income section. Nonetheless, where sufficient numbers of cases do exist, it seems that this function fits fairly well (table G.2.6 and figure G.2.3).

The age limits between first and ninth offense are, as was the case in the earlier discussions, rather small. That such is the case is illus-

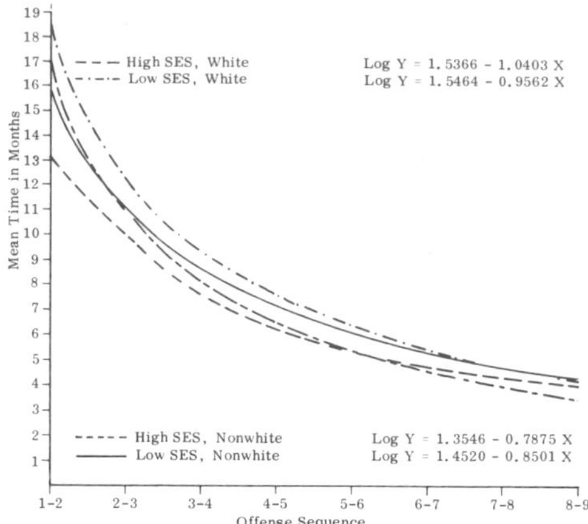

FIGURE G.2.3
Regression Estimate of Mean Time between Offenses by Race and SES

trated in table G.2.5. The mean age at commission of the first offense is lower for low SES nonwhites than for low SES whites for all offense types except damage. Generally, low SES white boys are 8 to 10 months older at this time than are the nonwhite delinquents. The ages at commission of the ninth offense for low SES whites and nonwhites offer no particular pattern except that both groups are about 2 years older on the average at this point in their delinquent careers. Roughly speaking, low SES nonwhite boys are almost 14 years old at the commission of the first offense, while low SES whites are about 14½ years old for the offenses of nonindex, injury, and theft. For the offenses of damage and combination, boys in both groups are about 13 years old.

High SES nonwhite boys began their delinquent careers later for the offenses of nonindex (3 months), theft (12 months), and combination (18 months) than did low SES nonwhites. For injury and damage, however, they began somewhat earlier (2 and 6 months respectively). High SES white offenders began later for all offense types except theft than did either low SES whites or high SES nonwhites. For the offense types of nonindex, injury, damage, and combination this differential was about one year, while for theft offenses high SES whites began about 1.3 months earlier than high SES nonwhites.

Both high SES groups were older at the ninth offense rank than both low SES groups. High SES whites were about 7 to 8 months older than were high SES nonwhites for the offenses of nonindex and theft, and about 14 months younger for offenses involving combinations of injury, theft, or damage.

TABLE G.2.5

Age at First and Ninth Offense by Race, SES and Type of Offense

	Low SES		High SES	
	White	Nonwhite	White	Nonwhite
1st Offense:				
Nonindex	14.0	14.7	14.3	15.2
Injury	13.9	14.7	13.8	14.7
Theft	13.6	14.5	14.6	14.5
Damage	12.7	12.4	12.2	13.2
Combination	13.0	13.7	14.5	14.9
9th Offense.				
Nonindex	15.8	16.2	16.0	16.6
Injury	16.2	16.9	–	16.6
Theft	15.6	13.9	16.2	16.8
Damage	14.8	–	–	–
Combination	15.2	14.9	17.3	16.1

If we were to typify these groups on the variable of age at commission, we would conclude that high SES boys are likely to be older at the first and ninth offense than low SES boys, and that within socioeconomic categories white offenders tend to be older than nonwhites.

The nonindex mean time regression lines cluster tightly (within about 2 months) from the third to fourth out to the eighth to ninth transition. The low SES white and nonwhite repetition rates are slightly slower than the high SES groups' rate; that is, their mean times between offense ranks are somewhat longer, although the mean-time regressions for all four race-income groups are similar, being about 17.25 months for the first to second mean time, 11.5 months for the second-to-third, and an even log decay to about three months at the eighth-to-ninth transition.

The mean times between injury offenses drop off very rapidly for high SES nonwhite offenders, from about 18 months for the first-to-second offense to about 10 months for the second-to-third to about 2 months for the eighth-to-ninth. The high SES white injury mean times are dramatically different, dropping only from about 11 months for the first-to-second offense to about 7.5 months for the eighth-to-ninth offense. Thus we observe a very rapid rate of injury offense repetition for high SES nonwhites when compared to high SES whites.

TABLE G.2.6

Mean Time between Offenses by Race and SES

Offense Sequence			Non-index[a]	Injury[b]	Theft[c]	Damage[d]	Combination[e]
1 – 2	White	L	20.31	22.29	17.99	18.83	18.27
	White	H	18.28	12.10	15.03	13.75	19.88
	Nonwhite	L	17.75	18.58	16.88	16.59	15.67
	Nonwhite	H	19.17	20.94	17.42	14.93	19.67
2 – 3	White	L	11.68	12.20	13.33	9.26	7.08
	White	H	10.73	10.90	13.00	5.58	11.37
	Nonwhite	L	10.50	11.49	8.58	7.26	9.13
	Nonwhite	H	6.64	15.17	6.68	0.80	5.84
3 – 4	White	L	8.87	6.04	7.09	2.63	6.17
	White	H	8.41	6.56	7.65	15.79	11.14
	Nonwhite	L	7.51	9.43	8.20	7.26	5.77
	Nonwhite	H	9.14	1.80	9.72	4.57	5.15
4 – 5	White	L	6.58	13.76	7.34	9.77	7.91
	White	H	6.28	5.90	5.56	3.53	1.50
	Nonwhite	L	7.27	6.23	6.16	4.76	6.73
	Nonwhite	H	5.53	4.05	5.67	0.0	4.15
5 – 6	White	L	5.72	9.40	12.72	0.0	6.09
	White	H	4.91	7.38	3.72	8.10	0.40
	Nonwhite	L	5.61	8.55	6.20	4.22	6.76
	Nonwhite	H	2.91	7.78	3.30	13.10	6.50

6 – 7	White	L	6.16	7.45	1.93	6.75	1.72
	White	H	3.96	12.05	5.26	4.95	8.41
	Nonwhite	L	5.48	5.27	6.56	6.80	6.32
	Nonwhite	H	3.69	2.08	6.60	0.0	2.30
7 – 8	White	L	5.81	1.40	3.19	36.10	3.67
	White	H	4.55	12.85	3.24	0.0	0.40
	Nonwhite	L	4.81	5.78	4.35	1.32	5.09
	Nonwhite	H	9.27	3.77	9.77	0.0	23.20
8 – 9	White	L	4.00	11.30	0.80	0.0	5.07
	White	H	3.75	4.40	1.55	0.0	5.45
	Nonwhite	L	4.87	4.84	2.66	6.36	4.82
	Nonwhite	H	4.49	0.0	1.85	0.0	6.65

Regression estimates:

White, High SES	[a]$\text{Log } Y = -1.0403 \text{ Log } X + 1.5366$,	[b]$\text{Log } Y = -.2449 \text{ Log } X + 1.0922$,	[c]$\text{Log } Y = -1.3500 \text{ Log } X + 1.6772$
White, Low SES:	[a]$\text{Log } Y = -.9562 \text{ Log } X + 1.5464$,	[b]$\text{Log } Y = -.9121 \text{ Log } X + 1.5588$,	[c]$\text{Log } Y = -1.6383 \text{ Log } X - 1.8873$
Nonwhite, High SES:	[a]$\text{Log } Y = -.7875 \text{ Log } X + 1.3546$,	[b]$\text{Log } Y = -1.5862 \text{ Log } X + 1.7461$,	[c]$\text{Log } Y = -.8933 \text{ Log } X - 1.4253$
Nonwhite, Low SES:	[a]$\text{Log } Y = -.8501 \text{ Log } X + 1.4520$,	[b]$\text{Log } Y = -.8418 \text{ Log } X + 1.4853$,	[c]$\text{Log } Y = -.9613 \text{ Log } X - 1.4848$
White, High SES:	[d]$\text{Log } Y = -1.5383 \text{ Log } X + 1.7234$,	[e]$\text{Log } Y = -1.4455 \text{ Log } X + 1.6598$	
White, Low SES:	[d]$\text{Log } Y = -.8519 \text{ Log } X + 1.3468$,	[e]$\text{Log } Y = -.9998 \text{ Log } X + 1.4560$	
Nonwhite, High SES:	[d]Too few cases,	[e]$\text{Log } Y = -.3442 \text{ Log } X + 1.0833$	
Nonwhite, Low SES:	[d]$\text{Log } Y = -.9536 \text{ Log } X + 1.4129$,	[e]$\text{Log } Y = -.6663 \text{ Log } X + 1.3087$	

The low SES white and nonwhite injury mean time regressions are similar, with both ranging from about 18 months for the first-to-second offense to 13 months for the second-to-third, down to about 5 months for the eighth-to-ninth.

The high and low SES nonwhite theft mean time regression lines are almost identical, starting from about 14.5 months between the first-to-second transition to 10.4 months for the second-to-third and evenly down to 3.5 months for the eighth-to-ninth. On the other hand, both the high and low SES white regression traces follow the same path, but at lower mean times than the nonwhites from the third-to-fourth transition on. At each theft offense rank the white mean time from the last offense is about one month less than the nonwhite mean time, regardless of socioeconomic level.

Damage offenses, because of their low incidence, present a difficult task for evaluation. We have presented regression estimates for only the high and low SES whites and the low SES nonwhites, as the number of data points was insufficient to enable any useful estimate to be considered for the high SES nonwhites. We can say that the regression estimates for both whites and nonwhites of the lower SES are essentially identical, ranging from 12.8 months for the first-to-second damage transition to about 7 months for the second-to-third, down to about 3 months for the eighth to ninth. The high SES white mean times average about one month less than the low SES estimates.

For combination offenses, the longest mean time regressions are generated by the high SES nonwhite group, ranging from about 10 months for the first-to-second transition to about 8 months for the second-to-third, down to about 5.7 months for the eighth-to-ninth. Although the low SES nonwhite regression estimates are longer than the high SES nonwhite estimates for the early offenses, they converge after the fifth offense. Both white SES groups produce lower mean time regression estimates than do the nonwhites, with the high SES whites taking the least time between offenses (17.2 months for the first-to-second transition, 10 months for the second-to-third, and about 1.7 months for the eighth-to-ninth).

In summary, the mean times between offenses when classified by race, income, and type of offense, under conditions of adequate category size, yield regression estimates which show no great difference between whites and nonwhites in either SES group for nonindex offenses, in the low SES group for injury, and in the low SES group for damage. Conversely, race negates the effect of SES in the mean time estimates between theft and combination offenses.

Index